A Biographical Dictionary of
Renaissance Poets and Dramatists, 1520-1650

A Biographical Dictionary of Renaissance Poets and Dramatists, 1520-1650

J.W. Saunders

Senior Lecturer in English Literature,
University of Leeds

THE HARVESTER PRESS · SUSSEX

BARNES & NOBLE BOOKS · NEW JERSEY

First published in Great Britain in 1983 by
THE HARVESTER PRESS LIMITED
Publisher: John Spiers
16 Ship Street, Brighton, Sussex
and in the USA by
BARNES & NOBLE BOOKS
81 Adams Drive, Totowa, New Jersey 07516

J.W. Saunders, 1983

British Library Cataloguing in Publication Data
Biographical dictionary of Renaissance poets and
  dramatists, 1520-1650.
  1. English poetry – Early modern, 1500-1700 –
  Biographies – Dictionaries   2. English drama
  – Early modern and Elizabethan – Biography –
  Dictionaries
  3. English drama – 17th century – Biography –
  Dictionaries
  I. Saunders, J.W.
  821'.3   PR535
  ISBN 0-7108-0325-7

Library of Congress Cataloging in Publication Data
Saunders, J.W., M.A.
  A biographical dictionary of Renaissance poets and
  dramatists, 1520-1650.
  1. English literature – Early modern, 1500-1700 –
  Bio-bibliography. 2. Authors, English – Early modern,
  1500-1700 – Biography – Handbooks, manuals, etc.
  I. Title.
  PR421.S33 1983   820'.9'003 [B]   83-6026
  ISBN 0-389-20271-1

Typeset in 11/12 Garamond by PRG Graphics Ltd
and printed in Great Britain by
The Thetford Press Ltd, Thetford, Norfolk

THE HARVESTER PRESS PUBLISHING GROUP
The Harvester Press Publishing Group comprises Harvester Press Limited (chiefly
publishing literature, fiction, philosophy, psychology, and science and trade books),
Harvester Press Microform Publications Limited (publishing in microform un-
published archives, scarce printed sources, and indexes to these collections) and
Wheatsheaf Books Limited (a wholly independent company chiefly publishing in
economics, international politics, sociology and related social sciences), whose books
are distributed by the Harvester Press Limited and its agencies throughout the world.

Contents

Preface

Samuel Johnson declared that biography was 'the most useful of the arts', because it can be applied most readily to an understanding of life. He agreed with his own forebears, our earliest literary historians, the dusty scholars who were the first to make a study of English literature: Thomas Fuller, Gerard Langbaine, Anthony Wood, William Oldys, and their colleagues, were all convinced that knowledge of a writer's life-pattern, all the things he did with his life, illuminated his canon. They believed that no single poem or play can be understood without reference to all the writer's other works in their social context. Further, they thought it useful to know who his friends and colleagues were, what they did, and what they shared with him.

This principle is particularly important in understanding the English Renaissance when writers – particularly poets and dramatists – worked in literary groups, their poems written in competitive rivalries, their plays written in collaboration, with the result that individual works were seldom isolated artefacts and more usually items flowing in a communal river, understandable best when we can identify the themes and currents that set them afloat.

The English Renaissance – part of a European revolution to which England came rather late – may be roughly dated 1520-1650. To be more precise, the beginning is 1528, the year Sir Thomas Wyatt brought back from Italy Castiglione's *Il Cortegiano*, a handbook of courtly manners of widespread influence. It was translated into Spanish in 1534, into French in 1537, into English in 1561 (by Sir Thomas Hoby), and into German in 1566. But since gentlemen in all countries were educated to be polylingual, the original Italian text had no need to wait for translation.

The end of the English Renaissance can be finally dated in 1642, the year the Civil War broke out and the playhouses were closed down. History is seldom tidy, and there is evidence that Renaissance values were already beginning to break down by 1630, or even a little earlier. But this is an identifiable period, the foundations laid in the reign of Henry VIII, and with the years 1580-1620 as the heart of the matter.

English did not emerge as a language until 1356 when it first became recognised in courts of law. Previously most literature was written in French, the language of our Norman conquerors, or in Latin, the international language of scholars. English emerged with England, the assumption of nationhood by our branch of the Norman empire, a process not completed until Henry VII's victory at Bosworth; and of its many dialects, it was not until Elizabeth's reign that a standard, Queen's English evolved, from the dialects of London and the southeastern Midlands – what George Puttenham described as 'the usuall speach of the Court, and that of London and the shires lying about London within 1x. myles, and not much above.' One other form of English survived with respect. The genocide inflicted by William I on northern England had left the Northumbrian form restricted to the area between Edinburgh and the borders and this became the Lallans of Burns, a language based on the Scottish court, entirely English, and quite different from the Gaelic of the Highlands. It was in no sense a dialect, and important because James I united both courts and their languages.

A dictionary of English Renaissance poets and dramatists can therefore exclude work written in Gaelic (Irish, Scottish, Welsh or Cornish), but it cannot exclude writers using the languages of either of the two courts. This dictionary therefore includes the 507 writers who come within this definition. It excludes writers whose major contribution was made before 1520 or after 1650, even though some of their work falls within 1520-1650, since properly they are not Renaissance writers, in any important sense, but are 'medieval' or 'Augustan', or whatever names one gives to the periods before and after the Renaissance. Also excluded are those who emigrated to the New World, and whose writings make up the first entries in a dictionary of American writers. The 507 writers included are comprehensive. No known writer, no matter how obscure, is excluded.

There remain a large number of poems, and some plays, we can only assign to *Anon*. Who, for instance, wrote that loveliest of all Renaissance poems, *There is a lady sweet and kind*?

In the medieval period poems were seldom attributed, since the
writer was unimportant, a man selected to scribe for the local
community. This tradition lived on, encouraged by a courtly
system in which names were not given in manuscripts, since
everyone in the group already knew the identity. But names
gradually became more important, not merely out of personal
ambition, but because the notion grew that poetry itself was a
means to immortality, an entirely new idea which encouraged
writers to think of posterity and leave their signatures to be
remembered. The probability, however, is that many of these
anonymous poems were written by writers in this dictionary,
and future scholars may achieve identification.

Renaissance means rebirth, a useful definition for a period
when new thinking co-existed with the old. Medieval certain-
ties were being replaced by revolutionary novelties. This is the
age of Copernicus, Kepler, Gassendi, Galileo, Paracelsus and
Napier. But nothing was determined absolutely: Plato co-
existed with Aristotle, Ptolemy with Copernicus, Hippocrates
with Paracelsus, Laud with Calvin. Shakespeare, for instance,
in *Hamlet* produces a Ghost capable of four different interpre-
tations, and in *Troilus and Cressida* postulates simultaneously
a Ptolemaic and a Copernican universe. A Renaissance portrait
shows eyes that are alert, wakeful and indeed suspicious. The
Renaissance man, even if given to a particular political or
religious dogma, tends to be essentially sceptical. Donne was
their voice when he said

> doubt wisely; in strange way
> To stand enquiring right, is not to stray;
> To sleepe, or runne wrong is. On a huge hill,
> Cragged and steep, Truth stands, and hee that will
> Reach her, about must, and about must goe.

We should not be surprised, then, if these biographies exhibit
sudden *volte-faces*. Indeed, one mark of the end of the Renaissance was the polarisation of the Civil Wars, when sides had to
be taken, and the sceptics were left in an untenable middle
ground.

One way of surviving cosmic uncertainty was to act one's
way through life, whether at court, on the stage, or in the

pulpit. Writers of the period were great hypothesisers, every poem or play a game of make-believe. Their work tends to be highly metaphorical, 'conceited' in their word, more and more 'far-fet' as time went on; dramatic and self-dramatising; egotistical and therefore erotic, since love was, for all its problems, more of a certainty than the political and physical cosmos; lyrical, catching transient moods; and patterned by metre and rhetoric, since the whole problem was to assert some kind of civilised order out of chaos.

The centre of order was the court, which after Henry VII established a specifically English nation and language. Castiglione had insisted that monarchs and their courtiers had prime responsibility for establishing national identity and civilised behaviour by writing in their native tongue and cultivating not only poetry, but music, dancing, fencing and other arts. This is why the Tudors set an example, and gathered round them courtiers proficient in the necessary skills. Augustans may have regarded the Elizabethans as primitive and barbaric, but emerging from the darkness of the Hundred Years War and the Wars of the Roses took longer than later critics imagined: there is no doubt that Elizabeth and her court advanced English civilisation in every way they could.

Those with the gift of golden speech were drawn to court by a complex *carrière ouverte aux talents*. Thomas Nashe expressed the general pride when he said that 'the Poets of our time . . . have cleansed our language from barbarisme, and made the vulgar sort, here in London . . . to aspire to a richer puritie of speach than is communicated with the Comminalty of any Nation under heaven.' Good livings could be won, if not in the Church after Henry VIII's reforms, but in law and medicine; but the magnet which drew Shakespeare from Stratford and Marlowe from Canterbury was the opportunity of putting their gifts of language to the service of the court. There were all kinds of ways of entering the system, in the service of one or other of the great noblemen. Spenser came in as a secretary, Daniel as a house-poet, Shakespeare as a liveried player, Herrick as a chaplain, Marlowe as a secret agent, Jonson as an antiquarian, Skelton as a tutor, Fraunce as a lawyer. Once within the system, the writer was expected to decorate and serve the court in more than one way. So many biographies in this dictionary reveal writers given to a bewildering variety of skills: we might call them polymaths.

It was a time when England was in conflict, at different times, with Ireland, Scotland, France and Spain, and various courtly groups were in conflict with each other. Intelligent young writers were therefore often involved in secret-service work for one group or another. Personal charm was also an important asset, so that there is more than a passing parallel with the popular notion of spies. Sir Francis Walsingham was certainly one of the great spy-masters, and many writers served him. It is difficult to identify agents positively, but these writers certainly served as agents: Sir Francis Bacon, Sir Francis Bryan, Sir Lodowick Bryskett, Sir William Cavendish, Sir George Buc, Samuel Daniel, Sir William Davenant, William Davison, Sir Edward Dyer, Richard Fermor, George Gascoigne, Sir John Gates, Edward Grimston, Richard Hakluyt, James Howell, Henry Herbert, first Marquess of Winchester, Ben Jonson, Christopher Marlowe, Thomas Morley, Sir Robert Naunton, Endymion Porter, Sir Walter Ralegh, Thomas Randolph the Elder, Richard Stanyhurst, Sir John Suckling, Cyril Tourneur, Sir Henry Wotton, Sir Thomas Wyatt. There were doubtless many more, as yet unidentified, and this list excludes the known recusants, conspirators, regicides and pirates. Such service exemplifies the willingness of the 'servant' to switch flexibly from battlefield to court, law court to theatre, pulpit to council.

Their biographies are shot through with twists and turns, and this is reflected in their writing. Sudden death is no stranger. There are writers who were shot, hanged, beheaded, hung, drawn and quartered; killed in battle, or brawls, stoned to death, assassinated, burned alive, poisoned, or drowned, driven insane, died of plague, smallpox, apoplexy, gaol fever, or sunstroke; died in prison, on the way to trial, of shock when suddenly reprieved; died in childbirth, committed suicide, flung over a cliff by a Cromwellian, killed by pirates, brigands, apprentices or peasants, and in one case *mirabile dictu* by Eskimos.

Against this backdrop it is a wonder that any kind of literary profession emerged. The beginnings were in the theatre, where Castiglione insisted courtiers should set an example and keep their own players. The rising Puritan tide totally disapproved of play-acting as defacing God's image, and Lord Leicester, who had joined the fashionable Puritan movement, had difficulty in explaining to critics like John Field why he kept his players; but fortunately for English literature his Renaissance instincts proved stronger than his Puritanism, and he maintained his patronage. In 1571 the Puritan majority on the London Council declared that 'all fencers, bearewards, comen players of enterludes and minstralles wandering abroad' were *ipso facto* vagabonds and liable to instant arrest, but players who wore the livery (that is were under the patronage of a nobleman) were exempt, so that every actor had an incentive to join one of the liveried companies. There were many such patrons, not only Leicester, but Effingham the Lord Admiral, Strange, Oxford, Pembroke, and Hunsdon the Lord Chamberlain. And as the Puritan tide rose, the companies sought even higher patronage in the King, Queen and Prince Henry.

But out of this ferment came the Elizabethan public – and later private – playhouse, successful until the Puritan victory in 1642. The first responsibility of a company was to its patron, performing for him at his home or on command at court. They could also be called in for other duties. Lord Hunsdon once called in Shakespeare and his company to act as supernumerary grooms to impress a visiting Spanish ambassador: for such functions the companies received handsome gratuities. But to augment their income, the companies also sought permission to play in town, or on tour. And as the tastes of the Queen and her court, and the butchers, bakers, and candlestick-makers were remarkably homogeneous, any play could be put on anywhere. When the Puritans closed the innyard theatres as centres of strong drink, prostitutes and plague, the companies built their own theatres, the Globes and Fortunes in which so much great drama was born.

It was a profitable business, attracting a diverse audience of young gentry, soldiers 'resting', students from the universities and Inns of Court, as well as the citizenry in the cheaper seats or standing in the yard. And there were ancillary awards: company-sharing made Edward Alleyn and Shakespeare prosperous; and there was a market for the printing of plays. An

actor could earn far more than the best of the skilled tradesmen, and, certainly by 1610, the best could earn over £100 a
year, in those days quite a fortune.

The printed-book market was nothing like so profitable.
The young gentry were as apt to buy a sixpenny book as go to a
play, but the general public, who could get into the Globe for a
penny, could afford for printed matter only the halfpenny
charged for broadside ballads and pamphlets. There was no
copyright system, and an author who sold all the rights in a
book for something like £6 would receive no more even if the
book proved successful, and ran into many editions. And
many printers published pirate editions leaving the author
without a penny. Attempts to augment their incomes by dedications – even multiple dedications – proved only of minimal
advantage. A writer like Thomas Churchyard, who published
many books over several decades, could not have earned more
than £10 a year; rather better than country vicars or Oxbridge
dons, but very much worse than 'solliciters and pettifoggers',
and actors.

The printed-book trade was in its infancy. Between 1500 and
1630 the total national book production of new books and new
editions rose from forty-five *per annum* to only 460, and many
of these books were not in English. And in a limited market
there were the added complications of the restrictive practices
of the Stationers Company and the censorship exercised by the
Bishop of London, where nearly all printers were established,
and the Puritan City Council. Moreover, courtly patronage
proved much less effective than in the theatre, because courtiers attached a stigma to print, as distinct from manuscript,
from which the theatre was relatively free.

In the theatre there was a decidedly ambivalent attitude to
players: despised by some as mountebanks, but admired by
others as royal servants, protected not only by their patrons
but by the discreet jurisdiction of the Master of the Revels,
who was responsible himself to the Lord Chamberlain, the
patron of Shakespeare's company. Some actors and playwrights found themselves in gaol from time to time, usually
because they had passed the bounds of tolerance and particularly at times of political sensitivity. No such balance was
available in the printed-book market, where the chief problem

was poverty and inadequate payments, so that many writers were imprisoned for debt.

Print was just *not* respectable. Gabriel Harvey, the don behind Sidney's 'Areopagus', expressed the fear in an extreme form when he asked Spenser 'What greater and more odious infamye, for on of my standinge in the Universitye and profession abroade, then to be reckonid in the Beacheroule of Inglish rymers?' The objection to the use of English occurs as late as Edmund Waller, who thought English poetry was writing in sand, a transient thing, compared with the permanence of Latin. But the real trouble was that the book market was chiefly associated with the works of the street balladists and homilectic reformers who sold at street prices. When Sir Thomas Bodley founded his great library at Oxford, despite his agreement with the Stationers Company to take whatever they had, he accepted very little in English, and positively refused to have on his shelves any street literature, which he called 'idle bookes, & riffe raffe'.

Most popular were the Bible, prayer books, the Sternhold–Hopkins psalter, and worthy, moral *vade-mecums* like John Norden's *The Pensive Man's Practice* (1584). Into this world most poets were fearful to venture, particularly those offering love-poems, popular at court, but regarded as not only frivolous but immoral by the book trade. There was a market for serious poetry, a few enlightened publishers, and others cashing in on a catchpenny noble title, assigning poems to the most worthy name in the private anthology at hand, which may well have been pirated. Some writers, seeking fame and patronage, were not averse to getting a book into print, hoping its wide circulation might net a good patron or preferment, and sometimes the ploy worked. Nevertheless, they usually blamed a friend for unauthorised publication, or found some other excuse for daring to use print. Today the question 'What have you published?' is a respectable inquiry about merit; then it was almost an insult, to be answered usually by a stout defence for going beyond the bounds of gentility.

It was a rare step when Ben Jonson not only printed but called his poems and plays *Workes*. The splendid Folio edition of Shakespeare (1623), which was accepted by the Bodleian, was a *rara avis*, justified only by the desire of his colleagues to do justice and preserve his canon. Spenser, and later Milton, defied the rules, anticipating the respectable print which, through subscription-patronage, gave later writers the chance of a profession in print. Towards the end of the period there first began to appear, from the best of the publishers, collected editions complete with portraits of the author, an act of *braggadochio* unthinkable in earlier times.

Thus, for most of the Renaissance we are dependent for most poems, and indeed many plays, on manuscripts. We know the titles of many poems and plays which, never reaching print, disintegrated in manuscript and have disappeared for ever. We cannot gauge the value of this loss, but at a time of such fertility it must have been very great indeed.

There were about 5000 writers in England at this time, many of them writing in Latin or French, and others concerned only with prose. In this dictionary are the 507 known poets and dramatists, the 10 per cent concerned with what we might call *belles-lettres*. Friendships, groups and collaborations are cross-referenced. The original spelling is used, except for *v* and *j* in their modern form, and the first preference for the spelling of names, as given in the *Dictionary of National Biography*, is generally adopted. Finally, to avoid confusion, Holland is referred to not as the Low Countries or the Netherlands, but as the 'United Provinces', the name most prevalent in the period; and Belgium is called as then the Spanish Netherlands.

I have omitted some leading courtiers, and the monarchs, Henry VIII and Elizabeth I, who wrote some poems it is true, but whose biographies do not belong in a dictionary of writers, whose chief contribution to history was in their writing.

J.W. Saunders

Classified List of Entries

Divisions of Classified System

Actors and men of the theatre (excluding dramatists)
Churchmen (Anglican, nonconformist and Roman Catholic)
Country gentry
Courtiers, diplomats and their agents
Dramatists
Historians and antiquarians
Lawyers and judges
Merchants, explorers, navigators, seamen and travel writers
Misfits (rebels, conspirators and criminals)
Musicians and composers
Physicians and surgeons
Poets
Printers, publishers and booksellers
Soldiers
Teachers (school, private and university)
Tradesmen (excluding printers)
Translators
Women writers

Classified Entries

All these writers were poets, dramatists or both. Nearly all had some connection with the court. Since the universities were intended to produce churchmen, and in smaller numbers lawyers and physicians, many writers were connected with one or more of these professions. Most writers could therefore be classified under more than one of the following classifications. Each writer, however, is included once only, in the occupation from which he made his primary earnings and for which he is now best known.

Actors and men of the theatre (excluding dramatists)

Alleyn, Edward
Armin, Robert
Barksted, William
Basse, William
Beeston, Christopher
Elderton, William
Field, Nathaniel
Henslowe, Philip
Kempe, William
Ogilby, John
Singer, John
Tarlton, Richard
Wilson, Robert, the elder

Churchmen (Anglican, nonconformist and Roman Catholic)

Abbot, John
Andrews, John
Arbuthnot, Alexander
Bale, John, Bishop of Ossory
Barry, Thomas de
Bastard, Thomas
Batman, Stephen
Baxter, Richard
Beeard, Richard
Bellenden, John
Boyd, Zachary
Bracegirdle, John
Brereley, Roger
Brice, Thomas
Carvell, Nicholas
Clarke, Samuel
Cocks, Roger
Corbet, Richard, Bishop of Norwich
Cosworth, Michael
Coverdale, Miles, Bishop of Exeter
Crashaw, Richard
Crashaw, William

Crosse, William
Crowley, Robert
Dod, Henry
Donne, John, Dean of St Paul's
Downe, John
Drant, Thomas
Earle, John
Evans, Thomas
Fisher, Fisher
Fitzgeffrey, Charles
Fletcher, Giles, the younger
Fletcher, Joseph
Fletcher, Phineas
Fletcher, Robert
Forrest, William
Fulwell, Ulpian
Goffe, Thomas
Gomersall, Robert
Gosson, Stephen
Grimald, Nicholas
Hall, Joseph, Bishop of Norwich
Harding, Samuel
Harvey, Christopher
Hausted, Peter
Herrick, Robert
Heywood, Jasper
Holland, Robert
Hopkins, John
Hume, Alexander
Huntington, John
Kethe, William
King, Henry, Bishop of Chichester
Knevet, Ralph
Lauder, William
Lever, Christopher
Loe, William
Marckant, John
Marshall, George
Mayne, Jasper
Melville, James

Neville, Alexander
Page, Samuel
Pestell, Thomas, the elder
Pestell, Thomas, the younger
Phillips, John
Pullain, John
Ramsay, Laurence
Roche, Robert
Ross, Alexander
Samuel, William
Sharpham, Edward
Slatyer, William
Smalle, Peter
Southwell, Robert
Strode, William
Wager, Lewis
Wedderburn, John
Wedderburn, Robert
Whittingham, William
Wilmot, Robert
Wisdom, Robert
Wykeham, William

Country gentry

Baker, Sir Richard
Barnfield, Richard
Beaumont, Sir John
Benlowes, Edward
Brathwait, Richard
Bryskett, Lodowick
Carew, Richard
'Cutwode, Thomas'
Daniel, George
Drummond, William, of Hawthornden
Fairfax, Edward
Habington, William
Hall, Arthur
Hawkins, Sir Thomas
Markham, Gervase
Marmion, Shackerley

Newman, Arthur
Puttenham, George
Puttenham, Richard
Salisbury, Sir Thomas
Scott, Sir Thomas
Stradling, Sir John
Vaughan, William
Wortley, Sir Francis

Courtiers, diplomats and their agents

Alexander, Sir William, Earl of Stirling
Aytoun, Sir Robert
Birkenhead, Sir John
Bryan, Sir Francis
Buc, Sir George
Carew, Thomas
Carlell, Lodowick
Cartwright, William
Chaloner, Sir Thomas, the elder
Clifford, Henry, Earl of Cumberland
Daniel, Samuel
Denham, Sir John
Dyer, Sir Edward
Fane, Mildmay, Earl of Westmorland
Ferrers, George
Fletcher, Giles, the elder
Fowler, William
Gorges, Sir Arthur
Greville, Fulke, Baron Brooke
Harington, John
Harington, Sir John
Hatton, Sir Christopher
Herbert, George
Herbert, William, Earl of Pembroke
Howard, Henry, Earl of Surrey
Lenton, Francis
Lindsay, Sir David
Maitland, Sir John, Lord Maitland of Thirlestane
Maitland, Sir Richard, Lord Lethington
Murray, Sir David

Overbury, Sir Thomas
Parker, Henry, Baron Morley
Porter, Endymion
Quin, Walter
Ralegh, Sir Walter
Roberts, Henry
Roydon, Matthew
Rudyard, Sir Benjamin
Sackville, Thomas, Earl of Dorset
Sheffield, Edmund, Baron Sheffield
Sidney, Sir Philip
Sternhold, Thomas
Stewart, William
Suckling, Sir John
Townshend, Aurelian
Vaux, Thomas, Baron Vaux of Harrowden
Vere, Edward de, Earl of Oxford
Waller, Edmund
Wotton, Sir Henry
Wyatt, Sir Thomas

Dramatists
Barry, Lodowick
Beaumont, Francis
Brandon, Samuel
Brome, Richard
Burnell, Henry
Chapman, George
Chettle, Henry
Cooke, Joshua
Daborne, Robert
Davenant, Sir William
Davenport, Robert
Day, John
Dekker, Thomas
Drue, Thomas
Fletcher, John
Ford, John
Gale, Dunstan
Garter, Bernard

Glapthorne, Henry
Greene, Robert
Hathway, Richard
Haughton, William
Heywood, John
Heywood, Thomas
Hooker, John
Hughes, Thomas
Inglend, Thomas
Jonson, Ben
Kirke, John
Kyd, Thomas
Lyly, John
Machin, Lewis
Marlowe, Christopher
Marston, John
Massinger, Philip
May, Thomas
Middleton, Thomas
Munday, Anthony
Nabbes, Thomas
Peele, George
Porter, Henry
Pound, Thomas
Rankins, William
Rowley, Samuel
Rowley, William
Sampson, William
Shakespeare, William
Sharpe, Lewis
Shirley, James
Smith, Wentworth
Stephens, John
Stevenson, William
Tailor, Robert
Tomkis, Thomas
Tourneur, Cyril
Wadeson, Anthony
Wager, William
Webster, John

Wedderburn, James
Wilkins, George
Wilson, Robert, the younger
Yarington, Robert

Historians and antiquarians
Adamson, Henry
Bolton, Edmund
Fleming, Abraham
Higgins, John
Howell, James
James, Richard
Kelton, Arthur
Lisle, William
Quarles, Francis
Warner, William
Weever, John

Lawyers and judges
Aylett, Robert
Beedome, Thomas
Brooke, Christopher
Chamberlain, Robert
Crane, Ralph
Davies, Sir John
Drout, John
Fraunce, Abraham
Fulbeck, William
Gardyne, Alexander
Hake, Edward
Hannay, Patrick
Hatcliffe, William
Hoskins, John
Hubert, Sir Francis
Kinwelmersh, Francis
Kynaston, Sir Francis
Lloyd, Ludovic
Norton, Sir Thomas
Parkes, William

Powell, Thomas
Rolland, John
Smith, Matthew
Warmestry, Gervase
Whitney, Geoffrey

Merchants, explorers, navigators, seamen and travel writers
Bagwell, William
Baker, Robert
Brinkelow, Henry
Gwyn, David
Hagthorpe, John
Hayman, Robert
Herbert, Thomas
Kidley, William
Mennes, Sir John
Neale, Thomas
Sandys, George

Misfits (rebels, conspirators and criminals)
Clavel, John
Constable, Henry
Copley, Anthony
Jenye, Thomas
Tichborne, Chidiock
Vennar, Richard
Walsingham, Edward

Musicians and composers
Bateson, Thomas
Bennet, John
Byrd, William
Dowland, John
Edwards, Richard
Farmer, John
Farrant, Richard
Ford, Thomas
Greaves, Thomas

Hilton, John
Hudson, Robert
Hudson, Thomas
Hunnis, William
Johnson, Robert
Lanier, Nicholas
Lawes, Henry
Leighton, Sir William
Morley, Thomas
Peebles, David
Redford, Henry
Robinson, Clement
Southern, John
Thorne, John
Tusser, Thomas
Tye, Christopher
Weelkes, Thomas
Whyhorne, Thomas
Wilbye, John

Physicians and surgeons

Barclay, William
Bullokar, John
Campion, Thomas
Graile, Edmund
Gwinne, Matthew
Hall, John
Mead, Robert
Moffett, Thomas
Shepherd, Luke
Twyne, Thomas
Vaughan, Henry, the 'Silurist'

Poets

This classification is very large, since it inevitably includes writers of whom we know nothing except a single book of poems. It includes however writers seeking a profession in poetry and these are asterisked.

Anton, Robert
Austin, Henry
Bancroft, Thomas
Bansley, Charles
*Barnes, Barnabe
Best, Charles
Bosworth, William
*Breton, Nicholas
Carliell, Robert
Chalkhill, John
Chester, Robert
*Churchyard, Thomas
Collins, Thomas
*Cowley, Abraham
Craig, Alexander
Cranley, Thomas
Davison, Francis
Day, James
Deloney, Thomas
Dennys, John
Dickenson, John
*Drayton, Michael
Edwards, Thomas
Elviden, Edmund
Felltham, Owen
Ferris, Richard
Fowler, Abraham
Freeman, Thomas
Gifford, Humphrey
Gordon, Patrick
Gosynhyll, Edward
Grange, John
Gresham, James
Grove, Mathew
Hanson, John
Hawes, Edward
Heath, John
Heywood, Robert
Holland, Hugh

Hornby, William
Howell, Thomas
Hutton, Henry
Jenynges, Edward
Kendall, Timothy
Kennedy, John
Lane, John
Lewicke, Edward
Lilliat, John
Linche, Edward
*Lodge, Thomas
*Lok, Henry
Lyon, John
Maxwell, James
Melbanke, Brian
Middleton, Christopher
*Milton, John
Moone, Peter
More, Edward
*Nashe, Thomas
Nicolls, Richard
Nixon, Anthony
Nugent, Richard
Parrot, Henry
Partridge, John
Petowe, Henry
Peyton, Thomas
Randolph, Thomas
Reynolds, Henry
Robinson, Richard of Alton
Rowlands, Samuel
Scoloker, Anthony
Scott, Alexander
Sempill, Robert, the younger
Sharpe, Roger
Shirley, Henry
Smith, William
*Spenser, Edmund
Steward, Sir Simeon
Storer, Thomas

Stubbs, Philip
Taylor, John, the Water Poet
*Turberville, George
Vaughan, Thomas
Walton, Izaak
Warren, Arthur
Warren, William
*Watson, Thomas
West, Richard
*Whetstone, George
*Wither, George
Woodhouse, Peter
Yates, James

Printers, publishers and booksellers

Awdelay, John
Baldwin, William
Copland, Robert
Crouch, Humphrey
Day, Angell
Fowler, John
Nelson, Thomas
Proctor, Thomas
Robinson, Richard, of London
Segar, Francis

Soldiers

Andrewe, Thomas
Blenerhasset, Thomas
Broke, Arthur
Chute, Anthony
Conway, Sir John
Gascoigne, George
Godolphin, Sidney
Grahame, Simion
Kyffin, Maurice
Lovelace, Richard
Lower, Sir William
Mercer, William

Montgomerie, Alexander
Mure, Sir William
Pricket, Robert
Rich, Barnabe
Rich, Richard
Sempill, Robert, the elder
Tooke, George
Ward, John
Willoughby, Henry
Wilson, Arthur

Teachers (school, private and university)

Aleyn, Charles
Browne, William, of Tavistock
Davies, John, of Hereford
Griffin, Bartholomew
Harvey, Gabriel
Hawkins, William
Jackson, Richard
Marvell, Andrew
More, Henry
Mulcaster, Richard
Peacham, Henry
Percy, William
Preston, Thomas
Radcliffe, Ralph
Richards, Nathanael
Rutter, Joseph
Sabie, Francis
Udall, Nicholas
Vicars, John
Wastell, Simon
Wharton, John

Tradesmen (excluding printers)

Burrel, John
Cotton, Roger
Huggarde, Miles
Johnson, Richard

King, Humphrey
Rawkins, Thomas
Vallans, William

Translators
Belchier, Daubridgcourt
Digges, Leonard
Golding, Arthur
Googe, Barnabe
Healey, John
Holland, Abraham
Newton, Thomas
Peend, Thomas
Phaer, Thomas
Saltonstall, Wye
Stanyhurst, Richard
Stapleton, Sir Robert
Studley, John
Sylvester, Josuah
Thorie, John
Tofte, Robert
Underdowne, Thomas
Weckherlin, George Rudolph
Young, Bartholomew

Women writers
Cary, Lady Elizabeth, Viscountess Falkland
Colville, Elizabeth, Lady Colville of Culros
Dowriche, Anne
Grant, Lilian
Grimston, Elizabeth
Herbert, Mary, Countess of Pembroke
Kello, Esther
Kyme, Anne
Primrose, Diana
Speght, Rachel
Whitney, Isabella
Wroth, Lady Mary

Note on Sources

This is a list of the most useful sources of *general* biographical information about the period. Wherever possible, further references are given at the end of each biography, for those sources of particular value for each writer, and these are given in reverse chronological order of publication, as the later works are those most accessible; although the works of P. Sheavyn and F.W. Bateson should be readily available.

F.W. Bateson: *English Poetry* (1934)
H.S. Bennett: *English Books and Readers 1558-1603* (1965)
G.E. Bentley: *The Profession of Dramatist in Shakespeare's Time, 1590-1642* (1972)
D.M. Bergeron: *English Civic Pageantry 1558-1642* (1971)
F.S. Boas: *An Introduction to Tudor Drama* (1933)
F.T. Bowers: *Elizabethan Revenge Tragedy 1587-1642* (1940)
J. Buxton: *Elizabethan Taste* (1963)
L.B. Campbell: *Divine Poetry and Drama in Sixteenth Century England* (1959)
A.J. Cook: *The Privileged Playgoers: Shakespearean Theater Audiences 1576-1642* (1981)
T.W. Craik: *The Tudor Interlude* (1958)
L. Hotson: *Shakespeare's Wooden O* (1959)
D. Javitch: *Poetry and Courtliness in Renaissance England* (1978)
R.F. Jones: *The Triumph of the English Language* (1953)
B. Joseph: *Elizabethan Acting* (1951)
T.J. King: *Shakespearean Staging 1599-1642* (1970)
L.C. Knights: *Drama and Society in the Age of Jonson* (1937)
J.W. Lever: *The Elizabethan Love Sonnet* (1956)
D.L. Petersen: *The English Lyric from Wyatt to Donne* (1967)
G.Parry: *The Golden Age Restor'd: The Culture of the Stuart Court 1603-42* (1981)
E. Rosenberg: *Leicester: Patron of Letters* (1956)
J.W. Saunders: *The Profession of English Letters* (1967)
P. Sheavyn (revised J.W. Saunders): *The Literary Profession in the Elizabethan Age* (1967)

R. Southall: *The Courtly Maker* (1964)

B. Travitsky (ed): *The Paradise of Women: Writings by Englishwomen of the Renaissance* (1981)

H.R. Trevor-Roper: *The Gentry 1540-1640* (1953)

C.V. Wedgwood: *Poetry and Politics under the Stuarts* (1960)

H. Weisinger: *Tragedy and the Paradox of the Fortunate Fall* (1953)

F.P. Wilson: *English Drama 1485-1585* (1969)

The outstanding reference work remains *The Dictionary of National Biography*, first compiled 1885-1913, and in course of constant revision. Another useful work, giving lists of writings and the chief commentaries on them, is the *Cambridge Bibliography of English Literature* (1940), now available in concise form (1958).

Acknowledgements

I am aware that this book is in a long tradition first pioneered four centuries ago. All concerned with literary biographies, and particularly biographical dictionaries, owe the pioneers a great debt and I should like humbly to acknowledge the inspiration and information they have given me: John Leland's itinerant researches (1534-43); John Bale's *Summarium* (1548), *Catalogus* (1557-9), and the great *Index*, not published until 1902; Thomas Fuller's *History of the Worthies of England* (1662), Edward Phillips's *Theatrum Poetarum* (1675); William Winstanley's *Lives of the Most Famous English Poets* (1687); Gerard Langbaine's *Account of the English Dramatick Poets* (1691); Anthony Wood's *Athenae Oxonienses* (1691); and the later work of scholars like William Oldys and Thomas Warton. There is even a sense in which we can be grateful to the often scurrilous notes of John Aubrey, who had a nose for scandal even if untrue, but who draws fine caricatures, which as Aldous Huxley once remarked, are sometimes truer than portraits. This dictionary would not be complete without this verbal toast in their honour.

J.W.S.

A

ABBOT, John (fl. 1623). Educated at Sidney Sussex College, Cambridge. He was an RC who spent much of his life in Antwerp, and whose one theological poem, *Jesus praefigured* (1623) was dedicated to the couple who never did marry, Prince Charles and the Spanish Princess, Maria de Austria.

ADAMSON, Henry (d. 1639). From Perth, the son of the Provost, his talents were encouraged by William Drummond of Hawthornden, and he was destined for the pulpit, but died young leaving only a local history and one published poem *The Muses Threnodia* (1638).

ALEXANDER, Sir William, Earl of Stirling (1567?-1640). Son of Alexander Alexander of Menstrie, educated at Stirling School, and the universities of Glasgow and Leyden, and one of the rising stars of the Scottish court under James VI, which he entered as tutor to Archibald, seventh Duke of Argyll, and then to Prince Henry. When James set up court in London, he was one of the thirty-two gentlemen-extraordinary of the private chamber of Prince Henry. He married a daughter of Sir William Erskine and thereafter had a royal pension of £100 p.a. and other benefits. When Prince Henry died in 1612 he transferred to Prince Charles. He was a good Master of Requests in 1614, and Secretary of State for Scotland from 1626 to his death, and a Scottish judge. On the accession of Charles, he won other titles: Viscount Canada, Earl of Dovan, Earl of Stirling, and based himself at Argyle Castle, Stirling. He was not popular but fair, taking a loyal line as an Episcopalian against the Covenanters, his general bias being constitutional:

> And in all ages it was ever seene,
> What vertue rais'd, by vice hath ruin'd been.

Writing mattered more to him than politics. He completed Sir Philip Sidney's *Arcadia* in 1613, and helped James I write his metrical psalter (not published until 1631, but Alexander had the publishing patent). His friends were Sir Robert Aytoun, Michael Drayton and William Drummond of Hawthornden,

to whom he had remarked 'Great men in this age either respect
not our toys at all, or if they do, because they are toys, esteem
them only worthy the kiss of their hand.' He was cautious
about the stigma of print, keeping out of a collected edition his
love-poems to *Aurora* (1604). But he made use of print to make
public his 'Monarchick Tragedies', *The Tragedie of Darius*
(1603), *Croesus* (1604), *The Alexandrian* (1605) and *Julius
Caesar* (1607). Between 1614 and 1637 he worked on an 11,000
line epic *Doomes-day*, which indicated his sympathy with
those who wanted a different, indeed Augustan, relationship
with the public, describing his collected edition, *Recreations
with the Muses* (1637), as *Workes*. But, as in Nova Scotia where
he had a charter, it was unremunerating work, and he died
insolvent.

ALEYN, Charles (d.1640). Educated at Sidney Sussex College,
Cambridge, he became a schoolmaster in Cripplegate, and
tutor for Sir Edward Sherburne. He published two historical
poems, *The Battailes of Crescey and Poitiers* (1631), and
another about Henry VII and the Battle of Bosworth (1638),
and a translation from Aeneas Sylvius, *The Historie of Eurialus
and Lucretia* (1639).

ALLEYN, Edward (1566-1626). Nobody fared more pros-
perously in the theatre than Alleyn, not even Shakespeare. His
first wife was the stepdaughter of Philip Henslowe, the leading
impresario, and his second the daughter of John Donne. He
played Tamburlaine, Barabas, Faustus, Greene's Orlando, and
Hieronimo. He started with the Earl of Worcester's Players in
1583, and moved on to the Lord Admiral's in 1589, where he
connected with Henslowe, helped build the Fortune (1600),
played at the Rose, Hope and Red Bull, and became with
Henslowe Joint-Master of the Royal Game of Bears, Bulls and
Mastiff Dogs (1604). Besides his shares in the Fortune and the
Bear Garden, he had property in Southwark, Kennington and
Sussex, and bought Dulwich Manor for £10,000 and founded
almshouses and Alleyn's School. He seemed to care more for
music than for words. We know of only one play, *Tambur-
cam*, in which he had a direct hand, though he may have
contributed to others.

　　G.L. Hosking: *Life and Times of Edward Alleyn* (1952).

ANDREWE, Thomas (fl. 1604). A soldier of fortune, who had fought at Nieuport (1600). He knew Samuel Rowlands and tried his hand at one undistinguished poem in rhymed heroics, *The Unmasking of a Feminine Machiavell* (1604).

ANDREWS, John (fl. 1615). A Somerset man, educated at Trinity College, Oxford, and a clergyman in Wiltshire. He wrote a number of religious poems interspersed in his works published between 1621 and 1655, the most important of which is *The Anatomie of Basenesse* (1615). Since satire was too vehement for self-respecting clergymen he published under the initials I.A.

ANTON, Robert (fl. 1616). Probably the son of a Lincoln Recorder, he went to Magdalene College, Cambridge, and published *Philosophers Satyrs* (1616) which refers to Beaumont, Spenser, Jonson, Chapman, Daniel, and Shakespeare's *Comedy of Errors*.

ARBUTHNOT, Alexander (1538-83). After education at St Andrews University, and studying civil law at Bourges, he became a clergyman in Aberdeen, principal of King's College, Aberdeen and Moderator of the General Assembly in 1573 and 1577. But James VI, taking offence at his political enthusiasm, sent him back to his college. He had wide interests as a mathematician, philosopher, lawyer, theologian, medico and wit, and was a gentle poet who circulated in MS *On Luve, The Praises of Women* and *Miseries of a Pure Scholar*. An ancestor of Pope's Arbuthnot, he lived at Arbuthnot, Kincardineshire.

ARMIN, Robert (fl. 1610). Apprenticed as a goldsmith, he was drawn by Richard Tarlton into the life of a comic actor with the companies of Lord Chandos, and then with Shakespeare, the Lord Chamberlain's, playing Dogberry (after William Kempe's departure), Feste, Autolycus and Lear's Fool. John Davies of Hereford describes him as honest and gamesome, but Armin had a shrewd business eye, rattling off pamphlets at £2 a time and becoming a sharer in his company. He probably contributed to many plays, but also wrote solo, for the Children of the Revels, at least one play, *The Two Maides of More Clacke* (1609).

AUSTIN, Henry (fl. 1615). Known as the author of *The Scourge of Venus* (1613), published under initials much to the annoyance of Thomas Heywood because Austin's poems plagiarised his own juvenilia from Ovid, and were reprinted, despite

Heywood's protest, by the dramatist's own publisher again in 1620.

AUSTIN, Samuel, the elder (fl. 1629). Son of a Lostwithiel Cornish squire. After studying at Exeter College, Oxford, he became a clergyman in Cornwall and wrote *Austin's Urania* (published 1629), a long religious poem in which he claims friendship with Michael Drayton and William Browne.

AWDELAY, John (fl. 1559-77). One of the writer-printers who lived in the Aldergate area. He was a Freeman of the Stationers Company, and augmented his earnings by writing news-sheets, tracts, anti-RC verse and ballads, the best of which, about the reigns of Edward VI, Mary and Elizabeth, is called *The Wonders of England* (1559).

AYLETT, Robert (1583-1655?). An LLD from Trinity Hall, Cambridge, he became one of the Masters of the High Court of Chancery and delighted in 'the relaxation of poetry'. His pastoral eclogues were published in 1653 and his religious verse (the 'idle wanton toys' of his youth) in instalments from 1622, collecting in 1654: *Divine and Moral Speculations, Susanna, Joseph, Peace with her Fair Gardens,* and *Thrifty Equipage.*

AYTOUN, Sir Robert (1570-1638). From an old Norman family, the de Vesseys of Northumberland, who took their surname from lands granted by Robert Bruce in Stirling. Son of the Captain of Stirling Castle, he studied at St Andrews University and civil law in Paris, travelled extensively, and returned home an accomplished writer in Latin, Greek and French, fit to be a gentleman of the bedchamber to James I and private secretary to his Queen. He was granted a pension of £500 p.a. in 1619, and became ambassador in Germany. He continued to serve Charles I, receiving £200 p.a. as Master of Requests, Master of Ceremonies and Privy Counsellor. He wrote English poems throughout his life, such as *Inconstancy Upbraided*, but not many survive. His many friends included Sir William Alexander and William Drummond of Hawthornden.

Ed. C.B.Cullens: *English and Latin Poems of Sir Robert Ayton* (1963).

B

BAGWELL, William (fl. 1593-1655). An unsuccessful London merchant who wrote, while in prison for debt, works on astronomy, and the lugubrious doggerel poem, *The Distressed Merchant, and Prisoner's Comfort in Distress* (published 1645).

BAKER, Sir Richard (1568-1645). His father was a disinherited son of the Baker family of Sissinghurst, Kent, but Richard did well at first. Educated at Hart Hall, Oxford where he shared rooms with Sir Henry Wotton, then Theobalds Inn, and travel as far as Poland. He was MP for Arundel (1593) and East Grinstead (1597) and High Sheriff of Oxfordshire (1620). But his marriage to Margaret Mainwaring, from a destitute Shropshire family, led to debts and the Fleet prison. He had been intimate with the theatre, and writers like John Donne, Sir John Davies, and other Inns of Court friends, but he did not write seriously until imprisoned. Besides theological prose and a popular *Chronicle*, possessed later in one of its many editions by Sir Roger de Coverley and Sir Thomas Booby, he dabbled in verse, for instance translating *Cato Variegatus* (1636).

BAKER, Robert (fl. 1563). One of the gold-seekers in Guinea (1562 and 1563), but neither of his voyages was successful: in the first he got wounded in a fight, and in the second he finished up after a storm in a French prisoner-of-war camp. He left verse accounts of both ventures in Richard Hakluyt's *Voyages* (1589).

BALDWIN, William (fl. 1547). A west-countryman who studied at Oxford but found his niche as corrector of the press to Edward Whitchurch, who encouraged and published his writings. His first book, *A Treatise of Morall Phylosophie* (1547), was popular for a century, and his first poetry, *Canticles or Balades of Salomón* (1549), hardly less so. This success seems to have won him the post of organising theatrical entertainments at court for Edward VI and Queen Mary. He edited on behalf of a group including Sir Thomas Sackville, George Ferrers and John Day, the popular *Myrroure for Magistrates* (which was augmented by later writers). He also wrote four poems himself about four dead heroes, Richard, Earl of Cambridge, Thomas Montague, Earl of Salisbury, William de la Pole, Earl of Suffolk, and Jack Cade. The general theme of the whole book is to discuss the limitations imposed upon rulers by moral considerations and to lean towards constitutional monarchy. At this time he seems also to have worked as a schoolteacher and clergyman. He also wrote the elegy, *Funeralles of King Edward the Sixth*, and with his group the anti-RC satire, *Beware the Cat* (1560).

Ed. L.B. Campbell: *Myrroure for Magistrates* (1938-46).

BALE, John (1495-1563). From a poor Suffolk home, he went from a Carmelite convent in Norwich to Jesus College, Cambridge. He later converted to Protestantism, married, and met much opposition as a clergyman in Thornden, Suffolk. He was supported by Thomas Cromwell who had been attracted to him by his plays, and on Cromwell's fall fled to Germany, where he published fierce theological tracts, earning him from Thomas Fuller the name of 'Bilious Bale'. He returned to England in 1547, was again a clergyman, in Bishopstoke, Hampshire, and Swaffham, Norfolk, and was promoted in 1553 as Bishop of Ossory in Ireland, where he wrote more plays for a children's company in Kilkenny. On the accession of Mary he fled again but en route a storm drove his ship into Cornwall, where he was imprisoned for treason, but released after paying a fine of £300 and then left for the United Provinces and Basle. He returned to England under Elizabeth and spent his last years quietly as a prebendary at Canterbury.

His first writings were all plays: *A Brefe Comedy or Enterlude of Johan Baptyste Preachynge in the Wildernesse* (1538); the most famous, *Kynge Johan* (written 1534-47); and *The Three Lawes of Nature, Moises and Christe, corrupted by the Sodomytes, Pharysees and Papistes* (of uncertain date). But he spent his years in exile, most profitably for posterity, by compiling from the notes of John Leland which he borrowed from Sir John Cheke, first a *Summarium* (1548), then a *Catalogus* (1557-9), and finally an *Index* (not published until 1902). His list of 1400 English writers over fifteen centuries, including writers from the sixteenth century and the Scots, provided a literary history not surpassed until Dryden's time. Oddly for a man so 'bilious' against RCs, what moved him to anger was the destruction of the monastic libraries when besides 'popashe bellygoddes', there perished 'the worthy workes of men godly mynded, and lyvely memoryalles of our nacyon'.

T.B. Blatt: *The Plays of John Bale* (1968); H. McClusker: *Bale: Dramatist and Antiquary* (1942).

BANCROFT, Thomas (fl. 1633-58). A Derbyshire man, he was educated at Catherine Hall, Cambridge with James Shirley; Sir Aston Cokayne was his friend and neighbour. A small poet in more ways than one, he was driven by a younger son's fortune to seek preferment through print, publishing *The Gluttons Feaver* (1633), *Two Bookes of Epigrammes and Epitaphs* (1639) (in which he mentions many writers of the day), and *The Heroicall Lover* (1658).

BANSLEY, Charles (fl. 1548). Known only for his rhymed satire bitterly attacking women's fashions, *Smels of papery and develyshnes* (1548).

BARCLAY, William (1570?-1630?). One of those who praised tobacco, which was very good for the health if we do not try 'as the English abusers do, to make a smoke-box of their skull' in *Nepenthes* (Edinburgh, 1614). His authority as a Scottish doctor rested on his MA MD from Louvain, and his years as Professor of Humanity in Paris.

BARKSTED, William (fl. 1611). He started his career as a child-player in the companies of the children of the Chapel Royal and children of the Queen's revels, playing in *Epicoene*. With his colleagues, including Nathaniel Field, he went on to join the Lady Elizabeth's company in 1611 and Prince Charles's in 1613, becoming a sharer. There is no trace of any playwriting, unless he was involved with John Marston in *The Insatiate Countess*, but we have his published poems, *Mirrha* (1607) and *Hiren* (1611).

BARNES, Barnabe (1559?-1609). He was born in Yorkshire, a younger son of a Bishop of Durham, and was educated at Brasenose College, Oxford (1586). He was a soldier with Essex at Dieppe (1591). John Florio was his servitor at Oxford, his best friend was William Percy, and he knew Thomas Bastard, John Marston and John Ford. Gabriel Harvey supported him against Thomas Nashe. Along with Nashe, Gervase Markham, Florio, John Minshew, Samuel Daniel and Shakespeare, he was a protégé of Henry Wriothesley, Earl of Southampton. I still think he is the strongest candidate for the role of rival poet for the favours of Southampton in Shakespeare's *Sonnets*. What we have extant is good: *Parthenophil and Parthenophe* (1593), *A Divine Centurie of Spirituall Sonnets* (1595), and one tragedy, popular with James I, *The Divil's Charter* (1607); but there must have been a great deal more.

BARNFIELD, Richard (1574-1627). Son of a landed family from Shropshire, he went to Brasenose College, Oxford (1589) and proceeded BA in 1592, despite a temporary rustication. Friendly with Spenser, Thomas Watson, Michael Drayton and Francis Meres, his idol was Sir Philip Sidney to whose mistress, Penelope, Lady Rich, he dedicated his first book. He published three books: *The Affectionate Shepherd* (1594) (variations on Virgil's second eclogue), *Cynthia* (1595), and four pamphlets in one: *The Encomion of Lady Pecunia, The Complaint of Poetry, Conscience and Covetousness*, and *Poems in Divers Humours*, but whatever ambition this indicated dried up suddenly, and he retired to his estate at Stone, Staffordshire, and was not heard of again. His poetry is full of the country: wethers and curtail dogs, birds crying *fie* and *teru*.

BARRY, Lodowick (1580-1629). An Irish gentleman who wrote one comedy for the Revels Children, *Ram Alley* (1611), and who promised to write more, but didn't.

BARRY, Thomas de (fl. 1560). A canon of Glasgow and chief magistrate of Bothwell who wrote a MS poem on the Battle of Otterburn, but, it seems, nothing else.

BASSE, William (d. 1653?). An Oxfordshire man in service with Sir Richard Wenman and Francis Lord Norris, Earl of Berkshire, at Rycote near Oxford. He was a company-sharer, but there is no reference in Henslowe or elsewhere of any dramatic writings. He saw print as a channel for poetry, and published *Sword and Buckler* (1602), *Three Pastoral Elegies* (1602), and an elegy for Prince Henry in 1613; he also prepared for print but did not publish *Polyhymnia*. With only these tantalising facts we urgently need more information about a man who, from a sound base, had a commercial eye on literature.

BASTARD, Thomas (1566-1613). Born at Blandford, he went to Winchester School and New College, Oxford (1586) a 'perpetual fellow' (1588) but the title didn't prevent him from having to leave, as Wood says, 'being much guilty of the vices belonging to poets and given to libelling.' He won the lifelong patronage of the Lord Treasurer, Thomas Howard, Earl of Suffolk, but his livings as a clergyman were poor, and he died in a debtors' prison in Dorchester. We only have some psalms and his epigrams, *Chresteleros*, published in 1598, which were much ridiculed, but defended by his friend Sir John Harington. He found the world 'an huge task and labour infinite'.

BATESON, Thomas (1580?-1620?). A composer, who published madrigals in 1604 and 1618, and sometimes wrote his own lyrics. A B. Mus., he was organist at Chester Cathedral (1599), vicar and organist as vicar-choral of the Cathedral of the Holy and Undivided Trinity, Dublin, and had the support of Francis Leigh, first Earl of Chichester.

BATMAN, Stephen (d. 1584). A Cambridge DD from Bruton School who was domestic chaplain to Archbishop Matthew Parker (whom he helped in his library) and to the Lord Chamberlain, Henry Cary, Lord Hunsdon. He was a clergyman at Merstham and Newington Butts, Surrey. Best-known for his theological prose (1569-83), he also persisted with fourteeners in verse, particularly in *Travayled Pilgrims* (1569), a history covering the monarchs from Henry VIII to Elizabeth.

BAXTER, Richard (1615-91). We know almost everything about him thanks to his prolific MS, *Reliquiae Baxterianae*, which includes an autobiography, and copious printed work after 1650. We have a clear picture of his youth in Shropshire, the son of a squire who gambled away his inheritance. He went to Wroxeter School, with Sir Richard Newport and Richard Allestree, but not to university, having a private tutor instead. Sir Henry Herbert tried to introduce him to a courtly career, but he withdrew, preferring to be a schoolmaster at Dudley and later, by the invitation of the parish, a clergyman at Kidderminster. Though he was anti-Covenant and against the abolition of the episcopacy, he thought nonconformists had the best ministers. He refused to wear a surplice, never administered communion, nor used the sign of the cross in baptism, and thought the Anglican liturgy lawful but defective. He ultimately became a chaplain in the parliamentary army at Naseby. Though much of his writings were completed after 1650, he contributed to the Renaissance by pioneer-work in popular Christian literature and by poems in which he des-

cribes his own contradictions as an Anglican with nonconformist leanings.

BEAUMONT, Francis (1584-1616). One of the brightest stars of
his time, for whose brief life there is only Bishop Corbet's
explanation: 'Wit's a disease consumes men in few years.' He
was the son of a judge, and was born at the family seat of
Grace-Dieu in Leicestershire. He went to Broadgates Hall,
Oxford, but left on the death of his father. For a time his
circumstances were somewhat reduced and he turned to
writing, under the influence of friends at the Inner Temple and
the Mermaid group which included, besides Jonson, his
brother Sir John, William Browne and Michael Drayton.

He wrote much courtly verse, including *Salmacis and
Hermaphroditus* (1602), and one masque for the wedding of
Princess Elizabeth in 1613. But his main career was in the
theatre, to which he contributed fourteen plays in eight years.
Before he teamed up with John Fletcher, neither dramatist had
been successful. Beaumont's best previous play was *The
Knight of the Burning Pestle* (published 1613), a gentleman's
amused dismissal of a middle-class audience who, despite the
censures of the City fathers, were taking an increasing interest
in the playhouses. He thought their taste for romantic comedy
a dream-fantasy. But once the team of Beaumontn Fletcher had
been established (about 1608 in the King's company) their
plays were immediately successful. They complemented each
other's writing: while Beaumont liked run-on lines, rhyme and
prose, and disliked feminine endings and extra syllables in the
blank line, Fletcher's tastes were exactly the reverse. They
became inseparable companions. As Aubrey relates, 'They
lived together in the Banke Side, not far from the playhouse,
both batchelors, lay together, had one wench in the house,
between them, which they did so admire, the same cloaths and
cloaks &c, between them.'

They seemed to contrive a formula for the current taste in
tragi-comedy, most successfully in *Phylaster* (1608), sub-titled
Love Lies a Bleeding (it bled but did not die), and *King and No
King* (1609). But they also wrote one superb tragedy, *The
Maides Tragedy* (1611). Their characters typify the age: the
Kings have absolute power and a right to loyalty in all circum-
stances, but are bound by the laws of conscience, friendship

and honour; the heroes are wronged but gullible, faithful but vulnerable to gossip; the heroines are less stupid, but still wronged and faithful; the villain is an openly discredited instrument of evil. Available for rescue are always a blunt but reliable soldier-friend, and reference to the common sense of the public, earthy but sound. The plots are always about hypotheses: assume that these terrible events come about, what can be done to resolve the issues? In the tragedy, Evadne's murder of the King who has wronged her is the only solution, but it is nevertheless sacrilege and so deserves her death.

Beaumont was relieved from financial necessity by the death of his brother, Sir Henry, so that he and Sir John could share the estate. He continued writing, but did not publish his poems or plays in his lifetime, and he was not therefore a professional like his partner.

W.W. Appleton: *Beaumont and Fletcher* (1956); J.F. Danby: *Poets on Fortune's Hill* (1952); L.B. Wallis: *Fletcher, Beaumont and Company: Entertainers to the Jacobean Gentry* (1947).

BEAUMONT, Sir John (1583-1627). His early path is the same as his brother's Francis: to Broadgates Hall, Oxford, the Inner Temple and the Mermaid. Perhaps in 1605 it was his elder brother's lot to take main responsibility for the Leicestershire estate. He published anonymously a mock-heroic poem, *Metamorphosis of Tobacco* (1602), but all the rest stayed in MSS till published by his son, also Sir John, in 1629 under the title *Bosworth Field, with a Taste of the Variety of other Poems*. He wrote all his life, but his major work, *Crown of Thorns in eight books* is lost. He contrived to be both a Royalist courtier, in the Buckingham camp, and a religious, indeed Puritan, poet.

BEEARD, Richard (fl. 1553-74). Rector of St Mary Hill, London 1560-74 and publisher of verse with prose in theological broadsides and pamphlets, including *A Godly Psalm of Mary Queen* (1553).

BEEDOME, Thomas (d. 1641?). Only known by *Poems Divine and Humane*, posthumously published by Henry Glapthorne in 1641, a collection of songs, epitaphs, elegies, epigrams and devotional poems. He seems to have known Sir Henry Wotton, George Wither and John Donne, and so may have been an Inns of Court man.

BEESTON, Christopher (d. 1635). A comic actor and manager with the Lady Elizabeth's company, the Queen's company and 'Beeston's boys' at the Cockpit which was remodelled as the Phoenix. His writing is untraced apart from commendatory verses.

BELCHIER, Daubridgcourt (1580?-1621). Son of a Northamptonshire squire, he went to Corpus Christi College and Christ Church, Oxford, and settled in Utrecht. We have lost his poems and translations, except for one translation from the Dutch, *Hans Beer Pot* (1618).

BELLENDEN, John (fl. 1533-87). From Lothian, educated at St Andrews University and in Paris. He became Archdeacon of Murray and canon of Ross. At the court of James V he was given the task of translating Boece's *Historia Scotorum* (published 1536) and Livy, as part of the education of the Prince, and he wrote poems about his work. As an RC he fled abroad where he died.

BENLOWES, Edward (1603?-76). A gentle soul nicknamed 'Benevolus', who, after Cambridge and foreign travel, inherited the estate of his father and, according to Wood, generously helped out poets, poor scholars, debtors, ladies in need of a dowry, musicians, buffoons, flatterers and the sellers of curiosities. He was quite happy to study in the Bodleian and write religious poems, including *Theophila* (published 1652). His friends included Phineas Fletcher, Sir William Davenant and Francis Quarles.

BENNET, John (fl. 1600). A popular writer of madrigals, published with the work of others in 1599, 1601, 1614, 1616, and memorable for his cries of ecstasy – the equivalent of our pop music.

BEST, Charles (c. 1570-1627). We know nothing about him, but he was one of the talented group concerned with Francis Davison's *Poetical Rhapsodie* (1602).

BIRKENHEAD, Sir John (1616-47). The son of a Northwich saddler of genteel stock, he was educated at Northwich School and Oriel College, Oxford. He caught the eye of Archbishop Laud and served him as secretary, becoming Fellow of All Souls, and later an MP and founder-member of the Royal Society. He edited the Oxford Royalist journal, *Mercurius*

Aulicus, and is known for his wry Renaissance poetry and the encouragement he gave to other Oxford men in their 'petite employments' (Wood), and for his poems, songs and epistles.

BLENERHASSET, Thomas (1550?-1625?). Son of a Norfolk squire, he went to Cambridge and into the army, becoming captain of Guernsey Castle, and in 1610 one of the instigators of the Ulster Plantation. Apart from his MS translation of Ovid's *De Remedio Amoris* and a panegyric for Queen Elizabeth, he is best known for his continuation of the work of William Baldwin and John Higgins, published without his authority in 1578 as the 'Second Parte' of the *Myrroure for Magistrates* when he was a soldier in Germany. A friend of Sir Thomas Leighton, Governor of Guernsey, to whose wife he dedicated his panegyric, *A Revelation of the true Minerva,* which was intended as part of a greater work, not completed.

He was most interested in early heroes such as Uther Pendragon, Cadwallader and Harold, but he followed Baldwin in preferring those born to be King, and is critical of 'the present estate of *England,* in which ther be more by three parts which serve like Carpite Knightes, *Venus,* & her darlinges, then god and their Prince: who I feare are so fast seazed upon *Beauties* firste, that this example wyl be little available unto them.'

BOLTON, Edmund (1575?-1633?). Son of an RC landed family of Leicestershire, Buckingham was a distant relative. He went to Trinity Hall, Cambridge, and the Inner Temple. He is primarily known as a hard worker in historical MSS, in the age of Camden, Selden and Spelman. He was considered for the appointment of Chronologer of London, but Jonson was preferred. There was no money in history or his love-poetry, and he survived in minor courtly employment with Buckingham, falling into debt and being imprisoned in the Fleet and Marshalsea prisons. His Augustan ambitions are seen in his frustrated proposal to set up a Royal Academy, including all KGs, Chancellors, and leading noblemen and gentlemen. His poetry survives in his pastoral contributions to *England's Helicon,* Ling's book of 1600, and a few occasional pieces elsewhere. His best poems, like so many in the Renaissance, read like lists or catalogues.

BOSWORTH, William (1607-50?). From Boxworth, Cambridgeshire, he started writing when young, influenced by

Ovid, Marlowe, Sidney and Spenser, and we have a collected edition, published by a friend known only by the initials R.C. in 1651, including his *Arcadius and Septa*, *Bacchus and Diana* and *Sonnets to Aurora*.

BOYD, Zachary (1585?-1653). A Presbyterian from an Ayrshire family, he was educated at Kilmarnock School, Glasgow University (1601), St Andrews University (1603-7), settling at the Protestant college of Saumur in France, where he stayed sixteen years, but refused the post of Principal. Driven out of France by the Religious Wars, he returned to Glasgow, first as minister, then as Dean of Faculty, Rector and Vice-Chancellor. Besides theological prose, he published verse (1640-52), including the *Psalms of David in Meeter* (1648), and more in MS, including long biblical narratives such as *Zion's Flowers*.

BRACEGIRDLE, John (d. 1614). Possibly the son of a Stratford vicar, he went to Queen's College, Cambridge, and, through the agency of Thomas Sackville, Lord Buckhurst, he became vicar of Rye, Sussex, where he died. In MSS he left a blank-verse translation from Boethius, and a rhymed *Psychopharmacon*, an earnest of further endeavours which were interrupted.

BRANDON, Samuel (fl. 1598). Known only for his *Tragicomoedi of the Virtuous Octavia* (1598), an interesting play because it poses the ambivalence of a lady torn between love of Antony and jealousy of Cleopatra.

BRATHWAIT, Richard (1588?-1673). His father was Recorder of Kendal, of an established Westmorland family. He was intended for law and went to Oriel College, Oxford, Pembroke College, Cambridge, and then London. He married two Teesside ladies, first Frances Lawson of Hurworth, then a daughter of Roger Crofts of Kirtlington. He became head of the family in 1618, army captain, Deputy-Lieutenant of the county, JP, Lord of the Manor of Catterick, and a Royalist in the Civil War, surviving to the age of 85.

He appeared in print in 1611, 1614, 1615, 1617, 1618, 1619 (twice), 1620, 1621 (twice), 1625, 1630, 1631, 1632, 1634, 1635 (twice), 1636, 1638 (twice), 1640 (twice), 1641, and again after 1655; but he was not interested in earning money, and published anonymously, or under a multitude of pseudonyms, including R.B., Blasius Multibus, Musophilus, Corymbacus, Philogenes Panedonius, Museaeus Palatinus, or R.B. Gent. We might single out *The Golden Fleece* (poems of 1611); *The Poet's Willow* (pastorals of 1614); *A Strappado for the Devil* (satires modelled on Wither, of 1615); *Nature's Embassie* (odes and pastorals collected in 1621); and the doggerel account of travels in England, *Barnabees Journal* (1638).

M.W. Black: *Richard Brathwait: An account of his life and Works* (1928).

BRERELEY, Roger (1586-1637). This fiery son of a Rochdale farmer set up as a Puritan preacher at Grindleton Chapel, Mitton-in-Craven: hence his group of Calvinists was known as the Grindletonians. He was tried in an ecclesiastical court, but the charge against him was not proved. True to the age, besides his sermons, we have theological verse, not published in his lifetime.

BRETON, Nicholas (1545?-1626?). One of the first writers to seek out, unsuccessfully, a profession in print; his interest in poetry declined after 1600. He was the son of a wealthy London merchant who died when Breton was only thirteen, leaving him substantial property and land.

Unfortunately his mother married George Gascoigne who spent most of the estate. Breton probably went to Oriel College, Oxford, married a Cripplegate girl, and settled down to find preferment. He tells us that in his youth he shared, with courtly dames, all the pleasures of the court, 'music, steeds, rapier and arms, all gallant games', and was much in demand:

> The next day after he had written this passion of Love, dyvers Gentle-women being then in the house: he was intreted by two or three of them at once, to make some verses: and one among the rest, being very desirous to have her request fulfilled, brought him a Pen and ynke, and Paper: with earnest intreaty, to make some verses, upon what matter he thought best himselfe.

He never forgot his gentility, stressing in title-pages his rank of *Gentleman*. He used his name openly, or at least the initials N.B. or B.N., or the anagram Salochin Treboun, only rarely adopting pseudonyms (Bonerto or Pasquil) for satire. He attributed his failure in about 1592 to 'the indiscretion of his youth, the malice of envy, and the disgrace of ingratitude', but it is difficult to relate these terms to any precise events. He received no courtly preferment of any kind, and was dependent on occasional patronage, his only substantial patron being Mary Sidney, Countess of Pembroke.

He appeared voluminously in print, in 1577, 1582, 1592, 1595, 1600 (four times), 1601 (twice), 1602 (thrice), 1604, 1605 (twice), 1614, 1616 and 1626. His own publisher, Richard Jones, purloined poems which appeared in various anthologies: *Bryton's Bowre of Delights* (1591) (interesting that Jones should think Breton eminent enough to put in the title, though there were only four poems by Breton, and Jones included poems by Edward de Vere, Earl of Oxford, Henry Howard, Earl of Surrey, Sidney and probably Ralegh), *The Arbor of Amorous Devices* (1597), *England's Helicon* (1600), *Phoenix Nest* (1593), and song-books. Breton was one of the few writers to be respected by Jonson, and he was praised by Francis Meres and Sir John Suckling.

But the printed-book market was no substitute for preferment, providing only £6 per book, or £2 per pamphlet plus dedication fees, if any. Breton was not gregarious, and had few friends. Nashe derided him as too commercial. In one of the Countess of Pembroke's poems, which remained in MSS, he summed up a disappointing career:

> My infant's yeares myspente in chilidishe toyes,
> My riper age in rules of little reasone;
> My better yeares in all mistaken joyes,
> My present time, – Oh most unhapie seasone! –
> In fruiteles labours and in ruthles love:
> Oh what an honor hath my harte to prove

But like many others he found consolation in religion:

>   I seek no prince's power,
> No miser's wealth, nor beauty's fading gloss,
> Which pamper sin, whose sweets are inward sour,
> And sorry gains that breed the spirit's loss:
> No, my dear Lord, let my Heaven only be
> In my love's service, but to live to thee.

Ed. J. Robertson: *Nicholas Breton: Poems not hitherto reprinted* (1952).

BRICE, Thomas (d. 1570). A Protestant who was a wanted man under Queen Mary because he imported books from Wesel. He came into his own with Queen Elizabeth, being ordained in 1560, and publishing in 1559 *A Compendious Register in Metre* of martyrs of the period 1555-8. His *Courte of Venus Moralized* (1567) and *Songs and Sonnettes* (1568) are lost.

BRINKELOW, Henry (d. 1646). Son of a Berkshire farmer, he began life as a Franciscan friar but, on conversion to Anglicanism, he married and became a mercer in London. He wrote verse satire on socio-religious subjects under the name Roderigo Mars. When driven into exile in Turin and Nuremburg, he published in Geneva *The Complaynt of Roderigo Mars* (1545?).

BROKE, Arthur (d. 1563). A soldier who died young 'drownded in passing to New Haven' for service overseas, presumably a scion of the Brooke family. All we have is his translation of Launay and Belle-Forest's version of the Bandello story, *The Tragicall Historye of Romeus and Julieit* (1562), a source Shakespeare revised.

BROME, Richard (d. 1652?). A long life beginning as Ben Jonson's servant before 1614. Not all of Jonson's friends liked him: Thomas Randolph, for instance, didn't. But his privileged position brought him into contact with Francis Beaumont, Thomas Dekker, John Ford, James Shirley and Sir Aston Cokayne. He wrote for the theatre, either solo, or with Jonson's son Benjamin or Thomas Heywood, and probably others. He wrote for the Globe and Blackfriars and the King's company; for the Cockpit and Salisbury Court and the Queen's company and Beeston's Boys: in all twenty-three comedies in thirteen years. He thought of himself as a *playmaker*, taking starting ideas from Shakespeare and Jonson's comedies of humours. Perhaps the most successful were *The Northern Lass* (published 1632), *The Sparagus Garden* (published 1640), *The Antipodes* (published 1640) and *A Jovial Crew* (published 1652). Many plays not printed have been lost. He also wrote occasional verses.

R.J. Kaufmann: *Richard Brome, Caroline Playwright* (1961).

BROOKE, Christopher (d. 1628). Son of a rich merchant and Lord Mayor of York, he went to Trinity College, Cambridge

and Lincoln's Inn, where he shared chambers with John
Donne, and became a bencher and summer reader; he then
moved into Parliament, as MP for York (1604-26) and Newport, Isle of Wight (1624). Besides Donne, his brilliant circle
included William Browne, John Selden, Michael Drayton, Ben
Jonson, John Davies of Hereford, and many others, all with
some attachment to Prince Henry. He married Mary Jacob and
lived in Drury Lane. His MS verse was all occasional: elegies,
eclogues, an epithalamium, commendatory verses.

BROWNE, William, of Tavistock (1591-1643?). Son of the Latin
playwright and poet who was also headmaster and canon of
Westminster. He went to Tavistock School, Exeter College,
Oxford, Clifford's Inn and the Inner Temple. He returned to
Oxford in 1624 as the tutor of Robert Dormer, and then moved
to a comfortable position as tutor in the family of William
Herbert, third Earl of Pembroke. He had an antiquarian interest in writers from Devon. He is most remembered as one of
the brilliant company at Lincoln's Inn. He published *Brit-
tania's Pastorals* (1613-16) and wrote a masque, *Ulysses and
Circe*, produced in 1615. With Christopher Brooke, George
Wither and John Davies of Hereford he published *The Shepheards Pipe* (1614), dedicated to Edward, Lord Zouche. He
wrote everything: sonnets, epistles, elegies, visions, Bac-
chanalian verses, epigrams and epitaphs, of which perhaps the
most famous is his tribute to Mary Sidney:

> Underneath this sable hearse
> Lies the subject of all verse;
> Sidney's sister, Pembroke's mother:
> Death, ere thou hast slain another
> Fair and learned and good as she,
> Time shall throw another dart at thee

BRYAN, Sir Francis (d. 1550). Born into the highest society, his
grandfather was a Chief Justice, his father a Buckinghamshire
knight, his mother was a Bourchier and sister of Lord Berners
(and at one time governess to the Princesses Mary and Elizabeth), and Anne Boleyn was a relative, probably a cousin. For
some reason history has not regarded him highly, but he was a
brilliant leader at the court of Henry VIII.

After Oxford, he was a naval captain under Sir Thomas
Howard, and at court a cupbearer, Master of Entertainments,

Master of the Toyles, and a secret agent earning a pension in 1520 as a cipherer. He was knighted for courage in Brittany under the Earl of Surrey in 1522. One of the Sheriffs for Hertfordshire and Essex 1523, and a dissolute companion of his King's leisure hours, he was sent on many missions. He failed to get the agreement of the Pope to Henry's divorce from Katherine of Aragon. He was ambassador in France, with Sir Nicholas Carew, his sister's husband. He willingly faked a quarrel with George Boleyn to enable Henry to get rid of Anne Boleyn and acted as intermediary with her successors, Jane Seymour and Anne of Cleves. He loyally supported his monarch against the Pilgrimage of Grace in 1536, and was MP for Buckinghamshire (1542-4) and a Privy Counsellor. He was the chief mourner at the funeral of Henry VIII.

Afterwards, he transferred his loyalty to the Duke of Somerset, and served him as a commander, becoming Lord Marshal of Ireland and Chief Justice; he was even willing, his first wife having died, to marry for his patron the Countess of Ormonde. Still sturdy, despite advancing years, he died suddenly, nobody knows of what.

Looking back, we know that Sir Thomas Wyatt was the leader of the poets at the court of Henry VIII. Some Elizabethans were misled by the higher rank of Henry Howard, Earl of Surrey, who was Wyatt's pupil. But Michael Drayton thought that, of the poets preserved in Tottel's *Songes and Sonettes* (1557), Bryan was the chief: Wyatt certainly held him in high regard. He was also keen on Guevara, who influenced Lyly towards Euphuism, and translated one of his books, *A Dispraise of the Life of a Courtier*, and persuaded his uncle, John Bourchier, to do another translation of Guevara. It has proved impossible to identify which poems were whose in Tottel.

BRYDGES, Grey, fifth Baron Chandos (1579-1621). The friend of Essex and Southampton who survived, despite arrest, the Essex insurrection of 1601 and who became a favourite courtier with James I, and served in the United Provinces (1610). His main interests were literary and dramatic. He kept his own players, held great state at Sudeley Castle as 'King of the Cotswolds', and doubtless had a hand in many masques and entertainments.

BRYSKETT, Lodowick (1547-1612?). Son of an Italian merchant with relatives in Florence, he went to Tonbridge School and Trinity College, Cambridge (1559). He was clerk of the council under Sir Henry Sidney in Ireland, and accompanied Sir Philip Sidney abroad (1572-4). He had successive promotions in Ireland, held large estates in Dublin, Cavan and Cork, and was secretary of the Munster Council at £200 p.a., with Spenser as his deputy. Spenser not only taught him Greek but involved him in an Irish literary group, which also included Dr Long, Archbishop of Armagh, Captain Christopher Carleil, Captain Thomas Norris, Captain Warham St Leger, and others. When he fled in the rising of Tyrone in 1598, he received a pension from Queen Elizabeth, and served Sir Robert Cecil as secretary and agent in Flanders, being taken prisoner there by the Spaniards. He subsequently retired to Ireland. His writings were occasional, including an elegy for Sidney, but he also translated Giraldo's *A Discourse of Civill Life* (not published for twenty years, in 1606).

BUC, Sir George (d. 1623). His family were on the Yorkist side at Bosworth, but the Howard influence converted this family with large estates in Yorkshire and Suffolk to the Tudor cause. He was educated at Chichester School, becoming Master in 1570. He was at Thavies Inn and the Middle Temple (1585), and was fortunate in his attachments: Sir Edward Stafford, ambassador in Paris; Sir Francis Walsingham, who trained him as an agent; and Sir Robert Cecil. He was on the Cadiz expedition (1596), an MP, and envoy. He served James I as first Deputy Master of the Revels under Edmund Tylney; he was appointed Master in 1608, but he went mad and was replaced by Sir John Astley. Unfortunately, his MSS were destroyed by fire, and we have nothing extant by him in drama, but we do have his eclogue, *Daphnis Polystephanos* (1604), a history of Richard III, and a treatise in which he advocated for London *The Third Universitie of England* (1615).

BULLOKAR, John (fl. 1622). A Chichester doctor, chiefly known as the lexicographer of *An English Expositor* (1616), he also wrote a life of Christ in verse, *A True Description* (published 1618).

BURNELL, Henry (fl. 1641). The son of a landed Leicester family, he married the daughter of Sir James Dillon, Earl of

Roscommon, and appears to have been one of the writers for Ogilby's theatre in Dublin. His *Landgartha* was acted there in 1639, and published in Dublin in 1641. Probably a casualty of the 1641 troubles.

BURREL, John (fl. 1690). A goldsmith of Edinburgh who became a printer in the King's Mint and is known for two poems, the printed *Description* of Queen Anne's entry to Edinburgh (1590) and the MS *Passage of the Pilgrims*.

BYRD, William (1540-1623). The greatest of the Elizabethan composers was probably born in Lincoln, and studied music under Thomas Tallis. He became organist of Lincoln Cathedral as early as 1563 and a gentleman and organist of the Chapel Royal (1569). He held the monopoly, with Tallis, of music publishing from 1575, was connected with Henry Cary, Lord Hunsdon and the Earl of Worcester, and was therefore a playhouse sharer. His madrigals, psalms and songs poured into print in 1587, 1588, 1589, 1591, 1610 and 1611, and more was left in MSS. He wrote or translated his own lyrics.

C

CAMPION, Thomas (1559?-1634). Son of a Chancery clerk of Hertfordshire, he went to Peterhouse, Cambridge, won an MD abroad, and then proceeded to Gray's Inn, where he became involved in drama, writing four masques which were presented there or in Whitehall or other courtly venues, to which he contributed not only words but music. He published his *Ayres* in 1601, 1612, 1613 and c. 1617, and only had recourse to a medical practice late in his life. His songs express the age, even though as an RC, he lived a harassed life, particularly about the time of the murder of Sir Thomas Overbury.

E.Lowbury, T.Salter and A. Young: *Thomas Campion, Poet, Composer, Physician* (1970); M.M. Kastendieck: *England's Musical Poet: Campion* (1938).

CAREW, Richard (1555-1620). At eleven years already at Christ Church, Oxford, and took over responsibility for his Cornish landed estates while still in his teens. He was at Middle Temple in 1574. He was JP (1581), Sheriff (1582), High Sheriff (1586), MP for Saltash (1584) and for St Michael's (1587), Deputy Lieutenant, and also served as an army colonel under Ralegh. As one of the founder-members of the Society of Antiquaries, he contributed a Survey of Cornwall. He was the friend of Sir Henry Spelman and William Camden. He translated part of Tasso's *Godfrey of Bulloigne* (1594), and was familiar with Greek, Italian, German, French and Spanish. He left many lyric poems in MS.

A.L. Rowse: *Tudor Cornwall* (1949).

CAREW, Thomas (1595?-1640). Richard Carew's cousin, and son of a Master in Chancery; his mother was a Rivers. After Merton College, Oxford and the Middle Temple, he was taken up by Sir Dudley Carleton, whom he served as secretary in Venice and Turin, but who dismissed him for making aspersions about himself and his wife. He was in Paris with Lord Herbert of Cherbury in 1619, and in 1628 became a Gentleman of the King's Privy Chamber and sewer-in-ordinary. He was intimate with many writers, including Sir William Davenant and Sir John Suckling. He wrote songs, occasional verses, psalms and masques.

CARLELL, Lodowick (fl. 1629-64). Gentleman of the Bows and Groom of the Chamber at the court of Charles I, he wrote plays – eight of them for the King's company at the Blackfriars, though he claimed they were not 'design'd to travel so far as the common stage.' However that may be, they were published a few years later. One might single out his tragi-comedy, *The Deserving Favourite* (1629), his most popular effort, *The Fool who would be a Favourite*, and the tragedy *Osmond*.

Ed. C.A. Gray: *Lodowick Carlell* (1905).

CARLIELL, Robert (d. 1622?). We know nothing of him but for his long patriotic and Anglican work, which attacks heathens, Turks, Papists, sectaries and tobacco, *Britaines Glorie* (1619).

CARTWRIGHT, William (1611-43). Dr John Fell said of him that he 'was the utmost man could come to'. Educated at Cirencester School, Westminster School, and Christ Church, Oxford, he was ordained, and became junior proctor at Oxford, and a member of the Council of War when, much to the grief of King Charles, he died of camp fever. A linguist, orator, poet and playwright, he was much commended by those who knew him: Jasper Mayne, Alexander Brome, Henry Vaughan. Izaak Walton produced a collected edition of his works in 1651. He wrote elegies, love-verses, epistles, translations and at least four plays, of which the tragi-comedy, *The Royal Slave*, acted before the King and Queen at Oxford in 1636, was the most promising.

CARVELL, Nicholas (d. 1566). Or 'Master Cavyl'. He was educated at Eton and King's College, Cambridge. He contributed to the 1563 edition of *Myrroure for Magistrates*, which supported the general line that

the Scriptures do forbyd us to rebell, or forcibly to withstand Princes, though they commaund unjust thinges: yet in any case we may not do them, but receyve quietly at the prince's hand whatsoever punishment God shall suffer to be layed upon us for our refusall: God will suffer none of his to be tempted above their strength.

CARY, Lady Elizabeth, Viscountess Falkland (1586-1639). While her husband, Lucius's lyrical poems were a minor part of his large career, as was their son's, another Lucius, Lady Elizabeth found writing a necessary refuge from a tyrannical mother when her husband was abroad. She wrote plays and poems as a pastime; her tragedy, *Miriam the Fair*, was published in 1613.

CHALKHILL, John (fl. 1600). A friend of Spenser, who wrote a talented pastoral history, *Thealma and Clearchus*, edited for print in 1678 by Izaak Walton who knew him in his youth and thought highly of him.

CHALONER, Sir Thomas, the elder (1521-65). Son of a London mercer, he studied at Oxford and the Inns of Court, started courtly service in 1541 with Sir Thomas Knyvet, who was then ambassador to the Emperor Charles V. Remarkably, he had an unbroken service through the reigns of Henry VIII, Edward VI, Queen Mary and Queen Elizabeth: clerk of the Privy Council, MP for Wigan (1545), Lancaster (1547), Knaresborough (1555), envoy, ambassador to Spain (1561-4), and a soldier with Cromwell in Scotland. His friends were Sir John Cheke and Sir Walter Haddon; his chief mourner was Lord Burghley. Among his poems are his contributions to the 1559 *Myrroure for Magistrates*, in which he makes Richard II an unmitigated monster. Henry Peacham held him as a model of ideal nobility in *The Compleat Gentleman* (1662).

CHAMBERLAIN, Robert (fl. 1640-60). Son of a gentleman from Standish, Lancashire, he became clerk to Peter Ball, Queen Henrietta Maria's Solicitor-General. Ball sent him, at the age of thirty to Exeter College, Oxford, where he became a leading member of the wits of Royalist Oxford, writing epigrams, epitaphs and occasional verse, reaching print in 1638 and 1640, and publishing a comedy, *The Swaggering Damsel*, in 1640.

CHAPMAN, George (1559?-1634). From Hitchin, he may have been educated at Oxford or Cambridge. He seems to have entered courtly service via the army, serving under Sir Francis de Vere in the United Provinces, and perhaps also under Ralegh, in whose camp he certainly appears, with his friend Matthew Roydon. Like Marlowe, whom he much admired, and Shakespeare, his first efforts, on a path which won him the patronage of the Countess of Walsingham, and Lucy, Countess of Bedford, the talented niece of Sir John Harington, were in printed poetry: *The Shadow of Night* (1594), from Ovid's *Banquet of Sence* (1595) – the book which influenced Robert Allot in *England's Parnassus* (1600) to put him in the first ten of his quoted poets – and a completion of Marlowe's *Hero and Leander* (1598).

By 1595 he had found his way into the theatre, where he wrote twenty-one plays, either solo or in collaboration, in fifteen years. He seems to have worked with Paul's Children, the King's company, with Henslowe's group, and with the Children of the Revels and the Queen's company. Among his collaborators were William Rowley, and Ben Jonson with John Marston (producing the play *Eastward Hoe* (1605), which offended the Privy Council and got them all into prison). His great plays were both two-part: *Bussy d'Amboise* and the *Conspiracie and Tragedie of Charles Duke of Byron* (which offended the French ambassador and got him into trouble again). His lighter touch is evidenced in *All Fools* and *The Gentleman Usher*. (All these plays date between 1604 and 1608.)

He was a better scholar than many of his fellow-writers and, as a sewer-in-ordinary to Prince Henry, he was socially higher, though in financial terms he was not much better off. He produced the famous translation of Homer's *Iliad* (issued in parts from 1598, and as a complete edition in 1609, with multiple dedications), and the *Odyssey*, complete in two stages by 1614; a complete Homer appeared in 1616. There is no evidence that his work brought him any financial security in the way that Homer made Pope's fortune. He wrote a masque for the wedding of the Princess Elizabeth in 1613, and another, *Andromeda Liberata*, for the wedding of the Duke of Somerset in 1614 (both Inns of Court performances). He also translated Ovid, Hesiod and Juvenal. He produced much romantic and religious verse between 1610 and 1614, some of which was published. As the years went on, both poems and plays become much less frequent and more didactic.

Like Marlowe, he specialised in drama with heroes to whom 'tis immortality to die aspiring.' They tend to be arrogant stoics, above fear and authority, whom only fate can overcome. He embroiders his stories with the supernatural; and there is a tendency, on the death of a main character, for forgiveness all round. He states a case for supermen who will restore a proper harmony. The more stridently he asserted this theme, the less logical his plots.

Farewell, brave relics of a complete man,
Look up and see thy spirit made a star;
Join flames with Hercules, and when thou sett'st
Thy radiant forehead in the firmament,
Make the vast crystal crack with thy receipt;
Spread to a world of fire, and the aged sky
Cheer with new sparks of old humanity.

C. Spivak: *George Chapman* (1967); M.MacLure: *George Chapman: A Critical Study* (1966).

CHESTER, Robert (fl. 1586-1601). He was in the household of Sir John Salusbury, in Denbighshire, and his *Love's Martyr* was published in 1601 in the anthology, *The Phoenix and the Turtle*, and reissued in the *Anuals of Great Britaine* (1611).

CHETTLE, Henry (d. 1607?). The son of a London dyer, he was apprenticed to and then became a stationer, in partnership with William Hoskins and John Danter, but he was unhappy in the trade. Having published Greene's *Groats-worth of Wit* (1592), he felt bound to apologise for Greene's slur upon Shakespeare 'because myself have seene his demeanour no lesse civill than he excellent in the qualitie he professes.' Nashe saw him as a scholarly ally of Gabriel Harvey. He took to the theatre to earn money, was in prison for debt (1599), and had a hand in as many as fifty plays in five years for Henslowe and the Admiral's company. Of his solo plays only *The Tragedy of Hoffman* survives, in an unsatisfactory text, (1631); few of his plays reached print, exceptions are *Robin Hood* (with Anthony Munday, 1601), *Patient Grissill* (with Thomas Dekker and William Haughton, 1603), and *Lady Jane* (with Dekker, Thomas Heywood, Wentworth Smith and John Webster, 1607). He also collaborated with Michael Drayton, Robert Wilson the younger in *Black Batman of the North*, and John Day, Ben Jonson and Richard Hathway.

CHURCHYARD, Thomas (1520?-1604). A Shrewsbury man, he entered courtly service as a page in the household of Henry Howard, Earl of Surrey, at the court of Henry VIII. He was a soldier in Scotland, Ireland, the United Provinces and France, where he was captured twice. Courtly preferment, however, was denied him, but he was given a pension in 1592 from Queen Elizabeth. In the meantime, he tried to make a living as a professional writer, but of his sixty books written in fifty years, through the reigns of Edward VI – James I, he probably earned only about £10 a year. He was much respected as an ancient of literature: to Spenser he was 'Old Palaemon' and Nashe thought him an 'aged Muse that may well be grandmother to our grandeloquentest poets at this present.' And he knew Surrey, Burghley, Ralegh, Whetstone, amongst others. He was published in Tottel's miscellany in 1557; his *Shore's Wife* in the 1563 *Myrroure for Magistrates* was probably the best piece in the entire work, while his best work was in 1593, *Churchyards Challenge*. Unfortunately, his verse had more in common with Skelton than with the Renaissance, in which he was at best a 'royster'.

CHUTE, Anthony (d. 1595?). An attorney's clerk and then soldier in Portugal, he was Gabriel Harvey and Thomas Churchyard's satellite in his occasional verse and writings on heraldry.

CLARKE, Samuel (1599-1683). Son of a Wolston, Warwickshire, clergyman, he went to Coventry School and Emmanuel College, Cambridge. He married the daughter of a clergyman and had livings in Warwickshire and Cheshire. He was attached to Fulke Greville, and so it is not surprising that he was one of fifty-seven ministers who in 1649 protested against regicide, for all his Puritanism. Earlier he was an industrious writer of biography; in verse we have his *Saints Nosegay, or a Poesie of 741 Spiritual Flowers* (1642).

CLAVEL, John (1603-42). The son of a landed family, he was disowned by them and took to highway robbery. When caught and condemned to death in 1627, he was saved by King Charles and his Queen who wanted to see published his verse *Recantation of an ill-led Life* (1628). He subsequently wrote a play for the King's company at Blackfriars, *The Soddered Citizen* (c.1630).

CLIFFORD, Henry, fifth Earl of Cumberland (1591-1643). After education at Christ Church, Oxford, he became a leading courtier, marrying Lady Frances Cecil, daughter of Robert, Earl of Salisbury; his sister Margaret married Sir Thomas Wentworth, who was his lifelong friend. He supported the Royalist cause, was MP for Westmorland, a member of the Council for the North, Joint Lord Lieutenant of Northumberland with Cumberland and Westmorland, and

Governor of Carlisle. But he was not of a 'martial temper', was rather disastrous in the field and in council, and should have been left alone with his horses, hunting, and his interests in architecture, poetry and mathematics. We have his *Poetical Translations of some Psalms and the Song of Solomon*.

COCKS, Roger (fl. 1635). A Suffolk clergyman, educated at Trinity College, Cambridge, he published in 1630 *Hebodo- mada Sacra*, seven poetical meditations on Matthew 2.

COLLINS, Thomas (fl. 1615). He knew Samuel Rowlands and Joseph Beaumont, admired Sidney, Spenser and Drayton, and had the Countess of Huntingdon as a patron, but we know nothing of his origins. He published *The Penitent Publican* (1610), and a pastoral elegy, *The Teares of Love* (1615).

COLVILLE, Elizabeth, Lady Colville of Culros (fl. 1603). As Elizabeth Melville she wrote *Ane Godlie Dreame*, possibly a retelling of an old story, published in 1603.

CONSTABLE, Henry (1562-1613). The son of Sir Robert Constable of Newark, he went to St John's College, Cambridge, and became the agent in Paris of Sir Francis Walsingham, and later Essex, who knighted him unofficially. At some stage he was converted to Roman Catholicism, and joined the French, hoping to detach the English from the Spaniards, receiving a pension from the French King; he was papal envoy in Edinburgh. He was unable to detach James I from the English Presbyterians, and died in exile in Liège. He was the friend of Sir Philip Sidney, and his mistress, Penelope Rich, as well as other ladies at court, and Sir John Harington and Edmund Bolton. His *Diana* (published 1592, revised 1594) was probably fictional, but nevertheless these lyrics, and other published in miscellanies, were much respected, although some think the true Constable is preserved in his MS *Spirituall Sonnettes*.

J. Grundy: *Poems of Henry Constable* (1964).

CONWAY. Sir John (d. 1603). Son of a Warwickshire knight, his mother was a Verney. He married Eleanor, the daughter of Fulke Greville. His experiences as a commander with Leicester, and Governor of Ostend, and particularly as a prisoner of war, turned him to religion, and he published *Meditations and Praiers* and *Poesie of floured Praiers* (1611).

COOKE, Joshua (fl. 1614). He wrote for Greene, who played

Bubble, the *City gallant*, and for the Queen's company, *Greene's Tu Quoque* (1614) and probably also *Fyftie epigrams* (1604).

COPLAND, Robert (fl. 1508-47). Trained by Caxton and Wynkyn de Worde, he became a bookseller and stationer as well as a printer. He wrote fifteen books, chiefly prose, philosophical and translated romances, but also coarse but entertaining verse, *The Hye Way to the Spyttel House* and *Jyl of Brentford's Testament* (dates not known).

COPLEY, Anthony (1567-1607?). Son of Sir Thomas Copley, one of the most eminent RC exiles, he was left at Furnivalls Inn but 'stole away' to join his parents in Rouen. He was employed by the Prince of Parma and then the King of Spain until 1589. When he returned to England he was of course highly suspect, frequently imprisoned on various charges, and his character didn't help: he was impetuous, a skilled duellist, and he once threw his sword at a parish clerk. He was loyal to Queen Elizabeth, disliked Jesuits, and was a patriotic RC, but finally he ruined himself by backing a conspiracy to get Lady Arbella Stuart on the throne, and had to spend the rest of his life in exile. He published *Wits, Fittes and Fancies* (1595) and *A Fig for Fortune* (1596).

CORBET, Richard, Bishop of Norwich (1582-1635). Son of a Surrey nurseryman who could afford to send him to Westminster School and, in 1598, Broadgates Hall and Christ Church, Oxford. He was a wit at the university and in the pulpit, perhaps timid and nervous in matters of state, but fun-loving, good-humoured, and a member of Ben Jonson's group; much the most literary of the churchmen. Thanks to Buckingham, he rose from the posts of Dean of Christ Church and vicar of Cassington in Oxfordshire, to a royal chaplaincy and the bishoprics of Oxford (1628) and Norwich (1632). His friends collected and published in 1648 his *Certain Elegant Poems*, in which *Fairies Farewell* laments the departure of fairies under Puritanism.

COSWORTH, Michael (b. 1568). Son of a London mercer, cousin of Richard Carew, he was educated at St John's College, Cambridge, and he circulated verses, particularly psalms, in his Cornish parish.

COTTON, Roger (fl. 1596). One of five bright sons of a Whitchurch squire (another became Lord Mayor of London), after Whitchurch School he became a draper in London. A friend of Hugh Broughton, who turned him towards religious scholarship, he published two poetic tracts: *An Armor of Proofe* (1596) and dedicated to Drake *A Spirituall Song (1596)*.

COVERDALE, Miles, Bishop of Exeter (1488-1568). A North Yorkshireman and Augustine friar at Cambridge, he was editor of Cranmer's Great Bible of 1539 After pastoral service in Europe when Thomas Cromwell fell, he rose rapidly in the Church with Cranmer's support, became chaplain to the King, almoner to Queen Katherine, and then Bishop of Exeter, and lived to the age of 81. Among his voluminous publications on theology and translations, he converted German hymns into *Goostly Psalmes and Spirituall Songes* (c.1540).

COWLEY, Abraham (1618-67). Son of a London stationer, he went to Westminster School and Trinity College, Cambridge, from which he was expelled to the benefit of St John's College, Oxford. He was essentially an Augustan poet, foundermember of the Royal Society (despite the fact that he was old-hat for Pope: 'Who now reads Cowley?'). Spenser inspired him to start writing at the age of ten, and he contributed to the Renaissance *Poetical Blossoms* (published in 1633 when he was only fifteen) and *Sylva* (1636) as well as a play performed for a royal visit to Cambridge, *The Guardian,* a pastoral drama, *Love's Riddle* (1638), love poems (probably fictional) *The Mistress* (1647), and other Latin and English verse. His epic *Davideis* and *Pindaric Odes*, so representative of Augustanism, were composed at university.

D. Trotter: *The Poetry of Abraham Cowley* (1979); A.H. Nethercot: *Cowley: the Muse's Hannibal* (1931).

CRAIG Alexander (1567?-1627). A Banff man, educated at St Andrews University, he went to London to seek preferment, with the help of Sir Robert Aytoun. His *Poetical Essayes* (1604) secured a pension of £400 p.a. from James I. The pension appears to have been paid irregularly and he went on publishing, in London, Edinburgh and Aberdeen: *Amorose Songes, Sonets, and Elegies* (1606), *Poetical Recreations* (1609), chiefly religious epigrams, and further *Poeticall Recreations* (1623).

CRANE, Ralph (fl. 1625). Son of a well-to-do merchant taylor, brought up in law, clerk to Sir Anthony Ashley, he only turned to poetry late in life when impoverished and sick. He dedicated to John Egerton, Earl of Bridgwater, *The Workes of Mercy* (1621). He seems to have made more money copying out rare MSS for patrons.

CRANLEY, Thomas (fl. 1635). A friend of George Wither, and brother-in-law of Thomas Gilbourne, he wrote from prison *Amanda or the Reformed Whore* (1635).

CRASHAW, Richard (1613?-49). The son of a Puritan London BD (see below), he lost his mother in infancy and a stepmother when he was only seven. From Charterhouse he went to Pembroke College, Cambridge, became skilled in Greek, Hebrew, Latin, Italian, Spanish, music and drawing, and would have taken orders but was expelled for refusing to take the Oath. After Oxford, London and Paris, he rejected his Puritan upbringing, converted to Roman Catholicism and eked out a living with Cardinal Palotta in Rome, who sent him to Loretto. We have his *Steps to the Temple* and *Delights of the Muses* (religious and secular verse) published in 1646, and a mass of other poetry in MSS.

A. Warren: *Crashaw: a study in Baroque Sensibility* (1939); R.C. Wallerstein: *Richard Crashaw* (1935).

CRASHAW, William (1572-1626). Richard's father, of Handsworth near Sheffield, and educated at St John's College, Cambridge. A clergyman of Puritan leanings who was prebendary of Ripon, preacher at the Inner Temple, and rector of Burton Agnes, Yorkshire, and St Mary Matfellon, Whitechapel. In addition to his sermons and theology, we have *A Handful, or rather a Heartfull of Holy Meditations* (published 1611 and popular) and the *Complaint* (1616), a dialogue between the author, his departed soul and the devils.

CROSSE, William (fl. 1630). Of 'sufficient parents' in Somerset, he went to St Mary Hall, Oxford, but never rose higher than military chaplaincies, with Sir John Ogle in the United Provinces, Sir Edward Horwood at Cadiz, and others. His chief work, *Belgiaes Troubles and Triumphs* (published 1625), is pretentious, and perhaps explains why.

CROUCH, Humphrey (fl. 1635-71). In the seventeenth and eighteenth centuries the Crouch family became notable publishers of popular literature. Humphrey was a balladist in broadside and pamphlet, publishing carols and *inter alia Love's Court of Conscience* (1637) and *A Whip for the back of a backsliding Brownist* (1640).

CROWLEY, Robert (1518?-88). A Gloucestershire man, educated at Magdalen College, Oxford, he spent his life as a printer – at one time a Master of the Stationers Company – and as a Puritan clergyman. In Queen Mary's reign, he was an exile in Frankfurt. Later he was Archdeacon of Hereford and vicar of St Giles-without-Cripplegate and St Lawrence Jewry. Though very much opposed to RCs, particularly surplices, he spent much of his time talking with RC prisoners. He put almost everything into metre, including sermons and treatises, was the first in 1549 to produce a whole metrical Psalter, printed *Piers Plowman*, and among many publications contributed *One and Thyrtye Epigrammes* (1550) and the satire *Opening of the Wordes of the Prophet Joell* (1567).

CUTWODE, Thomas (fl. 1599). A pseudonym for the author of *Caltha Poetarum* (1599), a work considered not only licentious but politically dangerous, and burned by the Archbishop of Canterbury with the books of Marlowe and Marston. According to Leslie Hotson, he was Tailboys Dymoke, of a landed Lincolnshire family and a brother of Sir Edward Dymoke (a patron of Samuel Daniel, and Queen's champion at the coronations of Mary and Elizabeth).

D

DABORNE, Robert (d. 1628). A Guildford MA who wrote for Henslowe, particularly the Queen's Revels. He collaborated with Cyril Tourneur, Nathaniel Field and Philip Massinger, but all his plays, except the tragedy, *Christian turn'd Turke* and tragi-comedy, *The Poor-Mans Comfort* are lost. In later years he gave up the stage for the Church, becoming – under the patronage of Lord Willoughby – Chancellor of Waterford, and prebendary and Dean of Lismore.

DANIEL, George (1616-57). Son of an East Yorkshire knight, he fought in the Civil War as a Royalist, but, supported by a lucrative marriage, much preferred to be left alone with his books. He kept neat MS collections of poems written in his 20s and 30s, *Occasional Poems, Scattered Fancies*, chronicles, eclogues, a versification of *Ecclesiasticus* etc.

DANIEL, Samuel (1562-1619). One of the most interesting writers of the period, unique in that he achieved lifelong patronage, and had much to say about the value of his experience. A Somerset man, after education at Magdalen Hall, Oxford, he went into courtly service with Sir Edward Stafford, ambassador in Paris. He worked in France as an agent for Sir Francis Walsingham, and had connections with Essex and Mountjoy. But his real entry to court was as tutor to Mary Sidney's son, William Herbert, later third Earl of Pembroke (Daniel was very much a house-poet at Wilton) and Lady Anne Clifford, daughter of the Countess of Cumberland. Among other patrons were Fulke Greville and Southampton. His sister married John Florio, the lexicographer. He was known and admired by Spenser and Nashe; Ben Jonson did not think much of him – but then Jonson rarely approved of anybody.

A pirate edition of his poems induced him to publish his sonnets *Delia* (1592), to a west-country lady (probably fictional). He married but had no children. He produced meticulously revised later editions of *Delia*, adding in 1592 *The Complaynt of Rosamund* and, in 1594, *Cleopatra*, one of his closet-dramas, designed to be read, not presented. In 1595 appeared his long historical poem, *Civile Wars between the two Houses of Lancaster and Yorke*, reaching, like other poets of the time, towards epic. In 1599 came *Musophilus* and a collected *Poeticall Essayes*, which in a second edition (1601) became his *Workes*. *Panegyrics and Epistles*, which followed, enabled him to print a few folio editions for special patrons, a practice which anticipates Augustan subscription patronage. A second play, *Philotas* (1605), broke his rules: 'my necessity, I confess, hath driven me to do a thing unworthy of me, and much against my heart, in making the stage the speaker of my lines', and he regretted his lapse: though written before the Essex conspiracy, his *Alexander the Great*, when played in 1601, was too like Essex and he needed the support of Mount-joy to assuage suspicious authorities. He produced revised collecteds in 1607 and 1611, and the prose *History of England*, from 1612, for which he was granted a printing patent in 1618.

Quite apart from the fees of patrons and printers, he earned courtly attention: he was a groom of the Queen's Privy Chamber in 1607, licenser of plays for the children of the Queen's Revels, and held a similar post with the Youths of Her Majesty's Royal Charter of Bristol. He was involved in many courtly festivities: a masque at Hampton Court in 1604, a tragi-comedy at Christ Church, Oxford in 1604, a Whitehall entertainment with Inigo Jones in 1610, and a masque for the Queen at Somerset House in 1614.

Even he found patronage uneven. He reached towards a Miltonic and Augustan solution. His audience though 'few, is all the world.' One understanding reader was 'a Theater large enow'. He saw a great future in English letters:

> who, in time, knowes whither we may vent
> The treasure of our tongue, to what strange shores
> This gaine of our best glory shall be sent,
> T'inrich unknowing Nations with our stores?
> . . . This is the thing that I was borne to doo,
> This is my Scene, this part must I fulfill.

Even in his prime he used to 'lie hid at his garden-house in Old Street . . . as the tortoise burieth himself in the winter in the ground.' When older he was happiest farming near Devizes, Wiltshire.

J. Rees: *Samuel Daniel* (1964).

DAVENANT, Sir William (1606-68). His father ran one of Shakespeare's haunts, the Crown tavern at Oxford, and Shakespeare may have been his godparent, but hardly his father, as Davenant hinted. Davenant was educated at the school next to Magdalen College, Oxford, became a Fellow of St John's College, and started writing at the age of twelve – in praise of Shakespeare, of course. He lost his nose as a result of syphilis, and may well have needed to romanticise himself!

He was an attorney from the Middle Temple, and entered court early as a page to Frances, first Duchess of Richmond, later becoming attached to Fulke Greville. He was the friend of Endymion Porter and men of the theatre. In poetry his most important work before the Civil War was *Madagascar and other Poems* (1635): there was no official Poet Laureate in his day, but he regarded himself as the unofficial successor in this role of Spenser, Daniel and Jonson. He made a greater stir in the theatre though, with plays at the Blackfriars for the King's company, including the tragedy, *The Cruel Brother* (published 1630), the tragi-comedy, *The Platonick Lovers* (published 1636), and his best comedy, *The Wits* (1635). There were also several masques for Whitehall or the Middle Temple, notably, with Inigo Jones, *Britannia Triumphans* (1637) in which the King himself played. He became governor of the King and Queen's company at the Cockpit, and had authority to build a playhouse in Fleet Street, a plan cut short by war. He was one of the most persistent in finding devious ways and means to keep drama in being during the Civil War, an effort rewarded by a monopoly at the Restoration.

A.H. Nethercot: *D'avenant: Poet Laureate and Playwright-manager* (1938); A. Harbage: *Sir William Davenant, Poet, Venturer 1606-1688* (1935).

DAVENPORT, Robert (fl.1623). Little is known about this talented writer, who in poetry contributed *A Crowne for a Conqueror* (1623) and a MS collection made for William, Earl of Newcastle, and in drama several plays, of which we have the tragedy *King John and Matilda* (published 1655), and two comedies, *The City Night-Cap* (1624) and *A New Trick to Cheat the Divell* (1639).

DAVIES, John, of Hereford (1565?-1618). A writing-master who taught the most eminent pupils in the land and ultimately

Prince Henry, but who found it difficult to earn a living, and poured out prolific poetry in print, supported by the friendship of Jonson and his group. He started with a verse treatise *Microcosmus* (Oxford, 1603), and continued with a long poem on the plague, *Humours Heav'n on Earth* (1603), *The Holy Roode* (religious, 1609), and all kinds of satires, epigrams, panegyrics, eclogues and other works, including *Wit's Bedlam* (1617).

DAVIES, Sir John (1569-1626). An outstanding man of his generation, from Chisgrove, Wiltshire, he was educated at Winchester School and Queen's College, Oxford, and won entry to court by his legal gifts. He was a barrister from the Middle Temple (1595), a member of the Inns of Court group which included John Donne, Sir Henry Wotton and John Hoskins. He married Eleanor Touchet, daughter of George, Lord Audley, who after her husband's death offended the authorities by publishing strange prophetical books. He was MP for Corfe Castle (1601), and, on his accession, King James I sent him to tackle the Irish problem, as Solicitor-General, later Attorney-General, MP for Fermanagh, and Speaker of the Irish Commons. He decided Rome was much more efficient in Ireland than Canterbury, studied Irish history, was a good administrator, but could find no better solution to the problem than the Ulster Plantation. He had had enough of Ireland by 1619, and returned to England to become MP for Newcastle-under-Lyme. He was to have been Lord Chief Justice but died of a sudden apoplexy.

He was founder-organiser of the Society of Antiquaries. But at court he was most respected for his poetry: *Orchestra* (1596), a 'Poeme of Dancing'; epigrams; entertainments for Queen Elizabeth; and *Nosce Teipsum* (1599), of which King James had a high opinion, a poem written while rusticated from the Middle Temple after an affray with his friend Richard Martin. His best poems are logically constructed, the points made piece by piece, facet after facet, metaphor after metaphor. A collected edition appeared in 1622, but much of his work from later years remained in MSS.

Ed. R. Krueger: *The Poems of Sir John Davies* (1976).

DAVISON, Francis (fl. 1602). The eldest son of Queen Elizabeth's Secretary of State, William, his mother was a Spelman.

He entered Gray's Inn in 1593 and spent 1595-7 abroad with his tutor, Edward Smyth, who found his charge extravagant with his £100 p.a. allowance. He was charged with, but exonerated from, complicity in the Essex rising. In 1608 his father left him £100 p.a. from the office of *Custos brevium* of the Queen's bench. He contributed to a masque at Gray's Inn (1605) and left psalms, but his claim to fame was made by one of the great miscellanies, *A Poetical Rapsody* (1602, reprinted 1608, 1611, 1621). Besides his own poems the most important contributor to this was his brother, Walter (1581-1608?), a soldier in the United Provinces, from whose life we surmise that both brothers were at King's College, Cambridge.

DAY, Angell, (fl. 1586). Son of a London parish clerk, he was apprenticed to a stationer, and prospered. He wrote as well: a popular manual on letter-writing, a pastoral romance, perhaps the first report on UFOs, *Wonderfull Strange Sightes seene in the Element, over the Citie of London and other Places* (c.1585), and poems, including one about Sidney.

DAY, James (fl.1637). A youthful poet known only for *A New Spring of Divine Poetry* (1637).

DAY, John (fl. 1606). A farmer's son from Norfolk, he went to Caius College, Cambridge, but was expelled for stealing a book. After travels in Scotland and Ireland, he settled with Henslowe, for whom he wrote twenty-five plays in ten years, some in collaboration with Henry Chettle, William Haughton, Thomas Dekker, Wentworth Smith, Richard Hathway, William Rowley and George Wilkins. We have his *Ile of Guls* (1606), for the Revels Children, and the two witty and vivacious comedies of 1608, *Law Trickes* and *Humour Out of Breath*, as well as a masque, *The Parliament of Bees*. Most of his plays and poems are lost.

DEKKER, Thomas (1570?-1632). A Londoner, probably originally a merchant taylor, whose life we can only determine from his prolific writings. He is one of the best sources of evidence about the life of writers. He was in the lower ranks of status, little above the travelling players who trudged 'upon the hard hoofe from village to village for chees & buttermilke', or the balladists and almanac-makers whom often he had to join for an extra pound or two. He gives a vivid picture of the book-stalls, St Paul's, backstage, the ways of rogues. Jonson, of course, did not approve his reckless want of art, but anyone so irrepressibly vivacious was bound to leave his mark.

He seems to have started with the Lord Chamberlain's company, writing plays like *The Shoemaker's Holiday* (1599), but he was soon writing for Henslowe, the Admiral's and Worcester's companies; forty-four plays in the first five years, sixty-four altogether in his career. He collaborated with Michael Drayton, Robert Wilson, Henry Chettle, Anthony Munday, Ben Jonson, John Day, William Haughton, Thomas Middleton, John Webster, Thomas Heywood, Wentworth Smith, and Philip Massinger, including *Patient Grissel* (1603), *The Honest Whore* (1604), *If it be not good the Divell is in it* (1612), *The Witch of Edmonton* (n.d.), and *The Virgin Martyr* (1622).

In verse he published *Canaans Calamitie* (1598), a popular religious piece, and *Dekker his Dreame* (1620). He was involved with Jonson in a *Magnificent Entertainment Given to King James* (1604). In the 1620s, he held briefly the post of writer of Lord Mayor's pageants. But he was in prison for debt 1613-16(?) and probably again later, where he may have died.

G.R. Price: *Thomas Dekker* (1968).

DELONEY, Thomas (1543?-1600). From Norwich. He was a silk weaver in London and succeeded William Elderton as the most prolific balladist and pamphleteer of his age, successful with prose 'novels' about craftsmen, but also known for historical and contemporary news-ballads, which were particularly in demand with the coming of the Armada.

DENHAM, Sir John (1615-69). We think of him as a Restoration courtier, but he was a brilliant member of the court of Charles I. Son of an Irish judge, and born in Dublin, he was educated in London and at Trinity College, Oxford, entering Lincoln's Inn in 1631. He married Anne Cotton, from a Gloucester family, who brought him £500 p.a.; he squandered thousands in gambling. When his father died in 1638 he inherited the family estate at Egham, Surrey. He became Governor of Farnham Castle and High Sheriff of Surrey, and once pleaded for the life of George Wither, then a parliamentary commander, since while Wither lived, he 'should not be the worst poet in England'. During the Renaissance he wrote much satirical verse against the Puritans, a verse paraphrase of the second book of the *Aeneid*, the Blackfriars tragedy, *The Sophy* (1642), and published *Coopers Hill* (1642).

DENNYS, John (d. 1669). A Gloucester man, devoted to the River Boyd, he published in 1613 the beautiful verse *Secrets of Angling*, praised by Izaak Walton.

DICKENSON, John (fl. 1594). Known only for the graceful lyrics in his romances *Arisbas* (1594) and *Greene in Conceipt* (1598), and the eclogues, in experimental English hexameters, *The Shepheardes Complaint* (c. 1594).

DIGGES, Leonard (1588-1635). Son of an army muster-master-general, his mother was a St Leger. He went to University College, Oxford, travelled abroad, then returned to Oxford, where he died. Apart from his commendation of Shakespeare in the Folio, he is best known for the verse translation from Claudian, *The Rape of Proserpine* (1617).

DOD, Henry (1550?-1630?). From Cheshire, he became a silk weaver and probably then a clergyman. He was very Puritan, and published *Certain Psalmes* (1603), then *Al the Psalmes* (1620), with a metrical version of the Act of Parliament ordering a Gunpowder Plot thanksgiving service!

DONNE, John (1572-1631). He was the son of a well-to-do London RC ironmonger, his mother was the daughter of John Heywood, and niece of Sir Thomas More. He went to Hart Hall, Oxford, at the age of twelve and was therefore too young to have to take the Oath of Supremacy. Though his mother's brothers, Elias and Jasper, died abroad as RC exiles, and though his mother was a pro-Jesuit activist, there is no evidence that Donne was fundamentally RC, and therefore frustrated by life. If anything he was a rebel against the family's Jesuitism, because it was neither humane nor subtle. His career is that of a normally ambitious wit. He was at Lincoln's Inn in 1592, and Izaak Walton described him as 'not dissolute but very neat, a great visiter of ladies, a great frequenter of playes, a great writer of conceited verses.' A typical satellite courtier, he attached himself to Essex, with whom he was at Cadiz (1596-7), and by 1598 he was chief secretary to Sir Thomas Egerton. His friends were Inns of Court men, and included Christopher Brooke, Sir Henry Wotton, Sir John Davies and Sir Henry Goodyere. Like them he seemed set on a career starting in Parliament as MP for Brackley, later Taunton. To this period belong his love-poems, his *Songs and Sonets,* most of his *Elegies* and *Heroical Epistles.*

In 1601 he eloped with Anne More, daughter of Sir George More, Lieutenant of the Tower, and the niece of Egerton's second wife, for which his father-in-law had him thrown in the Fleet prison, and out of his job. Although he had a private fortune of about £750, supporting his wife and later twelve children presented a problem. An obvious opening was in the Church, but when Bishop Morton pressed him in 1607 he pleaded unfitness due to 'irregularities' in his life. He toyed with law, but it was only his 'best entertainment and pastime'. What he really wanted, like his contemporaries, was political preferment, and he tried for the posts of secretary to Virginia, clerk to the Privy Council, diplomat in Venice: all without success. He was in Paris 1605-6 with Sir Anthony Chute. He enlisted support from his fellow-MP, Lord Edward Montagu (who married three consecutive members of the Rich family), and Sir Robert Rich, the second Earl of Warwick, who persuaded him to write poetry for his sisters Lady Cary, and Essex Rich (both daughters of Penelope Devereux and therefore related to Elizabeth Vernon, wife of the Earl of Southampton). but not all this tangled web of support could dissuade Morton (influential with King James as a stalwart of the proposed Chelsea College for controversy) or the King, who decided that Donne 'has the abilities of a learned divine, and will prove a powerful preacher, and my desire is to prefer him that way.'

Urged by the King, Donne published two prose treatises, *Pseudo-Martyr* (1610) about the controversy on the Oath of Supremacy, and *Ignatius His Conclave* (1611). Like Shakespeare, he also advertised his talents in verse, with the *Anniversaries,* dedicated to Sir Robert Drury, a friend also unsuccessful in getting high office (Donne's sister, Anne Lily, was Elizabeth Drury's best friend). Some find his poetry of this period his worst: like Shakespeare's *Venus and Adonis,* it strains too much. Far better was his epitaph for the four-year-old Dorothy Drury, probably the most perfect tribute in this age so familiar with love and death:

> She, little, promis'd much,
> Too soone untyed:

> She only dreamt she liv'd,
> And then she dyde.

Therefore I would faine do something, but that I cannot tell what is no wonder. For to chuse is to do; but to be no part of any body is to be nothing. At most, the greatest persons are but great wens and excrescences, men of wit and delightfull conversation, but as moales for ornament, except they be so incorporated into the body of the world that they contribute to the substantiation of the whole.

He discussed, as his son says, this dilemma in *Essays on Divinity*, his MS debates 'betwixt God and himself'. In 1615 he took orders as a curate in Paddington, became royal chaplain, DD of Cambridge, Reader at Lincoln's Inn, and in 1621 the greatest of the Deans of St Paul's. Ironically, his secular door was opened thereby, and he became a JP in Kent and Bedford, Governor of Charterhouse, and member of the council of the Virginia company. Nor did he regret his decision: 'I date my life from my ministry, for I received mercy as I received the ministry as the Apostle speaks.' The pulpit was his stage, just right for his self-analysis, his desire, like that of Marlowe, for the infinite, his flair for drama and exhibitionism and eloquence, and his objective metaphysical wit. We remember Walton's picture of him 'weeping sometimes for his auditory, sometimes with them, always preaching to himselfe, like an angel from a cloud, though in none.' Above all, his religious and secular verse share the same scepticism:

> On a huge hill,
> Cragged, and steep, Truth stands, and hee that will
> Reach her, about must, and about must goe.

He gained a tranquillity which enabled him to weather his wife's death in 1617, a serious illness in 1623, his daughter's death in 1625, and when he drew near death in 1631 he wrote his last sermon and last poem, designed his own monument and epitaph, and then 'disposed his hands and body into such a posture as required no alteration by those that came to shroud him.'

His early 'pagan Muse', 'love-song weeds, and Satyrique thornes', are remarkably like the later religious poetry which also circulated in MSS. The urge to outsoar the mind's boundaries is the same; Christ is like a mistress; Anne More was a cosmic rock in a divine universe. Perhaps he, and certainly his imitators, pushed metaphor to its limits, searching through contemporary technology to find new images, and later writers, like Thomas Traherne, rejected curling metaphors that gild the sense, or which, according to Thomas Hobbes, expressed 'more than is perfectly conceived'. But Augustans, and the Romantics who also thought little of his poetry, rewriting history in their own image, could not see that in this, above all, Donne was true to the Renaissance.

J. Carey: *John Donne: Life, Mind and Art* (1980); R.C. Bald: *John Donne, a Life* (1972); A. Alvarez: *The School of Donne* (1961); J.B. Leishman: *The Monarch of Wit* (1951).

DOWLAND, John (1563?-1626?). Probably an Irishman, and educated at Oxford he was internationally known as a lutanist, and played for instance at Elsinore; once attached to Lord Walden, son of the Earl of Suffolk, and composer of most of the Elizabethan melodies still sung today. We know that he wrote sonnets, and in *Songs or Ayres* (1597, 1600 and 1603) and *Lachrymae* (1605) the lyrics are probably his own.

DOWNE, John (1570?-1631). A Devonian whose mother was a Jewel. He was educated at Emmanuel College, Cambridge and became vicar of Winsford, Somerset and Instow, Devon. He left much MS verse, psalms, religious verse, and a verse translation of Antonius Moretus's *Institutia for Children*.

DOWRICHE, Anne (fl. 1589). From an Edgcumbe family, she married first Hugh Dowriche, a Honiton vicar, and then Richard Trefusis of Cornwall. She published *The French Historie* (1589), an account in alexandrines of recent bloody events.

DRANT, Thomas (d. 1578?). A Lincolnshire man, he was educated at St John's College, Cambridge, and became chaplain to Archbishop Grindal, prebendary of St Paul's, rector of Slinfold, Sussex, and Archdeacon of Lewes. He was a courtly Puritan who disliked the vanities of dress. While skilled in Latin and Greek, he wrote much English verse, including *A Medicinable Morall* (1566), translations of Homer's *Iliad*, and Horace's satires (1567), which he found harder than Homer, the *Wailingyes of the prophet Hieremiah*, and a lost *Book of Job*. In his *Arte of Poetrie* (1567), he set out rules for versification, which Sidney took into account, but which Gabriel Harvey referred to contemptuously as 'Dranting'.

DRAYTON, Michael (1563-1631). He started in his native Warwickshire as page to Sir Henry Goodyere; Ann Goodyere was his Platonic *Idea* (1593). As he told Drummond, 'where I love, I love for years', and significantly he never married. He devoted a lifetime to professional poetry; his avenue print. He sought patronage with mixed success: Lucy, Countess of Bedford was helpful; Sir Walter Aston made him an esquire; Prince Henry gave him a pension of £10 p.a.; but King James bitterly disappointed him:

> He next my God on whom I put my trust,
> Hath left me troden lower than the dust.

He had wanted to be a poet from an early age: at ten he begged his tutor 'Make me a Poet, doe it, if you can.' He saw himself as Spenser's chief heir, and loved in Marlowe and others 'those brave translunary things that the first Poets had.' His acquaintances included Shakespeare, Jonson, Chapman, William Browne, George Wither, William Drummond, Sir William Alexander, Donne and other writers. He tried every form – sonnets, eclogues, erotic epyllia, tragic legends, odes, satires, religious and historical poems. But sadly at the end of sixty-eight years of writing and revising volume after volume, he had only £5 when he died.

From his own description he was 'swart and melancholy'. And he was regarded as a sober man: he did not swagger in taverns or 'dominere in a pot-house'. He was at odds with the literary world round him. On the one hand, he thought his age 'lunatique' because it prized only manuscript poetry: 'What is kept in Cabinets and must passe only by transcription.' On the other hand, he abhorred the 'beastly and abominable Trash (a shame both to our Language and Nation)', the bulk of the poetry that appeared in print. He put his hope in posterity, which will

> Out of dust reduce our scattered rimes,
> Th' rejected jewels of these slothfull times.

He took an early interest in heroic historical characters –

Piers Gaveston, Matilda and Robert, Duke of Normandy. What impressed him about King David was Marlovian:

> A valour so invincible and hie
> As naturally enabled him to flye
> Above all thought of peryll.

His way ahead was presaged by *Mortimeriados* (1596, becoming *The Barrons Wars*, 1603), and by his most readable and often reprinted *England's Heroical Epistles* (1597). His ambition led him to writing epic poetry. He had difficulty in finding a printer, and additional harassment from the censorship, for the successive parts, from 1613, of *Poly-Olbion*. But he persevered and produced successive collected editions in 1605, 1619, 1622 and 1629. He turned his attention to the theatre, but of all the twenty plays in which he had a hand, as part of Henslowe's company, perhaps the only important work was *Sir John Old-castle*, written in collaboration with Richard Hathway, Anthony Munday and Robert Wilson. He carried much respect with all (except Jonson, of course) and was second only to Spenser in the number of quotations used by Allot in *England's Parnassus* (1600). B.H. Newdigate believed that his 'gatherings of shepherds and shepherdesses who met for song and dance on Cotswold, on the banks of the Trent and Avon, or on the Elizian plains, were not just fictions of Drayton's muse, or echoes from Theocritus or Mantuan.' These courtly groups represented his poetic audience in his earliest courtly years, which culminate in *Idea* (1593) and *Ideas Mirrour* (1594). Thereafter his literary ambitions led him to different scenes, less felicitous in achievement, important chiefly because, like Spenser, he pioneered Augustan modes and principles.

J. Grundy: *The Spenserian Poets* (1969); B.H. Newdigate: *Michael Drayton and his Circle* (1961).

DROUT, John (fl. 1570). An attorney of Thavies Inn who published in fourteeners, from the Italian, *Gaulfrido and Barnardo* (1570).

DRUE, Thomas (fl. 1631). We know nothing but his published play, *The Life of the Dutches of Suffolke* (1631), but he probably wrote other plays.

DRUMMOND, William, of Hawthornden (1585-1649). Son of the laird, distantly related to the royal family, his mother was a daughter of the private secretary of James I's Queen. He went to Edinburgh High School and Edinburgh University and studied law in Bourges and Paris, but was most impressed by London. He gave up law when he became laird in 1610, after which he rarely left Hawthornden.

These Scottish poets lived in more secure ambience than their English counterparts. He had a large library of 552 volumes, and his reading led to writing. He knew well Sir William Alexander, Sir Robert Kerr, Sir Robert Aytoun and Sir Robert Murray, and many Englishmen including Michael Drayton. Ben Jonson walked from London to Edinburgh to visit him, followed by John Taylor the Water Poet. Sadly, his fiancée Mary Cunningham died on the eve of their wedding in 1615, and maybe this was the main reason why he was a recluse, writing many poems to her memory. He did not marry till he was forty-seven.

An ingenious man, he invented military appliances, a new box-pistol, pike, battering-ram and telescope. He tried to be neutral in the Civil War, signing the Covenant, but advising wisely against war, believing it would lead to military dictatorship, backing Montrose and after him the Duke of Hamilton.

He published in Edinburgh *Meliades* (1613), and other elegies, his love-poems in 1616, a panegyric on King James's visit in 1617, and his religious verse, *Flowers of Zion* (1623), which reflects bad years in Edinburgh, of sickness, fire and famine. His *History of Scotland* was printed posthumously.

D. Masson: *Drummond of Hawthornden* (1873).

DYER, Sir Edward (d. 1607). Just as we know little about Bryan, the third of an earlier trio with Wyatt and Surrey, so we have had to neglect this third member of the triumvirate with Sidney and Greville. Of his many poems in MS, there are only at best a dozen we can assign with any certainty to him. Many doubtless appear in anthologies as by *Anon*. But, like Bryan, he was the senior and most energetic member of his group. Son of a Somerset knight, his mother was a Poyning, he went to Oxford (Wood says either Balliol College or Broadgates Hall), became a skilled lutanist, travelled abroad, and settled in the group at court of Burghley and Leicester. In his will Sidney divided his books between Dyer and Greville. According to Oldys, he never would 'fawn or cringe', but once he climbed a tree to recite verse, while the Queen walked underneath, to regain her lost favour. He was steward of the royal manor of Woodstock (1570), contributing to a royal entertainment there; served as a diplomat in the United Provinces and Denmark; was Chancellor of the Order of the Garter; MP for Somerset (1589 and 1593); and served Essex as a secret agent in Scotland, and the Queen in a very strange mission to Bohemia, connected with Edward Kelly the alchemist, an associate of John Dee.

R.M. Sargent: *At the Court of Queen Elizabeth* (1935).

E

EARLE, John (1601?-65). Born in York, son of an ecclesiastical lawyer, he went to Christ Church, Oxford, becoming Fellow of Merton, chaplain to the Chancellor (then Philip, Earl of Pembroke), and is most known for the 78 characters, after Overbury, in *Microcosmographie* (1628, three editions in its first year, often reprinted). He wrote many 'witty fancies' in verse, elegies, epistles, commemorative verse, etc. He was with the Falkland group of writers at Great Tew, and was much respected by Charles I, who made him tutor to Prince Charles. He was a gentle soul, much astonished when appointed to the Westminster Assembly of Divines because as a Royalist he could not serve. When he returned at the Restoration he became Bishop of Worcester and Salisbury opposing all revenge against the nonconformists.

EDWARDS, Richard (1524-66). A Somerset man, he was educated at Corpus Christi College and Christ Church, Oxford, studied music under George Etheridge, and music prevailed after his entry to Lincoln's Inn. He became a gentleman of the Chapel Royal, and in 1561 Master of the Children, for whom he wrote plays which were performed in Richmond and Oxford: only one survives, *Damon and Pithias* (published 1571). Many of his poems found their way into the miscellany, *Paradyse of Daintie Devyces* (1576).

EDWARDS, Thomas (fl. 1595). A university man who published in 1595 two promising long poems, *Cephalus and Procris*, and *Narcissus*

ELDERTON, William (d. 1592?). He started in the theatre as a boy-actor, becoming a comic as an adult. He wrote comedy for his company, and is chiefly known for his printed ballads, trifles, news-stories, elegies, satires; this verse for print was much despised by the educated wits.

ELVIDEN, Edmund (fl. 1570). A north-countryman of whom we know nothing, except that he published three books, *The Closit of Counsells* (1569, a collection including some translations), *A Neweyeares gift to the Rebellious Persons in the North* (1570), and *Pesistratus and Catanea*.

EVANS, Thomas (d. 1633). After Corpus Christi College, Cambridge, he became rector of Little Holland (1618). His only known work is *Oedipus: Three Cantoes* (published 1615).

F

FAIRFAX, Edward (d. 1635). The natural son of Sir Thomas Fairfax of Denton, Yorkshire, he was brought up in Leeds and Newhall, Kewston. In 1600 he published *Godfrey of Bulloigne*, in 'heroicall verse' the first complete translation of Tasso's *Gerusalemme Liberata*, dedicated to Queen Elizabeth. King James I, King Charles I and Edmund Waller found it seminal, but, as usual, Jonson found fault with the translation. In MSS we also have his eclogues; his history of the Black Prince and other works are lost. A studious, retired man, he was helpful in the education of the children of his half-brother, Lord Fairfax; his own daughters, it was claimed, were bewitched.

FANE, Mildmay, second Earl of Westmorland (d. 1666). His mother a Mildmay, he went to Emmanuel College, Cambridge, and was MP for Peterborough and Kent. He was put in the Tower as a Royalist in 1642, but his estates were restored on taking the Covenant in 1644. There was nothing remarkable in his political life, but in poetry he published for private circulation *Otia Sacra* (1648), and kept in MSS, neatly edited, *Fugitive Poetry*, including epigrams, anagrams and acrostics.

FARMER, John (fl. 1591-1601). A musician attached to Edward de Vere, Earl of Oxford, he published a treatise on counterpoint, and madrigals (1599) of which the best known is *Faire Nimphes, I heard one telling* . . .

FARRANT, Richard (fl. 1564-80). A Gentleman of the Chapel Royal, at one time organist and master of the choristers of St George's Chapel, Windsor, where he earned, besides a free house, the sum of £81.6.8. a year, and also for each play put on at Windsor before Queen Elizabeth the usual fee of £6.13.4. He also composed anthems.

FELLTHAM, Owen (1602?-68). A Norfolk man who admitted he was no scholar, but who, attached to the Earl of Thomond at Great Billing, Northamptonshire, published moral essays, *Resolves* (1620?), to which in later editions he added strongly Royalist poems.

FENNER, Dudley (1558?-87). An 'heire of great possessions' in

Kent, after Peterhouse, Cambridge, he followed the Puritan Thomas Cartwright to Antwerp, and after a short spell as curate in Cranbrook was suspended, imprisoned, and forced into exile at Middleburgh, where he published his able *Song of Songs* (1587).

FERRERS, George (1500?-79). A St Alban's man, educated at Cambridge and Lincoln's Inn. He entered court life as page of the Chamber to Henry VIII, and when seized as surety for debt the King released him and jailed the sheriffs instead. He was attached at one time to Thomas Cromwell. He was given the estate of Flamstead, Hertfordshire, was MP for Plymouth at various times beginning in 1542, and served with distinction as a soldier in Scotland and France, being left 100 marks in the will of the King. Under Edward VI he was one of the army's commissioners of carriages, and in this reign he began a long connection with courtly pageants and pastimes, as Master of the King's Pastimes with William Baldwin and John Smyth to help. He wrote several masques, none of which survives, but on the strength of them was named a tragedian by George Puttenham. For resisting the Wyatt rebellion he was given £100 by Queen Mary, and was MP for Brackley in her reign. Though now a veteran he continued to serve under Queen Elizabeth, writing verses for her visit to Kenilworth (1575); he was escheator for Essex and Hertfordshire, and MP for St Albans.

His chief extant work is in the *Myrroure for Magistrates*, inspired after reading Lydgate. He wrote two tragedies for the 1559 edition, added another in 1563 and two more in 1578, an issue of which he appears to have been the editor. He seems to detect sorcery at work in his villains – natural in one who was prepared to inform against the young Princess Elizabeth about her connections with John Dee.

FERRIS, Richard (fl. 1590). One of the five messengers of the Queen's household, who without training rowed in a wherry from London to Bristol with two friends, and celebrated the feat in printed ballads published in 1590.

FIELD, Nathaniel (1587-1620?). Born in Cripplegate, the son of a clergyman who attacked in print theatrical entertainments. His brother Theophilus became Bishop of Hereford and a minor elegist, and his own career was determined by joining the Chapel Royal, where he became one of the principal comics and played in Jonson's *Epicoene* and *Poetaster*. When his voice broke, he acted with the King's and Lady Elizabeth's players, playing the lead in Chapman's *Bussy d'Amboise*. He wrote for the Whitefriars and Whitehall *A Woman is a Weathercock* (published 1612), for the Blackfriars, *Amends for Ladies* (published 1618), and with Massinger, *The Fatal Dowry* (published 1632).

R.F. Brinkley: *Nathan Field, the Actor-Playwright* (1928).

FISHER, Fisher (fl. 1639). Born in Bedfordshire, the son of a York deputy-auditor, he went to Magdalen Hall, Oxford, and then into the Church as rector of Wilsden. At university he published a blank-verse play, *The True Trojans* (1633), performed at Magdalen College.

FITZGEFFREY, Charles (1575?-1638). Son of a Fowey clergyman, he went to Broadgates Hall, Oxford, and became the rector of St Dominic, Eastwellshire. He knew many writers: John Davies of Hereford, William Vaughan, Josuah Sylvester, Thomas Campion, Robert Hayman. He published a commemoration, *Sir Francis Drake* (1596), and religious verse, *The Blessed Birth-Day* (1634). It is assumed that it was his son, Henry, who went to Westminster and Cambridge and produced, with Francis Beaumont and Michael Drayton, satires and epigrams in 1617.

FLEMING, Abraham (1552?-1607). A Londoner, educated at Peterhouse, Cambridge, and rector of St Pancras, who is best known for his work as an antiquarian; he also translated Virgil's *Eclogues* (1575) and *Georgics* (1589), and Reginald Scot's *Discoverie of Witchcraft* (1584).

FLETCHER, Giles, the elder (1549?-1611). Watford born, son of the vicar of Bishops Stortford (who subsequently went to Kent parishes at Cranbrook and Smarden), he was educated at Eton and King's College, Cambridge, and became deputy orator of Cambridge. His career covered many fields. In the Church he had Chancery posts at Ely and Winchester. At court, he was Sir Francis Walsingham's agent in Scotland, Germany and Russia. He didn't think much of Muscovy, but his account was suppressed by the Eastland company who feared damage to trade. He was MP for Winchelsea (1584), Master Extraordinary of the Court of Requests, treasurer of St

Paul's, and remembrancer of London 1587-1605. His brother became Bishop of London. Essex was a later patron, but he survived his master's fall. He wanted to write a history in Latin of the Tudors, but the Privy Council refused him permission. His Russian story eventually appeared in Hakluyt's *Voyages*, but his main contribution to the Renaissance was the book of poems *Licia* (c. 1593).

FLETCHER Giles, the younger (1588?-1623). Born in Watford, son of Giles the elder, brother of Phineas, he was educated at Westminster School and Trinity College, Cambridge. He became rector of Alderton, Suffolk, and published, besides translations of Boethius and Petronius, the poems written at Cambridge, *Christ's Victorie* (1610). Note the sensuousness of his Christ:

> His cheekes as snowie apples, sop't in wine,
> Hid their red roses quencht with lilies white,
> And like to garden strawberries did shine,
> Wash't in a bowle of milke, or rose-buds bright
> Unbosoming their brests against the light . . .

FLETCHER, John (1579-1625). Nephew of Giles the elder, born in Rye, Sussex, when his father, later Bishop of London, was minister there. After Corpus Christi College, Cambridge, he found his place in the theatre. He started with the Revels Children and the King's company. At first he was unsuccessful: *The Faithful Shepherdess* was published in 1610 because, though we now see it as the most famous and best of the period's pastoral plays, it failed in the theatre, and Fletcher needed the money from print.

He had a neo-classical definition of tragi-comedy: 'not so called in respect of mirth and killing, but in respect it wants deaths, which is enough to make it no tragedy, but brings some near it, which is enough to make it no comedy, which must be a representation of familiar people, with such kind of trouble as no life is questioned; so that a God is as lawful in this as in a tragedy, and mean people as in a comedy.' It is not surprising his audience were confused.

Fortunately he was one of the best collaborators of the time, needing the companionship of another writer to help him out of theory into reality. His first great friend was Francis

Beaumont with whom he made the team of Beaumontn-
Fletcher, in *Phylaster* (published 1620), *King and No King*
(published 1619), and *The Maides Tragedy* (published 1619).
In all, he had a hand in 69 plays; other partners were Jonson,
Field, Tourneur, Daborne, Middleton, Rowley and Shirley,
but his most fruitful friend was Philip Massinger, with whom
he was buried as plague victims in the same grave. The firm of
FletchernMassinger has been too long neglected. It produced,
with the help of Shakespeare, *Henry VIII* and *Two Noble
Kinsmen*, and other plays in the 1610s and 1620s, including the
tragedy of *Sir John van Olden Barnavelt, A Very Woman, The
Custom of the Country* and *The False One*.

C. Leech: *The John Fletcher Plays* (1962); W.W. Appleton:
Beaumont and Fletcher: A Critical Study (1956); E.M. Waith:
The Pattern of Tragicomedy in Beaumont and Fletcher (1952).

FLETCHER, Joseph (1582?-1637). Son of a London merchant
taylor, he went to Merchant Taylors School and St John's
College, Oxford, acted with Laud in a play there, and became
rector of Wilby, Suffolk. His religious ambivalence is displayed in his published verse treatise: *The Historie of the
Perfect, Cursed, Blessed Man: setting forth man's excellencie,
miserie, felicitie by his generation, degeneration, regeneration*
(1628, 1629).

FLETCHER, Phineas (1582-1650). Son of Giles the elder, he was
born in Cranbrook, Kent, and went to Eton and King's
College, Cambridge. He is well-known as a poet from his
university days. He seems to have left Cambridge in some
disgrace, but made his way in the Church, becoming chaplain
to Sir Henry Willoughby at Risley, Derbyshire, and rector of
Hilgay, Norfolk. His closest friends were Edward Benlowes
and Francis Quarles. He wrote a play, *Sicelides*, for performance at Cambridge (1614), and published a collected
edition of eclogues, epithalamia, elegies and epistles in *The
Purple Island* (Cambridge 1633), in the chief poem of which,
written in Spenserian cantos, the human body *is* the island. He
also published the anti-RC *Locustae* (1627), and lasciviously
about Venus and Anchises, *Brittain's Ida* (1627).

FLETCHER, Robert (fl. 1586). A Warwickshire man who
probably left Merton College, Oxford after a quarrel with a
new warden, and went on to be a schoolmaster and clergyman

in Taunton. He published *An Introduction to the Loove of God* (1581) and *The Song of Solomon* (1586).

FORD, John (1586-1639?). At his best the most interesting of the period's dramatists after Shakespeare. He was the second son of a gentleman of Ilsington, Devon, his mother was a Popham. After Exeter College, Oxford (1601) and the Middle Temple (1602), with friends at Gray's Inn, he had to leave the Inns of Court for debt. He quarrelled with his father and was left only £10 in his will. But from his first published poem, *Fames Memoriall* (1606) about the Earl of Devonshire, he wrote without mercenary motive. At this time like the other wits, he was writing eulogistic verse, for the King, Lord Mountjoy and Sir Thomas Overbury, but he did not seek patronage. After 1616 he had a pension of £20 p.a. from his brother, a partial explanation of his independence. He went into the theatre, writing seventeen plays in seventeen years, without any indication of professional pressure. He did not publish any plays until 1629, and then used the anagrammatic pseudonym Fide Honor. His plays seem primarily intended for the private playhouses, the Blackfriars of the King's company, and Phoenix of the Queen's company. He made enough money to retire, like Shakespeare in his last years, to his native Devon.

He collaborated with Dekker, Middleton, Webster and Rowley in plays, including *The Sun's Darling, The Bristowe Merchant* and *The Witch of Edmonton*, but his most remarkable plays were solo: *The Lovers Melancholy* (published 1629), *'Tis Pity She's a Whore* (published 1633), and *Loves Sacrifice* (published 1633). His interest in abnormal frailties and morbid repelling farce was misunderstood until it was learnt that he embodied intellectual problems in his plots, which can then be seen as the working-out of contradictions in the best theories of his time.

Medically, his characters are the embodiments of Robert Burton's humours theory in *The Anatomy of Melancholy* (1621), and emphasise the sicknesses caused by the thwarting of love. But, in conflict with medical opinion, the theories of the code of courtly love associated with Queen Henrietta Maria suggested that love overrode moral considerations, true love being of equal hearts and divine, and found most often outside the property-status of marriage. Ford describes what happens when the cold, clinical determinism of the scientists fails to cope with the exalted individualism and egotism of romantic love, deliberately selecting extreme examples of incest, jealousy and adultery. Puritans were outraged, as were nineteenth-century readers, but in the private playhouses these plays asked exciting questions about human nature and led to the exacting curiosity of the Restoration.

D.K. Anderson: *John Ford* (1972); M. Stavig: *John Ford and the Traditional Moral Order* (1968); C. Leech: *John Ford and the Drama of his Time* (1957); H.J. Oliver: *The Problem of John Ford* (1955); G.F. Sensabaugh: *The Tragic Muse of John Ford* (1944).

FORD, Thomas (d. 1648). One of Prince Henry's musicians whose pension went up from £30 to £40 then £80 p.a., and in whose *Airs* (1607) first appeared the songs *There is a lady sweet and kind*, and *Since first I saw your face*.

FORREST, William (fl. 1581). Educated at Christ Church, Oxford, he was one of the first pensioners of the new Wolsey's College in 1553. Chaplain to Queen Mary, he celebrated her accession in the broadside, *A New Ballade of the Marigold*, and left many MS poems, including *The Second Gresyld* (1558), psalms, panegyrics and religious poems. A friend of Alexander Barclay, he remained a patriotic RC, probably supported by Thomas Howard, Duke of Norfolk.

FOWLER, Abraham (fl. 1577). Educated at Westminster School and Christ Church, Oxford, he was a friend of Thomas Rogers and William Camden, and wrote poems with and for them.

FOWLER, John (1537-73). A Bristol man, he went to Winchester and New College, Oxford, but as an RC retired to Louvain, Antwerp and Douay to set up a printing press for controversial pamphlets and wrote epigrams and other verses, including *A Psalter for Catholics* (c. 1578).

FOWLER, William (fl. 1603). Son of the executor of the Countess of Lennox, he was at one time a clergyman in Hawick but was exiled to France whence he was driven out by the Jesuits. He became a prominent burgess of Edinburgh, secretary to Queen Anne and her Master of Requests in England. His friends were the Earl of Crawford, Sir James Balfour and other courtiers, and his nephew, William Drummond of Hawthornden. Among his MS sonnets and Petrarchan translations are *The Tarantula of Love* and *The Triumphs of Petrarch*.

FRAUNCE, Abraham (fl. 1587-1633). A Shropshire man, educated at Shrewsbury School and St John's College, Cambridge, supported by Sir Philip Sidney. He became a barrister at Gray's Inn, practising as a lawyer (thanks again to the support of Sidney and his sister Mary, Countess of Pembroke) in the court of the Marches of Wales, and was later appointed president under the patronage of John Egerton, first Earl of Bridgwater. He gradually abandoned literary work for legal, but started at college by writing and acting in Latin plays, and then joined Sidney's 'Areopagus', of which the leader was Gabriel Harvey, and whose other members included Dyer, Greville, Spenser (to whom he was 'Corydon') and Thomas Watson. He wrote in English hexameters and quantitative verse in his translation of Watson's version of Tasso's pastoral *Amyntas* (1587), his collected verse *Countess of Pembrookes Yvychurch* (1591), *Amintas Dale* (1592), and *Countess of Pembrokes Emmanuel* (1592), and even in *The Lawiers Logike* (1588).

FREEMAN, Thomas (fl. 1607-14). A Gloucestershire man, educated at Magdalen College, Oxford, who published two books of epigrams, *Rubbe and a Great Cast*, and *Runne and a Great Cast* (both 1614).

FULBECK, William (1560-1603?). Born in Lincoln, son of the Mayor, he went to St Alban Hall, Christ Church, Gloucester Hall, Oxford, and to Gray's Inn (1584). Before turning to a legal career he wrote a masque performed at Greenwich before the Queen by the Gray's Inn men, *The Misfortunes of Arthur* (1588).

FULWELL, Ulpian (fl. 1586). This Somerset man relates 'When I was in the flower of my youth I was well regarded of many men, as well as for my prompte wit in scoffing and taunting, as also for the comlynesse of my personage, beinge of very tall stature and active in many thinges, whereof I became a servitour.' But for all the attention given by Queen Elizabeth, Burghley, and his best patron and friend, Edmund Harmon, he had to settle, after St Mary Hall, Oxford, for obscurity as a rector at Naunton, Gloucestershire. He wrote one interlude,

Like Wil to Like (published 1568), and two prose-verse medleys, *The Flower of Fame* (1575) and *Ars Adulandi* (1576).

G

GALE, Dunstan (fl. 1596). Known only for his version of *Pyramus and Thisbe* (published 1597, 1617, 1626).

GARDYNE, Alexander (1585?-1634?). Educated at Aberdeen University, he became an advocate in Aberdeen, and published *Garden of Grave and Godlie Flowers* (Edinburgh, 1609), a collection of highly 'conceited' sonnets, elegies and epitaphs. In MSS he turned to *Theatres* of Scottish Kings and worthies (some lost), and to a metrical version of Boece's Latin biography of Bishop Elphinstone.

GARTER, Bernard (fl. 1570). A Londoner who published, in imitation of Broke's *Romeus and Juliet*, his own version of the story, *The tragicall and true historie which happened between two English lovers* (1563), and the anti-RC, *A New Yeares Gifte* (1579). He also wrote, with Henry Goldingham, a masque for the Queen's visit to Norwich in 1578, and probably others too.

GASCOIGNE, George (1542-77). He was the son of a Bedfordshire knight, his mother a Yorkshire Scargill, related to Sir Martin Frobisher. Brought up in Westmorland, he went to Trinity College, Cambridge and the Middle Temple, then Gray's Inn (1555), becoming an ancient (1557), and MP for Bedfordshire (1557-9). He travelled in France (1563-4), and was on familiar terms with his neighbours Francis Russell, second Earl of Bedford, and his special patron, Arthur, Lord Grey of Wilton. Among his many friends were Francis and Anthony Kinwelmersh, John Vaughan, Alexander Nevile, Richard Courtop, George Turberville and Sir Henry Wotton. He was MP for Midhurst (1572), and was at one time charged with being not only insolvent (which he was regularly), but also guilty of manslaughter, atheism and, the cruellest cut of all, of being 'a common rymer'. Extravagance was his vice. He was disowned by his father for his debts, and was still in trouble when he thought he had solved his insolvency by marrying a rich widow, Elizabeth Breton, much to the loss of her son Nicholas. He had to flee to the United Provinces, where, after a shipwreck, he served as 'The Green Knight' with the rank of captain with William, Prince of Orange, becoming a prisoner of war for four months. He returned to military duties when the Spaniards sacked Antwerp in 1576, but died the following year at the home of his friend George Whetstone.

Did 'old George' beat out 'the path to that perfection which our best poets have aspired to since his departure'? Did he show the way for Sidney and his friends? It is difficult sorting out what he himself calls 'Flowres' from the 'Hearbes and Weedes' published from financial necessity, but after the interregnum of Queen Mary he certainly helped put English letters back on their feet. His plays at Gray's Inn, *Supposes* (published 1573), after Aristo the first extant English comedy, and *Jocasta* (also 1573), after Euripides written with Francis Kinwelmersh the second extant English tragedy, break from the interludes into new Elizabethan modes. His 'tragicall comedies', *The Glasse of Government* (1575), and *Steele Glas* (1576) were the earliest verse satires. Elsewhere, he has claims to be the first English literary critic and importer of the Italian novella. With George Ferrers, Henry Goldingham and William Hunnis he wrote *Princely Pleasures* for the Queen at Kenilworth. There is a voluminous mass of other work, including, from Conti, *The Droome of Doomesday* (1576), and *A Delicate Diet for daintiemouthde Droonkardes* (1576). But in his major collection, published first by his friends as *A hundreth Sundrie Flowres* (1572, and revised by him as *The Posies of George Gascoigne Esquire*, 1575), there are very few poems which deal with central Renaissance dilemmas.

We must conclude that he was not 'old' in the sense of age, being only thirty-five when he died, but old-styled. For all his astringent economies with words, which savours of neo-classicism, he drops all too often into the sing-song homely rhythms of his contemporaries Richard Edwards and Thomas Churchyard.

C.T. Prouty: *George Gascoigne, Elizabethan Courtier, Soldier and Poet* (1942).

GIFFORD, Humphrey (fl. 1580). A Devon gentleman, in the service of Edward Cope of Edon, who published *A Posie of Gilloflowers* (1580). He was at one time an official at the debtors' prison, the Poultry Counter, and concluded:

Cease now your suits, and glose no more,
I mean to lead a virgin's life,
In this of pleasure find I store,
In doubtful suits but care and strife.

GLAPTHORNE, Henry (fl. 1639). A friend of Richard Lovelace and Thomas Beedome who published his *Poems* in 1639 and some of his plays (the others are lost): the tragedies, *Argalus and Parthenia* (for Whitehall and the Cockpit), *Albertus Wallenstein* (for the Globe), and the comedies *The Hollander* and *The Ladies Priviledge* (for Whitehall and the Cockpit) (all 1639-40).

GODOLPHIN, Sidney (1610-43). A bright star, killed in action at Chagford, from Godolphin, Cornwall; his mother was a Sidney. After a distinguished career at Exeter College, Oxford and the Inns of Court he entered parliament as MP for Helston (1628 and 1640) but left to raise Royalist forces in Cornwall strongly for Strafford. He was the friend of Falkland, Clarendon, Hobbes, and 'Little Sid' to Suckling; Edmund Waller completed his translation from Corneille, *The Passion of Dido for Aeneas*. He left many songs and poems in MSS.

GOFFE, Thomas (1591-1629). Son of an Essex clergyman, he went to Westminster School and Christ Church, Oxford, and became rector of East Clandon, Surrey. At Oxford he wrote plays, one of which, the tragi-comedy *The Careless Shepherdess* (published 1656), went straight from Christ Church to Salisbury Court; his tragedies, also posthumously printed, are *The Raging Turk, or Bajazet the Second*, *The Courageous Turk, or Armureth the First* and *Orestes*. He was a confirmed bachelor, but was inveigled into marrying the widow of his predecessor at East Clandon. The experience seems to have killed him.

GOLDING, Arthur (1536-1606). Son of an auditor of the Exchequer, whose half-sister Margaret married the sixteenth Earl of Oxford, John de Vere, so that in due time he became uncle and receiver of the wayward seventeenth Earl, Edward, and lived with him at the home of Sir William Cecil. He was thus well connected with Leicester, Essex, Sidney, Sir Christopher Hatton, Sir William Mildmay, Lord Cobham and the Earl of Huntingdon. He was one of the first members of

Archbishop Parker's Society of Antiquaries, and was granted landed property in Essex. He had Puritan leanings. He translated Julius Caesar, Beza and Calvin, and completed Sidney's translations of de Mornay's treatise on the *Trewnesse of the Christian Religion* (published 1589). But perversely he is best known for his ballad translation of Ovid's *Metamorphoses*, which went into nine editions (1565-1612).

L.T. Golding: *An Elizabethan Puritan: Arthur Golding* (1937).

GOMERSALL, Robert (1602-46?). A Londoner, he went to Christ Church, Oxford, and then into the Church, as 'a very florid preacher' according to Wood, becoming vicar of Thornicombe, Devon, faring well enough to leave £1000 to his son. He published *The Tragedie of Ludovick Sforza* (1628, maybe an Oxford play), and his poem *The Levites Revenge* (1628), both in a collected edition (1633).

GOOGE, Barnabe (1540-94). Son of the Recorder of Lincoln, his mother was a Mantell. He went to Christ's College, Cambridge, New College, Oxford, and the Staple Inn. He served his kinsman, Sir William Cecil, Lord Burghley in Ireland, becoming one of the Queen's pensioners (1563), and in 1574-85 Marshal of the Presidency Court of Connaught. He published a translation of Manzoli, *The Zodyake of Life* (1560), *Eglogs, Epytaphes, and Sonnetes* (1563), a translation from Kirchmayer, *The Popish Kingdome* (1570), and a translation from Heresbachius, *Four Bookes of Husbandrie* (1577). Of the last William Webbe remarked that Googe was 'a painfull furtherer of learning', an apt comment judging by the *Eglogs*, which is a homespun effort indicating how far Spenser had to go to improve English pastoral poetry.

GORDON, Patrick (fl. 1615-50). It is believed he was the Royalist son of Sir Thomas Gordon of Cluny, his mother a Douglas, an adherent of the Marquis of Huntly, and known for two narrative poems in heroic verse, published in 1615, about Robert the Bruce, and Pernardo and Laissa.

GORGES, Sir Arthur (d. 1625). His father was a vice-admiral, his mother a cousin of Ralegh, so that it is no surprise to learn that he commanded under Ralegh the first Warspite in 1597 against the Spaniards. The account is in *Purchas his Pilgrimes* (1625). His first wife was the great heiress Douglas Howard, aged twelve. When she died, Spenser wrote *Daphnaida* for his 'Alcyon'. To temporary royal displeasure his second wife was Elizabeth Clinton, daughter of the Earl of Lincoln, who brought him considerable property in Chelsea. He was a gentleman-pensioner of Queen Elizabeth and later of Prince Henry (James I didn't really like him). He was MP from 1584 for Yarmouth, Chelmsford, Dorset and Rye, and was a JP. He set up what was described as 'Britain's Burse', a 'Publike Register for Generall Commerce', but it failed. He translated Lucan's *Pharsalia* and left prolific poetry in MSS.

GOSSON, Stephen (1554-1624). Educated at Corpus Christi College, Oxford. We know him best for his attacks on the theatre in *Schoole of Abuse* (1579) and *Playes Confuted* (1582), an onslaught so severe Sidney was moved to defend Poesie. Later he entered the Church, becoming lecturer in Stepney at £30 p.a. and rector of Wigborough, Essex, and St Botolph, Bishopsgate. In London he was esteemed for his pastoral poetry and three plays, written in the early 1570s, the tragedy, *Catiline's Conspiracy*; the comedy, *Captain Mario*; and the moral, *Praise at Parting*, all lost. He may well have been an actor himself; certainly he was a lifelong friend of Edward Alleyn. Such sudden changes, of course, are not unusual in the Renaissance. We cannot gauge his true talents from his coarse satire, *Pleasant Quippes for Upstart Newfangled Gentlewomen* (1595).

GOSYNHYLL, Edward (fl. 1560). One of the writers against women, who published a verse attack, *Scole House of Women* (1541), recanted when William Myddylton produced in reply *Prayse of all Women* (1542), but continued the controversy into the 1560s with *A Dialogue betwene the Commune Secretary and Jealousye, touching the unstableness of Harlottes*.

GRAHAME, Simion (1570?-1614). Son of an Edinburgh burgess, he led a shiftless life, poor, licentious, exiled temporarily abroad, travelling and picking up a living as he could (chiefly as a soldier), writing poems about his *Pilgrimage*, and probably ending his days as a Franciscan. He published *The Passionate Sparke of a Relenting Minde* (London, 1604), and, before Burton, *The Anatomie of Humors* (Edinburgh, 1609).

GRAILE, Edmund (fl. 1611). A Gloucester man, educated at Magdalen College, Oxford, who became physician at St Bar-

tholomew's Hospital, Gloucester, and published a religious
metrical text, *Little Timothie, his Lesson* (1611).

GRANGE, John (fl. 1577). By his own account he was a
'Gentleman, Student of the Common Lawe of England'. What
is remarkable about his collections, *The Golden Aphroditis*,
and *Granges Garden* (1577), is their appeal to the genteel, or
those who would like to be. He dedicated to 'the Courtelike
Dames and Ladie-like Gentlewomen', and the poems are
headed 'A valiant yong Gentleman . . . bewayleth his former
life in this order', 'A Gentleman seeing his brother desirous to
goe to the seas, wrote these verses', 'The Description of the
love of a Gentleman and Gentlewoman', and so on.

GRANT, Lilian (d. 1643). Née Murray, the wife of John, laird
of Frenchie, she wrote poetry as a leisure pursuit, but the MSS
did not survive.

GREAVES, Thomas (fl. 1604). Probably from Derbyshire, a
composer and lutanist to Sir Henry Pierrepont, he published
Songes (1604), including 'Come Away Sweet Love . . .',
'Lady, the melting crystal of thine eyes . . .' and 'Sweet
nymphs . . .'.

GREENE, Robert (1560?-92). This Norwich man, son of a
respectable saddler, went to St John's College and Clare Hall,
Cambridge, and travelled in Italy, Spain, Denmark and Poland
from 1589, but led such a dissolute life that, as he says, he was
'so discontent that no place would please me to abide in.' He
had some vague idea of becoming a physician, but instead
married a gentleman's daughter, settled in Norwich, got her
pregnant, spent the dowry, and had left her for London by
1596. He rapidly went downhill, lodging with a shoemaker
and his wife, and owing them £10 on his death. His only
visitors were women, one of whom bore him Fortunatus
Greene (d. 1593). His enemies, including Gabriel Harvey,
made the most of this ignominious end, and stirred up a
controversy in which Chettle defended his dead friend.

Nobody tells us more about the miseries of an attempted
literary profession. He approached sixteen different patrons
for seventeen books, and went to great lengths to modify his
writings for the middle-class market. He found living with his
own failure very difficult, and lashed out at Shakespeare and
Marlowe, who had been successful, in his otherwise bitterly

repentant *A Groatsworth of Wit* (1592).

He started off with massive talents, a real skill in romances which combined verse, prose and Euphuism, notably *Mamillia* (1580), the popular *Pandosto* (1588), and *Menaphon* (1589), which contain excellent songs and eclogues. He was happiest as an actor and playwright, chiefly for Lord Strange's company, collaborating with Shakespeare in the *Henry VI* trilogy, (published 1594), with Lodge in *A Looking Glass*, and producing solo *Orlando Furioso* (which he slyly tried to sell to two companies), *Friar Bacon and Friar Bungay* (acted 1594) and *Greene à Greene*.

J.C. Jordan: *Robert Greene* (1915, repr. 1965).

GRESHAM James (fl. 1626). He published, from Ovid, a heroic-couplet poem, *The Picture of Incest* (1626).

GREVILLE, Fulke, Lord Brooke (1554-1628). Unlike his brilliant friend Sidney whom he knew from Shrewsbury School, he had a long life, which ended in violence at 74 when his servant, Robert Haywood, stabbed him and then committed suicide in a tiff about his will; typically Greville forgave his assassin on his death-bed. He was the steadying influence in Sidney's group, guardian indeed of his comrade. They were both deflected by the Queen from their rash plan to serve with Drake in the West Indies into service in Heidelberg and the United Provinces.

His father was a substantial squire of Warwickshire who had married Ann Neville, daughter of the Earl of Westmorland. After Jesus College Cambridge, Greville had long parliamentary service, representing from 1580 Southampton, Haydon, Yorkshire, and Warwickshire. His main power base was his post as secretary of the Marches of Wales, held from 1583 to his death, despite at one time the opposition of the President, Edward, Lord Zouche. He knew all the cabals of his time, was in Burghley's camp, but also with Essex, until in the end he had to join in the siege of Essex House. He thought Essex foolish, but also a victim of his foes and friends. Sir Robert Cecil, who became Chief Secretary of State, never forgave him for his defence of Essex, and he had to resign as a rear-admiral his post of secretary to the navy in 1604. But when Cecil died in 1612, he was able virtually to start a new political career at sixty, with Robert Carr, Viscount Rochester, and

Henry Howard, Earl of Northampton. He became Chancellor of the Exchequer in 1614. By his death he was a landowner in thirteen counties, earning £3635 p.a. from his lands, £3184 from fees and pensions (the post in Wales was worth £1000 alone), and £269 from leases.

He never found any dichotomy between his worldliness and his religious view of life, having an assured grasp of managing apparent disorder within the Paradise of order which could only be realised in 'the heart of Man'.

To his days with Sidney and Dyer belong the miscellany *Caelica* and the first closet plays *Mustapha* (published 1609) and *Alaham*. *Caelica* is a mix much like Donne's: love-poems which are sometimes religious, sometimes coarse, sometimes graceful, the lady is both chaste and sexually cynical, the lover both idealist and pirate. The sonnets are not sugared: Francis Bacon tells how Greville at court saw himself as like 'Robin Goodfellow' for 'when the maids spilt the milk-pans or kept any racket, they would lay it upon Robin.' There was no Anne More or Penelope Rich in his life, his ladies are fiction. He never married, and adopted a cousin as his heir. He was able to look objectively at the tangles Sidney achieved with long patience and the bemused tolerance of a man to whom, like Donne, the paradoxes of love were close to the paradoxes of God.

The typical courtier, he was always diffident about the status of literature. Within the group he could play: writing *Grace for Zenith* to match Dyer's *A Fancy,* or *Shepherd's Conceit of Prometheus* in competition with Sidney. He accepted some of the neo-classical theories, especially with drama, of the 'Areopagus', but when it came to changing the courtly system he was most hesitant. He loyally published a corrected edition for print (to anticipate pirate versions), of Sidney's *Arcadia* (1590-3), but was uneasy because he knew Sidney's efforts 'were scribled rather as pamphlets, for entertainment of time and friends, then any accompt of himself to the world.' He did not print his own poetry, and his consent even for a posthumous edition was lukewarm. He destroyed his play, *Antony and Cleopatra,* in case it was misread, after the downfall of Essex, as Daniel's *Philotas* was. This is a pity because by all accounts he had invented a striking Octavia, a lady, like himself, patient and long-suffering. He remained at the heart of literature, and in his later years was the friend of William Camden, Samuel Daniel, Francis Bacon, John Speed, Lancelot Andrewes and John Overall.

R.A. Rebholz: *The Life of Fulke Greville* (1972); J. Rees: *Fulke Greville Lord Brooke 1554-1628* (1971).

GRIFFIN, Bartholomew (fl. 1596). He died in Coventry, but his family was from Northamptonshire. He was probably an attorney from the Inns of Court. He may have been employed by Sir Thomas Lucy (Shakespeare's neighbour) at Charlecote as tutor to his grandchildren. We know little about him, but he published the charming sonnet-sequence *Fidessa* (1596), and other poems in the miscellany *The Passionate Pilgrim* (1599).

GRIMALD, Nicholas (1519-62). From Huntingdonshire, probably a son of the Grimaldi merchant family from Genoa. After Christ's College, Cambridge and Merton College, Oxford, he was chaplain to Bishop Ridley and was in prison with him in 1555. He wrote sermons, tracts and translations from Cicero and Virgil, and two Latin plays, but he is chiefly remembered for his poems in MSS, of the Wyatt school, of which forty were published in Tottel's *Songes and Sonnettes* (1557).

GRIMSTON, Elizabeth (d. 1603). A Bernye of Gunton, Norfolk, she married a Yorkshireman, lost all but one of her children, was made miserable by her mother, and turned for consolation, 'a dead woman among the living', to writing for her surviving son various meditative and religious essays, including odes and other poems, published the year after her death as *Miscelanea*.

GROVE, Mathew (fl. 1587). The publisher found a MS by this author, of whom we know nothing, and published in 1587 the ballad-poem, *Pelops and Hippodamia*, with appended songs, sonnets and epigrams.

GWINNE, Matthew (1586?-1627). Of Welsh descent, the son of a London grocer, he went to St John's College, Oxford, becoming junior proctor and lecturer in music. He supervised plays performed for the Queen at Christ Church, in 1592, and wrote Latin plays for King James, staged at St John's and Magdalen Colleges. He took up medicine, attended Sir Henry Lenton, ambassador in Paris in 1595, was the first Professor of

Physics at Gresham College, London (1597), and in the College of Physicians was Fellow, six times censor and twice registrar. He had a lucrative practice and in 1605 was physician to the Tower. He was also an expert on the healthy qualities of tobacco. His English poetry was confined to MS communication with his friend John Florio.

GWYN, David (fl. 1588). He suffered a long and cruel imprisonment in Spain, and described his experiences in verse published in 1588.

H

HABINGTON, William (1605-54). The son of an RC exile, he was educated by Jesuits at St Omer's and Paris, but settled in England, where he became a distinguished writer, friend of Jonson, Philip, Earl of Pembroke, Endymion Porter, Sir William Davenant, James Shirley, BeaumontnFletcher, and King Charles I, who encouraged him to write history. He married Lucy Herbert, the daughter of William Herbert, first Baron Powis, and wrote for her *Castara* (published anonymously 1634, and reprinted with additions in 1635 and 1640). There was also a tragi-comedy *The Queene of Arragon* (published 1640).

HAGTHORPE, John (fl. 1627). A Chester-le-Street man from Co. Durham, who at one time lived in Scarborough Castle and was involved in non-lucrative land deals before finding more security in the navy, as a captain at Cadiz and against the 'Dunkirkers'. He published *Divine Meditations and Elegies* (1622), *Visiones Rerum* (1623) and *Englands-Exchequeur* (1625).

HAKE, Edward (fl. 1579). Educated at Gray's Inn and Barnard's Inn, he attracted the attention of Leicester and gained preferment at Windsor, becoming under-steward, bailiff, Mayor in 1586, and MP for New Windsor in 1588. He thought it wrong that 'we should cloye the worlde with to many bookes of weake handling.' Nevertheless, he was involved in writing for Whitehall, and in several verse translations (he found verse a better translating medium than prose), and went ahead with his Puritan satires, *Newes out of Powles Churchyarde* (1567, 1579).

HALL, Arthur (fl. 1563-1604). Known as the first translator into English (fourteeners) of Homer's *Iliad* (published 1581), supreme until Chapman, and very much a fiery man of the court. Originally the ward of Burghley, he went to St John's College, Cambridge, travelled in Italy and the Balkans, and was a squire of considerable landed property, and MP for Grantham (1571-85). He needed Burghley's help: he had trouble with debts, affrays and contempt of the House of Commons.

HALL, John (1529?-66?). A Maidstone surgeon, member of the Worshipful Company of Chirurgeons, who published not only medical tracts against quacks, but also a string of verse works: *Solomon* and *Psalms* (1549), *A Poesie in the Forme of a Vision* (against necromancy, 1563), *The Courte of Vertue* (a counterblast to current Courts of Venus, 1565), songs, sonnets, ballads, biblical metrifications, etc.

HALL, Joseph, Bishop of Norwich (1574-1656). His father was the deputy of the Earl of Huntingdon in the North and his mother was a Puritan Bambridge. After Ashby-de-la-Zouche School, this brilliant wit was sent to Emmanuel College, Cambridge by family subscription, and justified their support by working his way up in the Church, via a rectory in Suffolk and a chaplaincy to Prince Henry (who had been impressed by his prose meditations circulating in MSS), prebendaries and deaneries, to the bishoprics of Exeter and Norwich. The Civil War halted his progress: his cathedral was sacked; he was given a meagre pension, because he was regarded as malignant, and he had to be content to live out his long life in Higham, Norfolk. His sons did well in the Church too, one becoming Bishop of Chester. He was low-Church, tolerant of the Puritans (taking the line that Rome was corrupt but Canterbury true, but not enough to save him from Puritan onslaught in the Smectymnuan controversy). It was a case of the biter bit, because in his youth, besides pastorals and panegyrics, he had produced biting satires *Virgidemiarum* (1597, 1598, 1599, 1602), which attacked almost everything, in particular the theatres, and which decided the authorities to burn his book, along with those of Marston, Marlowe, 'Cutwode' and others, and put satire out of favour for more than a decade.

    T.F. Kinloch: *Life and Works of Joseph Hall* (1951).

HANNAY, Patrick (d. 1629?). From Kirkcudbright, he rose in the legal service of Queen Anne to the posts of clerk of the Irish Privy Council, and Master of the Irish Court of Chancery, building up landed estate in Co. Longford. He knew Sweden, and London (from living some time near Croydon). He published *A Happy Husband* (1618-19), elegies on the death of his patron (1619), and a collected edition of his songs, sonnets and other poems, previously circulating in MSS, in 1622.

HANSON, John (fl. 1604). Educated at Peterhouse,

Cambridge, he is known only for a rather turgid book of verse commemorating James I's entry into London, *Time is a Turn-Coate* (1604).

HARDING, Samuel (fl. 1641). From Ipswich and educated at Exeter College, Oxford, he was a chaplain who published an unacted tragedy, *Sicily and Naples* (1640).

HARINGTON, John (fl. 1550). Born in Stepney of an old Cumbrian family, he was Henry VIII's agent and Treasurer of Camps and Buildings. He married the King's natural daughter, Etheldreda, who brought him an estate near Bath, and died early. He wrote much MS love-poetry, chiefly to Princess Elizabeth's ladies at Hatfield, singling out Isabella Markham whom he married in 1554. This earned the temporary displeasure of the Princess who imprisoned him in the Tower, but later relented and rewarded him by becoming godmother to his son.

HARINGTON, Sir John (1561-1612). Educated at Winchester School and Christ's College, Cambridge, he became a favourite with Queen Elizabeth like his father, but also earned the Queen's displeasure for corrupting the morals of her ladies by the MS circulation of erotic verse. She rusticated him for a while and sentenced him to translate Ariosto's *Orlando Furioso*, which he completed and published in 1591, defending his two- and three-syllable rhymes. But his wit would out: when he published satires, either anonymously or under the pseudonyms of Misodiaboles and T.C. Traveller, the Queen did not like their Rabelaisianism or possible aspersions against her favourite, Leicester. He weathered such storms, entertained the Queen at Kelston (where he instituted water closets – among the first in the country), became High Sheriff of Somerset, and served as Essex's commander-of-horse in Ireland. It took him some time to extricate himself from Essex's fall and financial problems led to a short imprisonment; he suggested that he should go back to Ireland (where he thought his natural sympathies with the Irish would help find solutions) as both Chancellor and Archbishop, but James I refused, and Harington had to be content with helping with the education of Prince Henry.

Some of his verse, including epigrams, reached print posthumously. Queen Elizabeth referred to him as 'that saucy poet, my godson'. James I, in a different light, said that Harington impressed his learning on him 'as made me remember my examiner at Cambridge.'

I. Grimble: *The Harington Family* (1958); T. Rich: *Harington and Ariosto: A Study in Elizabethan Verse Translation* (1940).

HARVEY, Christopher (1597-1663). Son of a clergyman from Bunbury, Cheshire, and educated at Brasenose College, Oxford, he became rector of Whitney, Herefordshire, briefly headmaster of Kington School, and vicar of Clifton-on-Dunsmore, Warwickshire. His devotional poems, *The Synagogue*, were appended to the 1640 edition of George Herbert's *The Temple,* and his emblem-book, *Schola Cordis*, was published anonymously in 1647.

HARVEY, Gabriel (1550-1631?). He was the son of a prosperous Saffron Walden master ropemaker, who sent his three sons to university. Gabriel, the eldest, went to Christ's College and Pembroke Hall, Cambridge, and was Professor of Rhetoric (1574). He was an ambitious, quarrelsome and arrogant man, who 'could hardly find it in his hart to commend any man', although Sidney and his friends, who accepted his 'Areopagus' which attempted to neo-classicise English letters, balanced his foibles with his worth. To Spenser he was affectionately 'Hobbinol'.

He was unpopular at Christ's College which is why he transferred to Trinity Hall where, with the support of Leicester, he hoped to get the Mastership after the death of his relative, Henry Harvey, but by royal mandate he was set aside for another candidate; and despite Burghley's backing he later failed to get the post of public orator. Perhaps his most unforgivable lapse was his attack on Greene after his death, which roused Nashe into a vitriolic reply; *Have with you to Saffron Walden* (1596) and Harvey's reply, *The Trimming of Thomas Nashe* (1597), caused such public scandal that both writers were silenced by the Privy Council.

His best verse is in *Foure Letters and certaine Sonnets,* which he published in 1592, despite his hesitation at appearing in the same market as the ragged-rhymers. The pity is that, at best, his attempt to patriate hexameters was doomed to failure, since the notion was alien to English verse rhythms and needed in addition phonetic spelling to make it at all presentable. He was better with Latin verse. In the end, he seems to have tired of his failures with poetry, preferring the 'expert artisan', and his last years were spent in sciences such as navigation and astrology.

V.F. Stern: *Gabriel Harvey: His Life, Marginalia and Library* (1979).

HATCLIFFE, William (1568-1631). From Lincoln, and educated at Jesus College, Cambridge, he became a leading light at Gray's Inn, where in 1586 he contributed much to the Christmas entertainments and was 'Prince of Purpoole'. He may have known Shakespeare; and certainly knew Thomas Campion. Whatever early promise he showed was obliterated as he squandered his inheritance and struggled with debt the rest of his life.

HATHWAY, Richard (fl. 1598-1603). A Warwickshire man, one of the least known of Henslowe's team of writers at the Rose, helping with eighteen plays in five years and collaborating with Dekker, Day, Chettle, William Haughton, Wentworth Smith and William Rankins. He wrote poems, and plays about King Arthur, Owen Tudor, Hannibal and John of Gaunt, as well as comedies, but all this work is lost, and one only play remains, written with Drayton, Munday and Robert Wilson the younger, *Sir John Old-castle* (published 1600).

HATTON, Sir Christopher (1540-91). From a Northamptonshire family, he went to St Mary Hall, Oxford, and the Inner Temple, where he acted on the same stage as Leicester in 1561, and by 1572 he was one of the Queen's bodyguard, her Gentlemen Pensioners, and a special favourite as her 'mutton', 'bellwether', 'pecora campi', earning thereby £400 p.a. by 1575.

He never married, and Mary Queen of Scots thought he was the Queen's lover. He was MP for Higham Ferrers (1571) and Northamptonshire (1571-86) and was Leader of the Commons. He was also a Privy Counsellor, Chancellor of Oxford, High Steward of Cambridge, and, in 1587, Lord Chancellor in the procession with Burghley on his right, Leicester on his left – the great triumvirate. He was a celebrated dancer, actor and writer of courtly verse. He knew Spenser, Churchyard, Christopher Ocland and Greene, and supported Drake, Frobisher and other adventurers. He was both an agent and commissioner as his Queen prompted. Unfortunately, he opposed the match with the Duke of Alençon, which enabled Ralegh to replace him as the Queen's favourite. Not all his poetry and court drama are firmly identifiable.

E. St J. Brooks: *Sir Christopher Hatton* (1946).

HAUGHTON, William (fl. 1598). Probably from Oxford, he was in the Henslowe team at the Rose, working with Day, Chettle, Dekker, Wentworth Smith and Hathway. He was in prison at least once for debt. We know little about him, and of his twenty-five plays, written in five years, we only have extant his solo comedy, *English-Men for my Money* (published 1616).

HAUSTED, Peter (d. 1645). From Oundle, Northamptonshire, and educated at Queen's College, Cambridge, he became curate of Uppingham, rector of Hadham, Hertfordshire, vicar of Gretton, Northamptonshire, and chaplain to the Earl of Northampton. He died during the siege of Banbury Castle. Beside Latin poems and plays, he produced heroic poems, *Hymnus Tabaci* (published 1650), and an English play *The Rival Friends* (published 1632), played at Cambridge for a Royal visit, and which, despite its good songs, got a mixed reception, being 'cryed down by Bayes, Faction, Envie and confident Ignorance'.

HAWES, Edward (fl. 1606). While only sixteen, and at Westminster School, he published *Trayterous Pireyes and Catesbye Prosopopoeia* (1606).

HAWKINS, Sir Thomas (d. 1640). An RC, he inherited the family estates in Kent; his mother was a Pettit and his brother John a Jesuit MD. He was a talented musician and poet, friend of James Howell and Edmund Bolton, and published *Odes and Epodes of Horace in Latin and English Verse* (1625, 1631, 1635, 1638), and wrote in MSS elegies, translations and biographies.

HAWKINS, William (d. 1637). Educated at Christ's College, Cambridge, he became curate of Hadleigh, Suffolk, and master at Hadleigh School, writing for his pupils, who included Joseph Beaumont, *Apollo Shroving* (published 1627).

HAYMAN, Robert (d. 1631?). A Devon man who went to Exeter College, Oxford at the age of eleven and then on to Lincoln's Inn. His poetical talents won him political promotion as Governor in Newfoundland and a privileged prospector in Guiana. His *Quodlibets,* a mix of epigrams, satire and religious verse, was published in 1625.

HEALEY, John (d. 1610). The translator of Philip Mornay (1609), Bishop Hall (1609), Epictetus (1610), and Vives's *St Augustine* (1610), in prose and verse. We know that with his friend John Coventry he 'long sayled in a deepe darke sea of misfortune' and death arrived before he reached harbour.

HEATH, John (fl. 1615). A Somerset man who went to Winchester and New College, Oxford, he published *Epigrams* and other verses from 1610 and also translated from French and Spanish. Jonson rated him on a level with John Taylor, the Water Poet.

HENSLOWE, Philip (d. 1616). Though he seems to have done next to no writing, he was the leading theatrical impresario of his time, getting together the talents of many writers, both famous and not so famous. From Southwark, he was known as a dyer, pawnbroker and money-lender, and at court was a groom (1593) and sewer (1603). His land investments paid off, and he was able to build the Rose in 1588 for Lord Strange's company, and made it the home of the Lord Admiral's company, with Edward Alleyn (1594-1600) and also owned the theatre at Newington Butts and the Bear Garden on Bankside. For the company, copying the rival Globe, he built the Fortune in 1600, and left Alleyn in charge there while he fostered the Earl of Worcester's company at the Rose. Later he pulled down the Bear Garden and erected on the site the Hope for Lady Elizabeth's and the Queen's Revels. With Alleyn he was Joint Master of the royal game of bears, bulls and mastiff dogs. He bought plays from Drayton, Dekker, Chapman, Jonson and most of the dramatists, recording transactions in a diary.

HERBERT, Edward, first Lord Herbert of Cherbury (1583-1648). The 'black' Lord Herbert is an archetype of the Renaissance courtly writer, whose learning was an adornment, who was cooperative not competitive, wit allowing him equivocation, always concerned with *decorum* or *decencie* or *seemelynesse* or, to use George Puttenham's words, '*beau* semblant, the chiefe profession as well of Courting as of poesie'. He expressed an essential self-deprecating *sprezzatura* and *disinvoluntara*, in a milieu civilised by women.

Eldest son of the rich and landed family from Montgomery Castle, his mother was Magdalen Newport (her mother a

Bromley). She became the friend of John Donne and re-married, at the age of forty, Sir John Danvers, twenty years her junior. The poet George was the fourth son; Edward's other brothers were soldiers, courtiers and scholars. He was at one time the ward of Sir George More. He went to University College, Oxford, at the age of fourteen. He married the heiress Mary Herbert, daughter of Sir William, who made her inheritance dependent on her marrying another Herbert.

Besides writing Edward was skilled at music, fencing, riding and all courtly arts. Indeed, he was such a skilled duellist he believed duels were much the best way of settling wars. He was Sheriff of Montgomery (1605), abroad with Aurelian Townshend (1608) and with Grey Brydges, fifth Lord Chandos in the military expedition to Juliers (1610). In 1614 he was again a soldier with the Prince of Orange, at Juliers and Cleves, visiting Cologne, Heidelberg and Italy, and was a military inventor. He was the favourite of Queen Anne. As a member of the Buckingham group he was made ambassador in Paris. He was a skilled secret agent, the friend of the Prince of Orange, the Elector Palatine and France, and always hostile to Spain. He tried to restrain the French against their Protestant rebels, and suggested the eventually successful match between Charles I and Henrietta Maria. He was stabbed and beaten by a jealous husband, Sir John Ayres, in 1611. He was one of those left trying to cling to an unstable, middle course in the Civil War.

The centre of a brilliant circle of patronage he knew not only Donne but also Jonson, Selden and Carew. He wrote a history of Henry VIII, an autobiography, and the philosophical *De Veritate*, a pioneer attempt at comparative religion. He believed from Aristotle that man's chief faculty was *nous*, a natural instinct direct from God at birth which for him took precedence over conscience, sensation and reason. He attributed sin to hereditary physical defects. Though always an Anglican, he was alert to and tolerant of other religions. In poem after poem he reconciled Love with the cosmos:

> Not here on earth then, nor above,
> Our good affection doth impair;
> For where God doth admit the fair,
> Think you that he excludeth love?

Ed. S. Lee: *The Life of Lord Herbert written by himself* (1906).

HERBERT, George (1593-1633). Walton thought him from youth 'marked out for piety', but his elder brother Edward knew he was not 'exempt from passion and choler', and he saw himself as frail but fierce. Perhaps in time self-deprecation was stronger than self-esteem. Born into the house which Donne saw as a 'a court, the conversation of the best', he moved with his protective mother to Oxford and then London, went to Westminster School and Trinity College, Cambridge (though the winds from Fenland were not good for his health). Cambridge had long been the centre of Puritanism – 500 Cambridge men having gone into exile in the reign of Queen Mary – and there was always there a constant effort at establishing a balance between Geneva and Canterbury.

George was the real scholar of the family, becoming public orator in 1620, influenced particularly by the gentle Lancelot Andrewes (who was a major contributor to the King James Bible, and was Bishop of Winchester). Yet George deliberately turned his back on Cambridge, 'peace with all but bookworms', and launched on a political career as one of the two Secretaries of State and MP for Montgomery (1624); he was supported by William Herbert, third Earl of Pembroke, and the Duke of Lennox and Richmond. He idealistically wanted international peace between the states and religions, was anti-Spanish like his brother, but the Catholic victories in Bohemia and elsewhere made peace impossible, and he retired from the scene to Little Gidding, Huntingdonshire. Nicholas Ferrar, another political failure from Virginia, had set up there a 'Sanctuarie and Temple of God', where George became deacon, seeking to give away the cash rewards of prebendaries. Like Donne he bore his disappointments hardly:

> I am no link of Thy great chain
> But all my company is a weed.

In 1629 he married Jane Danvers, from his stepfather's family, a marriage of equals, giving 'daily obligingness to each other'. He became rector of two Wiltshire parishes near Wilton, and friend of the unhappy Anne Clifford, whose two marriages – first to Philip Herbert, Earl of Pembroke, then to the Earl of Dorset at Knole, did not bring her the comfort he had. White-haired at thirty-nine, he was regarded in the neighbourhood, so says his brother Edward, as 'little less than sainted'. When he knew he was dying he was as composed as Donne: he sent Ferrar a beautifully ordered book of his poems, all ready for print; sang a song to his lute, wrote his will, sent the weepers to another room, and quietly faded away.

His *Temple*, published at Cambridge in 1633 by Ferrar, was highly popular, going into many editions (one reader was Charles I while in prison).

H. Vendler: *The Poetry of George Herbert* (1975); M. Chute: *Two Gentlemen* (1960); M. Bottrall: *George Herbert* (1954).

HERBERT, Mary, Countess of Pembroke (1561-1621). Mary Sidney, Philip's sister and Leicester's niece, wife of Henry Herbert, second Earl of Pembroke, Spenser's 'Urania', patron of Donne, Jonson, Daniel, Breton, and many other poets, the greatest literary lady of her time. She translated *Antonius* (1590), from the French of Robert Garnier, a popular dramatist at court, and wrote ceremonial and occasional verse, and her own psalms.

HERBERT, Thomas (1597-1642?). Another brother of Edward, page to Sir Edward Cecil, he served with distinction in the army at Juliers (1610), in the navy in the East Indies (1617), and was commander of the Dreadnought (1625). He was disgruntled to get no further. He trifled in verse, and elegies and songs were published in 1641, notably in *Newes out of Islington*.

HERBERT, William, third Earl of Pembroke (1580-1630). His mother was Mary Sidney; tutored by Daniel, he was at New College, Oxford at the age of thirteen, and a favourite at court with Queen Elizabeth. He was 'the greatest Maecenas' of the time, according to Aubrey, and was the friend of Donne, Browne, Jonson, Massinger, Chapman, Inigo Jones and many other talents. He offended the Queen by making Mary Fitton, one of her ladies, pregnant and refusing to marry her (the child only lived a month), for which he was put in the Fleet Prison and rusticated. But he came to favour again with James I, becoming Lord Warden of the Stanneries, Lord Lieutenant of

Cornwall, Warden of the Forest of Dean, Privy Counsellor, and Lord Chamberlain (1615-26). For all his *braggadochio*, he was a melancholy man, which he sought to cure by marrying Mary Talbot, daughter of the Earl of Shrewsbury.

His lively mind led him to develop waterworks in Monmouthshire, become Governor of the Society of London for Mineral and Battery Works, and he had interests in many companies – the Virginia, the North West Passage, the Bermudas, the Guiana, the East India. He was on the Council for New England (1620). He supported Ralegh's attempt to regain courtly respect, and Bacon in his troubles, and was a moderating influence on Buckingham. He was Chancellor of Oxford from 1617 to his death, and Broadgates Hall was renamed Pembroke College after him. In politics, like his family, he was anti-Spanish and pro-French, but opposed all extremists. Most observers have been confused by his mixture of gravity and libidiousness, loyalty and advocacy of liberty, but this is typical of the Renaissance. He was expert at jousting, but his main interests were drama and poetry. He wrote masques for courtly entertainments, Henry Lawes and Nicholas Lanier composing music for his songs; and some of his many poems were published by Donne's son, in a volume with some by Sir Benjamin Rudyard in 1600.

HERRICK, Robert (1591-1674). Born in Goldsmiths Row, Cheapside to a close-knit and long-lived Leicester family. The family business was in ironmongery, but Herrick's father (who committed suicide when Robert was only fourteen months old, devastated by the death of his first-born) set up as a goldsmith. Though technically a suicide's estate was forfeit to the Queen's Almoner, the family regained control with three administrators – Robert's uncle William, Sir Richard Martin and Giles Fletcher the elder. Of the £5000, Robert's share was £800, in an allowance at first paid £10 a quarter by his uncle, who apprenticed him as a goldsmith. It was not Robert's bent: he preferred Virgil, Horace and Martial, and he was released from contract to go to St John's College, Cambridge at the age of twenty-two, whence he moved to Trinity Hall, ostensibly to study law. With his college friend, John Weekes, he was ordained deacon in 1623, and with Weekes he was one of Buckingham's chaplains on the ill-fated expedition to Rhé

(1627). Two-thirds died and one aggrieved survivor, protesting against the fiasco, assassinated Buckingham. Like Weekes, who also survived, Robert finished up in a west-country living, at Dean Prior, Devon. The courtly vicar found 'A people currish, churlish as the seas', but the job was worth over £30 p.a., with fees and tithes, and Robert settled down with his housekeepers and innocent delight in the country. He kept an orphan lamb, a cat, a spaniel (Tracy), a pet hen, a goose, a pet sparrow (Phil) and even a pet pig. And he had in his local literary circle, Weekes, another Rhé survivor, James Smith, related to Sir Richard Grenville, and the local ladies whom he assiduously and with joy cultivated.

Few writers had so many friends. He was in Jonson's circle, and was particularly friendly with William Browne, John Selden, Adrian and Endymion Porter, Sir William Davenant, Thomas Carew and George Sandys, as well as musicians, who wrote for his songs: Henry and William Lawes, Nicholas Lanier, John Wilson, Robert Ramsay and John Hilton. He knew his Mitre and Devil, his Mermaid and Triple Tunne. He wrote poetry continuously all his life, much of it to 'my girls', ladies known as Julia, Lucia, Electra, Anthea, Diamenea, Perenna, and many other names. He always insisted on his 'cleanly wantonness', and it is wise to see them as chiefly fictional. After all, Abraham Cowley had twenty-one 'mistresses', but was too shy to speak of love to a single one of them! Poetry was to him a way of finding order. It is unlikely that such a man would involve himself too deeply in amorous disorder.

At first he never considered print, though a few pieces appeared accidentally in miscellanies. But as he grew older the more he was convinced that his growing MSS, 'begot of my immortal seed', would provide a memorial of his friends and times, and he offended his Bishop by a swift visit to London to negotiate in 1640 with the publisher Andrew Crooke. The poems *Hesperides* were eventually published in 1648 – more than 1400 in 477 pages, about love, society, nature, weddings, drinking, and one-fifth of them religious, a tumultuous jumble which was not reprinted for 175 years. The Herrick family was split by the Civil War, when he said 'the roof's a tottering', and Robert was ejected to London until 1660, but his poetry seems to have died with the Civil War.

G.W. Scott: *Robert Herrick 1591-1674* (1975); M. Chute: *Two Gentlemen* (1960).

HEYWOOD, Jasper (1535-98). Son of John. He was a page to Princess Elizabeth, and educated at Merton College, Oxford, aged twelve, where he was Lord of Misrule at Christmas festivities, and known for his translations of Seneca, *Troas* (published 1559), *Thyestes* (published 1560), and *Hercules furens* (published 1561). Staying staunchly RC, he was expelled from Merton College, and for a while he was Fellow at All Souls' College, but had to resign, becoming a Jesuit priest in Rome, and Professor of Theology for seventeen years in Dillingen. His one visit to England as a missionary led to imprisonment in the Clink and the Tower for seventeen months, and then final expulsion. His actor's presence, almost that of an apostolic legate, and his views, considered moderate for a Jesuit, encouraged the offer of an Anglican bishopric if he would only conform.

HEYWOOD, John (1497?-1580?). A Londoner and RC, he was an important writer who bridged into the Renaissance from medieval patterns. He started as a choirboy with the Chapel Royal at 8d a day in 1515, and may have been educated at Broadgates Hall, Oxford. He became a singer and 'player of the virginals' at £6.13.4 a quarter by 1526, and was later master of the Children of the Chapel Royal performing before Princess Mary, and Sir Thomas More at North Mymms, where he met and married Eliza Rastell, niece of Sir Thomas. He survived the reign of Edward VI and had his best period under Queen Mary, retiring abroad after her death to spend the rest of his days in exile, chiefly in Malines.

He was higher in social status than the court jesters, Henry VIII's Will Summers, or Mary's Jane, but he inherited the licence of the minstrels and his repartee was welcome even when Mary was dying. Out of this came epigrams which became a standard Renaissance form. His own were published in successive editions (1562-98) and influenced among others Sir John Harington and Sir John Davies. Some of his ballads also reached print and set a style for the street balladists. Even more important was his transformation of the medieval interlude into Tudor comedy: *The Pardoner and the Frere; Johan the Husband, Tyb the Wife and Syr Jhan the Priest,* (both published 1533); *The Four P.P.* (1543); and later, *The Play of the Wether,* and *The Play of Love.*

R.C. Johnson: *John Heywood* (1970); R. de la Bère: *John Heywood, Entertainer* (1937).

HEYWOOD, Robert (1574?-1645). From another Heywood family in Heywood Hall, Lancashire, his mother was an Asheton from Penketh; he was the friend of Richard James. He wrote for MS circulation five 'centuries' of poems: *Observations and Instructions, Divine and Morall.*

HEYWOOD Thomas (d. 1641). Yet another Heywood family, this time from Lincolnshire. He was probably a Fellow of Peterhouse, Cambridge. He was an utter professional, like Bernard Shaw setting himself a target of so much writing for each day. He was apparently deformed in some way, but this did not prevent him sharing the hurlyburly of London which he loved:

To see, as I have seene, Hercules in his own shape hunting the boare, knocking down the Bull . . . pashing the Lion, squeezing the Dragon, dragging Cerberus in chains . . . O, these were sights to make an Alexander . . . so bewitching a thing is lively and well spirited action.

And he was proud to be English: 'our country breeds no beggars' he has a heroine say to an Emperor of Morocco, and against Spaniards another says:

> These Englishmen,
> Nothing can daunt them. Even in misery,
> They'll not regard their masters.

Many of his plays are lost because he disdained printing them. He claimed to have had a hand – or at least a finger – in 220. From a huge canon, one might single out the domestic tragedy, *A Woman Killed with Kindness* (1603); *The Fair Maid of the West* (1617), *The English Traveller* (published 1633) and *The Wise-Woman of Hogsdon* (published 1638). There are unchronicled gaps in his life, for instance 1619-30 when his theatrical connections temporarily ceased, presumably while he could afford to undertake more serious work.

F.S. Boas: *Thomas Heywood* (1950); A.M. Clark: *Thomas*

Heywood, Playwright and Miscellanist (1931); O. Cromwell: *Thomas Heywood: a Study in the Elizabethan Drama of Everyday Life* (1928).

HIGGINS, John (fl. 1570-1602). Probably educated at Christ Church, Oxford, he was, according to Hearne, a poet, translator and antiquary of great industry, who revised Huloet's *Dictionarie* (1572), published with Nicholas Udall *Flowers, or Eloquent Phrases of the Latine Speach* (1575) and other works (much was left in MSS), including typically *A Discourse on the ways how to annoy the King of Spain* (1571). But he is chiefly known for his continuation, in 1574 and 1587, of the *Myrroure for Magistrates*, in which the first uses of some modern punctuation like the apostrophe comma, diaeresis and quotation comma are made. More importantly, he shifted the direction of the book – where Baldwin had started with Richard II, and had a contemporary reference in mind, the errors made by rulers, Higgins went back to Brute, the Romans, Lear and Cordila – and generalised his theme. His tragic heroes were apolitical, noble souls denied by destiny, fortune, reality itself. Shakespeare and his colleagues were much more influenced by Higgins than by Baldwin.

HILTON, John (d. 1657). Educated at Trinity College, Cambridge, he became parish clerk and organist at St Margaret's, Westminster in 1628, at £6.13.4. a year, and augmented his income by writing songs, madrigals, elegies, catches, rounds, including 'Come fellow . . .', 'Come let us all a-maying go . . .' and 'Turn, Amaryllis . . .' some of which were published (1601, 1627, 1648, 1652).

HOLLAND, Abraham (d. 1626). The son of Philemon, he went to Trinity College, Cambridge, settled in Chelmsford, and produced the narrative poem about the battle of Lepanto, *Naumachia* (1622). He was a voluminous translator. His other poems, including his own epitaph, were published posthumously by his brother Henry in 1626. Among his friends were Drayton and William Browne.

HOLLAND, Hugh (d. 1633). A Denbigh man, son of the Welsh poet Robert, he went to Westminster School and Trinity College, Cambridge, travelled in Europe and the Middle East, where he became an RC, and despite Buckingham's support and much to his discontent, never got preferment. A man from the Mermaid, he knew Jonson and Shakespeare, and published in English verse *Pancharis* (1603, about Owen Tudor), *A Cypres Garland* (1625, a lament for James I), and commendatory verse, including one poem in the Shakespeare Folio. He could also write Greek, Italian and Welsh.

HOLLAND, Robert (1557-1622?). Son of a Conway squire, he married Jane Conway and owned most of the town of Conway. He went to Clare, Magdalene and Jesus Colleges, Cambridge, was rector of successive parishes in Pembroke and Carmarthen, and published, besides his Welsh poems, *The Holie Historie of our Lord* (1594) in English.

HOOKER, John (fl. 1540). A Maidstone man, educated at Magdalen College, Oxford, who left in his MSS one English college play, *Piscator*.

HOPKINS, John (d. 1570). Oxford educated, he became the schoolmaster and rector of Great Waldingfield, Suffolk, and collaborated with Thomas Sternhold and others in the great psalter of 1549, which ran into over 600 editions by 1828.

HORNBY, William (fl. 1618). From Peterborough School, he cashed in as a reformed drunkard by publishing in prose-verse, *The Scourge of Drunkenness* (1618) and *Hornbyes Hornbook* (1622).

HOSKINS, John (1566-1638). A Herefordshire man, he went first to Westminster School, but after his father discovered a family connection with William of Wykeham, was transferred to Winchester, and thence to New College, Oxford. He was expelled for satire, but supported himself by teaching at Ilchester and Bath till he married a rich widow in 1601. He then immediately joined the Middle Temple and became a barrister, reader, MP for Hereford (1604 and 1614), Serjeant-at-Arms and then a Justice in Wales and a member of the Council for the Marches (a typical Inns of Court progression). His continuing satire, against the Scots this time, led to imprisonment in the Tower for the best part of a year.

He was the friend of Ralegh, whose *History* he revised, Jonson (he was called 'Ben's father'), and many Inns of Court men, including Donne, Sir John Davies, Selden, Camden, Daniel and Sir Benjamin Rudyard. He wrote much MS verse, including witty occasional poems, epigrams and epitaphs, very much following courtly modes:

we study according to the predominancy of courtly inclinations: whilst mathematics were in requests, all our similitudes came from lines, circles and angles; whilst moral philosophy is now a while spoken of, it is rudeness not to be sententious. And for my part I'll make one. I have used and outworn six several styles since I was first Fellow of New College, and am yet able to bear the fashion of the writing company.

L.B. Osborn: *The Life, Letters, and Writings of John Hoskyns 1566-1638* (1937).

HOWARD, Henry, Earl of Surrey (1517?-47). From the great Howard family, his father was the third Duke of Norfolk, his mother the daughter of Edward Stafford, Duke of Buckingham. With John Clerk, and probably John Leland, as his tutors, from an early age he could translate Latin, Italian and Spanish. He started in court as companion at Windsor to Henry VIII's natural son, Henry Fitzroy, Duke of Richmond, who married his sister Mary. He was married at fifteen to Frances de Vere, daughter of the fifteenth Earl of Oxford. His loyalty to Henry VIII was remarkable. He was sword-bearer at the coronation of Anne Boleyn (1533), Earl Marshal at her trial (1536), mourner at the funeral of Jane Seymour (1537), jouster at the marriage of Anne of Cleves, and mourner at the funeral of his kinswoman, Catherine Howard. He served his monarch with distinction, as a marshal in France (1543-6), as an agent and diplomat, and against the northern rebels in 1536. His chief difficulties were the RC loyalties of his family and a 'heady will', which got him into prison twice (in 1542 over a quarrel; in 1543 for breaking the windows of a London citizen with bolts from a crossbow) but he survived these handicaps. Finally however he fell foul of the stratagems of Edward Seymour, Lord Hertford, who caught him in an offence about quartering arms (to prove the Howards superior to the Seymours). Henry VIII saw this as a threat to the succession of Edward VI, and had him put in the Tower, tried for high treason and executed, only days before his own death.

He was one of the circle led by Sir Thomas Wyatt and Sir Francis Bryan, who adorned Henry VIII's court with brilliant ceremonial and poetry, and which also included Thomas Lord Vaux, John Heywood and Edward Somerset. He experimented in sonnets and *ottava rima*, knew well Petrarch, Boccaccio, Martial and Horace, translated two books of the

Aeneid into a 'straunge meter', which in fact was the first blank verse, and came to light when Tottel published in 1557 a MS anthology of verse by his group, *Songes and Sonnettes*, in which 96 were by Wyatt, forty by Nicholas Grimald, and forty by himself. He learned much from Wyatt, although they were not intimate friends, because of the age gap.

He pioneered many of the central qualities of Renaissance poetry, being particularly good and one of the first at splitting up a proposition or hypothesis into a catalogue of component parts, deriving from them a metaphorical pattern:

> Set me whereas the sun doth parch the green,
> Or when his beams do not dissolve the ice;
> In temperate heat, where he is felt and seen;
> In presence prest of people, mad, or wise;
> Set me in high, or get in low degree;
> In longest night, or in the shortest day . . .

In fact, he built his antitheses with such delight he did not notice that, for instance, in that last line there is no antithesis at all!

HOWELL, James (1594?-1666). Son of a clergyman from Llangammarch, Brecknockshire, his brother became Bishop of Bristol. After Hereford School and Jesus College, Oxford, and some time abroad representing a glass firm and becoming familiar with French, Spanish and Italian, he set himself on political preferment from 1622. He failed to get the embassy in Constantinople, was tutor companion to the sons of Lord Savage and Lord Altham, and secret agent for the Turkey company in Spain, where he was friendly with Endymion Porter and Sir Kenelm Digby. This didn't help his career, since Digby was so opposed to Buckingham.) Promotion came slowly; as secretary first to Emanuel, Lord Scrope, later the Earl of Sunderland (1626); secretary to Robert Sidney; MP for Richmond; attaché to Sidney in the Danish embassy and Strafford in Dublin. In the Civil War his royal connections got him imprisonment in the Fleet (1643-51), but Charles II rewarded him with £200 and the post, worth £100 p.a., of Historiographer Royal. From what he wrote, one would guess that he was simultaneously a supporter of both the King and Parliament. He did not start publishing until 1640, and his imprisonment accelerated his output: political and historical tracts, translations, a dictionary, and much verse before and after 1650.

HOWELL, Thomas (fl. 1568). A Somerset man in the service of the Earl of Shrewsbury, and later the Countess of Pembroke, he published rather rough poems in *The Arbor of Amitie* and *Newe Sonets and poetic Pamphlets* (both 1568) and *H. His Devises, for his own exercise and his Friends pleasure. Vincit qui Patitur* (1581).

HUBERT, Sir Francis (d. 1629). Probably the son of one of the clerks of Chancery, he went to the Middle Temple, and became a clerk in Chancery himself. He published the poems *The Historie of Edward the Second* (1629) and *Egypt's Favorite. The History of Joseph* (1631).

HUDSON, Robert (fl. 1600). Not a Scot (he was born in northern England), though his best friends were Scots, for instance, Alexander Montgomerie, who thought highly of his MS poems, of which only four sonnets survive. A musician of the Chapel Royal.

HUDSON, Thomas (fl. 1610). Robert's brother, who was master of the Chapel Royal in 1586, recommended by James VI to publish his *Historie of Judith*, translated from du Bartas, in 1584. He left poems in MSS, some of which are cited in *Englands Parnassus* (1600).

HUGGARDE, Miles (fl. 1557). A London hosier who opposed the Reformation, and loyally backed Queen Mary, publishing many verse tracts accordingly: *The Abuse of the Blessed Sacrament, The Assault of the Sacrament of the Altar, The Excellency of mannes nature, A Mirrour of Love*, and many others, spanning the years from 1547 to his death. Bishop Bale rudely called him 'Insanus Porcarius'.

HUGHES, Thomas (fl. 1587). From Cheshire and educated at Queen's College, Cambridge, he went to Gray's Inn and had the chief hand, with Sir Francis Bacon collaborating, in the play performed before the Queen at Greenwich in 1588, *The Misfortunes of Arthur*.

HUME, Alexander (1560?-1609). Son of Patrick, the fifth Lord Polewarth, founder of the Marchmont family, he was born in Berwick, and educated at St Andrews University and Paris. Failing to get preferment at court and in law, he became the

Puritan minister of Logie, near Stirling. He wrote a verse autobiography when he was thirty, and many poems, including in Augustan heroic couplets one celebrating the destruction of the Armada, and *Hymns and Sacred Songs* (Edinburgh, 1599).

HUNNIS, William (d. 1597). A musician and Gentleman of the Chapel Royal under Edward VI, he was opposed to Queen Mary and joined the Dudley conspiracy against her. He was put in the Tower in 1556 but managed to survive until his Lady Elizabeth became Queen, when his prosperity was assured. He married a grocer's widow (inheriting her first husband's membership of the Grocers' company), and he was restored to the Chapel Royal, succeeding Richard Edwards as master of the children, for whom he wrote plays, now lost (as are many of his songs, sonnets and roundlets, and his contribution to the entertainment at Kenilworth, 1575). Fortunately, some of his poems survive in the miscellanies, *Paradise of Dainty Devices*, and *Englands Helicon* (1600), otherwise we should only have his long sequence of homely religious works: *Certayne Psalmes* (1549), *A Hyve full of Hunnye* (a metrical *Genesis*, 1578), and his most popular work, *Seven Sobs of a Sorrowfull Soule for Sinne* (fourteen editions between 1581 and 1636). He was favoured by patents: Custodian of Gardens and Orchards at Greenwich, at 12d a day plus perks; toll-taker on London Bridge (which he sold back to the incumbent, as was the custom, for £40).

HUNTINGTON, John (fl. 1553). An Oxford Protestant clergyman, well-known for his sermons, he was arrested in 1553 but recanted and escaped to Germany, returning to be canon of Exeter in 1560. In his youth he published the doggerel poem *The Genealogy of Heretics* (c. 1540).

HUTTON, Henry (fl. 1619). From Durham, of the same family as Matthew, Archbishop of York, and probably an Oxford man, he is known only for his satire, *Follie's Anatomie* (1619).

I

INGLEND, Thomas (fl. 1566). Known only for his interlude *The Disobedient Child* (published c. 1560).

J

JACKSON, Richard (fl. 1570). A Lancastrian connected with the Stanley family, he was educated at Clare Hall, Cambridge, and was a teacher at Ingleton, West Yorkshire. A ballad-writer best known for his MS poem *Flodden Field*, written about 1570.

JAMES, Richard (1592-1638). From Newport, Isle of Wight, he was educated at Newport School and Exeter College, Oxford. He took orders but only had one living, at Little Mongeham, Kent in 1629. He acted in Russia as chaplain to Sir Dudley Digges, but most of the time he seems to have had his own resources to travel widely in Wales, Scotland, Shetland, Germany and Greenland. We know he had a devastating wit, but his reputation is that of a quiet and esteemed scholar, friend of Sir Robert Cotton (with whom he was imprisoned in about 1630 over a political MS), Sir Kenelm Digby, Sir John Eliot, Sir Henry Spelman, Ben Jonson and many others. He followed the example of his uncle Thomas, Bodley's first librarian, in looking after the library of Sir Robert Cotton and his son Sir Thomas. He had strong Protestant views, engaged in controversy, and left many MSS, some of which reflect his skill not only in classical but in Saxon and Gothic languages; an Anglo-Saxon dictionary; a Russian vocabulary; and many poems in Latin and English, religious and secular, written throughout his life.

JENYE, Thomas (fl. 1565-83). A professional conspirator, he was in service with Thomas Randolph, the most prominent secret agent in Scotland; with Sir Henry Norris, at the embassy in France, where he tried to get the Earl of Moray to England; and was a leading light in the northern rebellion of 1569 and fled abroad when attainted. He was plotting for Mary Queen of Scots in Brussels (1570); was a pensioner of the Spanish secret service until 1574; was with Egremont Ratcliffe in Norway (1578), when his leader was executed for a plot against Don John of Austria; and he was involved in the Throckmorton conspiracy of 1584. Understandably, he only wrote political poetry in MSS, *Maister Randolphes Phantasey* (1565) about Moray's revolt, and from Ronsard, *The Present Troobles* *in France* (published Antwerp, 1568).

JENYNGES, Edward (fl. 1574). We know only his ballad-poem, *Alfagus and Archelaus* (published 1574), founded on the story of Orestes and Pylades.

JOHNSON, Richard (1573-1659?). An apprentice, then a freeman of London and a romance writer best-known for his *Famous Historie of the Seaven Champions of Christendom* (1596), which mixes good blank verse with prose, and his earlier rhymed *Nine Worthies of London* (1592). He also published, before 1620, *The Golden Garland of Princely Pleasures and Delicate Delights* (songs and sonnets), and elegies.

JOHNSON, Robert (fl. 1626). A lutanist and composer who began with Sir Thomas Kytson in Suffolk, participated in the 1575 Kenilworth entertainments, and finally became musician to Prince Henry in 1611 at £40 p.a. and to Charles I in 1626 at £60 p.a. Before that he was musician to the Lord Chamberlain's company, second only on the flute, it was said, to John Dowland. He wrote the music for Shakespeare's *The Tempest*, Middleton's *The Witch*, Beaumont and Fletcher's *Valentinian*, and Jonson's *Masque of the Gipsies*.

JONSON, Ben (1573?-1637). A Londoner and son of a clergyman, his mother remarried a member of the Bricklayers and Tilers company, and he started work as an apprentice bricklayer. But his literary talents were displayed at an early age, and he was sent to Westminster School, but not to a university. Like other wits he had courtly ambitions and served as a soldier in the United Provinces. At different times he cultivated Sir Robert Townshend, Lord Aubigny, Sir Robert Cotton and Sir Walter Ralegh, with whose *History* he assisted. He had RC connections, and was therefore a useful Privy Council agent at the time of the Gunpowder Plot, but political preferment was always denied him, perhaps because he was by nature undiplomatic, quick-tempered and arrogant.

By 1597, *faute de mieux*, he had become an actor, later a playwright, touring with Lord Pembroke's men, later joining the Lord Chamberlain's, and then settling with the Lord Admiral's under Henslowe. His irascible nature was early shown when in a quarrel he killed a fellow-actor and was imprisoned in Newgate. He escaped execution by pleading clergy (as the son of a clergyman), but had his hand branded.

He was, with colleagues, twice gaoled for plays that offended the authorities, *Isle of Dogs* (1597) and *Eastward Ho* (1605), and he created public scandal by his bitter 'stage war' against Dekker and Marston. In 1610 he won a pension of 100 marks a year from James I, which he commuted to £100 and wine. He was nominated Master of the Revels, should Buc and Astley die, but he never filled the post. William Herbert, third Earl of Pembroke, at one time sent him £25 every New Year's Day. As the writer of City pageants, he became Chronologer of the City of London at £10 p.a. But he was disappointed by the rewards of playwriting. He told his friend, William Drummund, that twenty-eight plays in forty-one years had yielded him only £200, although at £7 a play he was better paid than most.

He was somewhat ashamed of the public playhouses, while at the same time showed skill and joy in exploiting their staging possibilities. He thought poetry a higher art altogether, valuing his songs, epigrams and other poems, which provide the heart of his *Workes* (1616), titled with typical pride and an Augustan self-assurance. He believed that 'Poets are of rarer birth than Kings': it was poetry that was the 'sacred invention', 'blessed, aeternall, and most true devine'. He referred to his plays as poems, as indeed some of them are, and has Ovid Junior say to Ovid Senior in *Poetaster:*

> I am not known unto the open stage,
> Nor doe I traffique in their *theaters*.
> Indeede, I doe acknowledge, at request
> Of some neere friends, and honourable *Romanes*,
> I have begunne a *poeme* of that nature.

What irked him more than financial distress though was the lack of proper dignity afforded by the theatre, and he disliked much of its cheap rabble-rousing.

After poetry, he esteemed scholarship, and thought of himself as a scholar. Indeed, he produced several scholarly books, including an English grammar, and was temporarily Professor of Rhetoric at Gresham College, London. He disapproved of plays which did not observe classical standards, did not obey the unities, mixed tragedy and comedy, and which were not properly constructed with a Chorus, acts and scenes, proper elocution and *sententiae*. For this reason he seldom had a good word for any contemporary poets or dramatists. Even Shakespeare he found 'careless', and for him Donne's accents didn't work while the metaphors were 'far-fet'. Bishop Fuller's description of the wit-combats at the Mermaid between Shakespeare and Jonson is worth repeating:

which two I behold like a Spanish Great Galleon, and an English Man-of-War; Maister Johnson (like the former) was built far higher in learning; solid, but slow in his performances. Shakespeare, with the English Man-of-War, lesser in bulk, but lighter in sailing, could turn with all tides, tack about and take advantage of all winds, by the quickness of his Wit and Invention.

Such a metaphor, with memories of the Armada still vivid, indicates that Jonson had less of the Renaissance in him than Shakespeare. Jonson's basic flaw was that he believed

> Men that are safe, and sure, in all they doe,
> Care not what trials they are put unto;
> They meet the fire, the Test, as Martyrs would,
> And though Opinion stamps them not, are gold.

He was a perfectionist, wanting 'A printed book without a blot! All Beauty, and without a spot.' He didn't like compromising between popular and closet drama, or between courtly and classical standards. This was why, seeking absolutes, he became connected with Roman Catholicism and envied the black-and-white world of Robert Southwell. His lyrical poems are the least affected by his neo-classical theories, the plays the most.

From his earliest comedies with the Lord Chamberlain's men at the Globe, *Every Man in his Humour* (first at the Curtain, 1598), and *Every Man out of his Humour* (1600), on to his later work, *Volpone* (published 1605) and *The Alchemist* (published 1612), he tried to establish a classical 'comedy of humours' dealing with

> Deedes and language such as men doe use,
> And persons such as comoedie would chuse,
> When she would shew an image of the times,
> And sport with humane follies not with crimes.

Rejecting Elizabethan bombast, irregularities and 'antikes', he was what Aldous Huxley calls 'one of the sobers, protesting with might and main against the extravagant behaviour of the drunks, an intellectual insisting that there was no way of arriving at truth except by intellectual processes, an apotheosis of the plain man determined to stand no nonsense about anything.'

He seriously believed few men were balanced (like his Crites in *Cynthia's Revels*, 1601): with most

> some one peculiar quality
> Doth so possesse a man that it doth draw
> All his effects, his spirits, and his powers,
> In their confluctions, all to runne one way.

The theory of the flesh made absurd by a dominant folly led to a theatre of caricature – plays beautifully constructed (one could draw a diagram of the plot of *Volpone*) but essentially critical, and little concerned with the reconciliation with absurdity which is the aim of Shakespeare's comedies and the English comic spirit: Jonson laughs *at*, not *with*. There are exceptions when he seeks to 'please not the cookes taste but the guests': *Epicoene* (Queen's Revels, Whitefriars 1609) and *Bartholomew Fair* (Hope 1614).

His tragedies are similarly handicapped, notably the best, *Sejanus* (Whitehall and Globe 1603), and *Catiline* (rejected by the Globe until 1611 but published by Jonson himself in 1605). His tragic heroes, unlike Shakespeare's, are wholly evil and cannot redeem themselves or their societies; and in both his comedies and tragedies he dismissed love as an irrelevant element. In a way he is almost a medieval, seeing tragedy as merely a story of downfall.

He drifted away from the theatre into what Dryden called his 'dotages'. In despair he longed for an illiterate audience, better than 'fastidious impertinents', finding a happier place for his theories and fantasies in masques, which he first attempted at Althorpe in 1603. He was a master in this medium, writing twenty-seven, as well as other courtly entertainments for performance at Whitehall, in noble houses and private playhouses. Court subsidies gave him free rein with casts, scenery, music, lighting and dancing. He knew these were mere 'disguisings', 'transitory devices' and totally ephemeral, but they gave him a truly lyrical outlet, and the conventions demanded uncritical drama of happy endings and reconciliations, order coming after disorder by delightful surprise.

For all his irascibility he built up several circles of writers who respected his learning and principles, just as he had several taverns which he visited (not just the Mermaid). They were known as 'Sons of Ben' or 'the right worshipfull Fraternitie of Sirenaical Gentlemen'. He was linked with all the major and many of the minor writers of his time, whether they were theatre men, Inns of Court men, antiquaries or scholars. He was certainly a giant, but in so many ways a misfit.

G. Parfitt: *Ben Jonson: Public Poet and Private Man* (1977); S. Orgel: *The Jonsonian Masque* (1965); W. Trimpi: *Ben Jonson's Poems* (1963); J.B. Bamborough: *Ben Jonson* (1959); M. Chute: *Ben Jonson of Westminster* (1953).

K

KELLO, Esther (1571-1624). Daughter of an Edinburgh schoolmaster from a Huguenot family, she became a celebrated calligrapher and miniaturist and made her living by presenting hand-illuminated works to patrons. Her poetry is religious in nature, as in *Octonaries upon the vanitie and Inconstancie of the World* (Edinburgh, 1609).

KELTON, Arthur (fl. 1546). From Shrewsbury, and educated at Oxford, he was a historian who 'must forsooth write and publish his lucubrations in verse'; and did, as proof of which we have his history (1547) which proved that the English and Welsh were descended from Brutus. He also published a *Book of Poetry in Praise of the Welshmen* (1546).

KEMPE, William (fl. 1600). A comic actor with the company whose successive patrons were Leicester, Strange and Hunsdon, the Lord Chamberlain, and after Tarlton acted Shakespeare's Dogberry. At one time he was a soldier in the United Provinces and Denmark. He devised contributions to many plays, merriments or extemporisations, *ad hoc* repartee, and the jigs, often obscene, that closed all performances, even the tragedies. He was one of the original sharers of the Globe. He 'daunst himself out of this world', as described in his *Nine Daies Wonder* (1600), when he morris-danced from London to Norwich.

KENDALL, Timothy (fl. 1577). From North Aston, Oxfordshire, he was educated at Eton, Magdalen College, Oxford, and the Staple Inn. His literary performance was poor, limited to the imitative *Flowers of Epigrammes* (1577).

KENNEDY, John (fl. 1626). A Scottish poet who published *The History of Calanthrop and Lucilla* (Edinburgh, 1626), reprinted in London as *The Ladies' Delight*.

KETHE, William (d. 1608?). A Scot who was in exile in the reign of Queen Mary in Frankfurt and Geneva, but later was rector of Okeford Superior, Dorset, and army chaplain with Ambrose Dudley, Earl of Warwick, in Le Havre (1563) and against the northern rebellion (1569). He published polemical religious broadsides, and psalms in Geneva (1561), some of which transferred to the English and Scottish psalters (1562), including his famous version of Psalm 100, 'All People that on Earth do Dwell'.

KIDLEY, William (fl. 1624). He was from Dartmouth and was educated at Exeter College, Oxford. His verse is lost, except for *A Poetical Relation of the Voyage of Sir Richard Hawkins, Knight, unto Mare del Zur* (1624).

KING, Henry, Bishop of Chichester (1592-1669). One of the more literary bishops, son of the brilliant John, Bishop of London, he went to Westminster School, Christ Church, Oxford, and on via the posts of prebendary of St Paul's, Archdeacon of Colchester and royal chaplain, to the bishopric of Chichester. He was the friend of Donne, Jonson, George Sandys, Sir Henry Blount, James Howell and Izaak Walton. He wrote poetry, particularly elegies, all his life, and a collected edition was published in 1657.

KING, Humphrey (fl. 1613). A London tobacconist who could present only 'a course homespun linsey woolsey of wit', but seeing his 'inferiours in the gifts of learning, wisedome and understanding torment the Print daily', published himself his *An Halfe-penny-worth of Wit* (by 1613).

KINWELMERSH, Francis (d. 1580?). From Essex, he proceeded, like his two younger brothers, to Gray's Inn where he wrote, with his friend George Gascoigne, *Jocasta* (1566), a blank-verse rendering of Euripides' *Phoenissae*. He may have been MP for Bossiney, Cornwall (1572).

KIRKE, John (fl. 1638). Possibly the godson of Spenser's friend Edward Kirke. A playwright, whose work is lost, except for the popular tragi-comedy *The Seven Champions of Christendom* (Cockpit and Red Bull), not published until 1638.

KNELL, Thomas the elder (fl. 1570), and
KNELL, Thomas the younger (fl. 1560-81). It is not always possible to disentangle who was who here. The father was a clergyman in Dorset, London and Middlesex, before becoming chaplain to Walter Devereux, first Earl of Essex. The son was a clergyman who had an LLB from Peterhouse, Cambridge. Both wrote polemic, anti-RC prose and verse, epitaphs, and one wrote *An Historical Discourse of the Life and Death of Dr Story* (1571).

KNEVET, Ralph (1600-71). A Norfolk man who was tutor and chaplain with the Paston family at Oxnead, probably later becoming rector of Lyng. He wrote many poems, religious and secular, and published *Stratisticon or a Discourse of Military Discipline* (1628), *A pastoral for the Florists Feast at Norwich, Rhodon and Iris* (1631), and elegies for Lady Katherine Paston (1637).

KYD, Thomas (1558-94). Son of a scrivener who went to Merchant Taylors School, but broke away from his scrivening apprenticeship to follow the other wits. He was briefly a notary, what Nashe called a 'noverint'. We have few details of his career at court, but by 1590 he was in the service of Essex as a secret agent. He followed courtly fashion in translating from Robert Garnier *Fair Cornelias Tragedy* (1595); other courtly closet plays, including a blank-verse *Pompey the Great,* have been lost. He also wrote for the public playhouse, chiefly for the Lord Chamberlain's company. It is likely that he wrote the originals of *Hamlet* and *Taming of the Shrew* adapted later by Shakespeare.

He ran into trouble with a campaign with which he was associated against the Dutch in 1593. When the Privy Council investigated and searched his lodgings, they found an essay which questioned the doctrine of the Trinity. He blamed the friend he was lodging with, Christopher Marlowe, and the rival group of Sir Walter Ralegh to which Marlowe belonged. Marlowe was exonerated, Kyd was not, and there was nothing more unemployable than a failed secret agent. Even his family disowned him and he died in poverty two years later.

Of his two plays which survive, *The Spanish Tragedy* (written c.1586) is quite extraordinary. It is the first revenge tragedy, posing the problem of why this genre was so popular in a Protestant society. It introduced so many new departures that perhaps the answer is among them. We have our first Machiavellian villain, Lorenzo, who lives only for the achievement of a selfish and exclusive ambition; it brings to the public playhouse Senecan horror, already familiar at court; it is episodic but, unlike Marlowe's plays, the plot is coherent and is about real people; it invents the antic disposition; it includes a play within a play, where death ceases to be fictional and becomes real, the first soliloquies, dumb-shows, supernatural appearances, and discovery scenes; it is full of irony and surprise: the title-page illustration of Hieronimo finding his son hanging in the stage-arbour, 'a place made for pleasure, not for death', indicates the shock suffered by the first audiences. Its popularity, which lasted well into the 1630s, was unrivalled by any other play, although Ben Jonson was commissioned to give it a new lease of life in 1600: he didn't really approve of it, added more mad scenes, duplicated the horror, and slyly subtitled it *Hieronimo is mad againe*.

P.B. Murray: *Thomas Kyd* (1970); A. Freeman: *Thomas Kyd: Facts and Problems* (1967); P. Edwards: *Thomas Kyd and early Elizabethan Tragedy* (1966).

KYFFIN, Maurice (d. 1599). From Denbigh, he was a tutor to the sons of Lord Buckhurst, and the friend of John Dee. Later in life he was successful as a financial officer in the army, Surveyor of Muster-Rolls in the United Provinces (1588), deputy treasurer of the Normandy expedition (1591), and Controller of the Muster-Rolls in Ireland (from 1596). He wrote a fine eulogy of the Queen, *The Blessednes of Brytain* (1587, 1588), an English translation of Terence's *Andria* (1588), and interested himself in translating into Welsh.

KYME, Anne (1521-1546). Born an Askew from the Lincolnshire family and forced into marriage by her father, she became a Protestant, which much offended her husband, and left her family to seek divorce in London. She may have served Queen Catherine Parr. She was arrested twice for heresy; she escaped in 1545, but was burned at the stake in 1546. She left a *Balade* in Newgate prison, preserved in MS.

KYNASTON, Sir Francis (1587-1642). From Shropshire, his mother was a Bagenall. He went to Oriel College, Oxford, and Trinity College, Cambridge, then Lincoln's Inn, where he was a barrister in 1611. He married the daughter of Sir Humphrey Lee, was MP for Shropshire (1522), and Esquire of the Body to Charles I on his accession.

He wrote a masque for a royal occasion (1636), translated Chaucer's *Troilus and Criseyde* (published 1635), and much verse including *Leoline and Sydanis* (published 1642, with some good sonnets appended). He founded the Musaeum Minervae (1635), an academy, of which he was regent, and which offered noblemen and gentlemen study in heraldry, common law, antiquities, coins, husbandry, music, dancing, writing, sculpture and behaviour, but which did not survive its founder.

L

LANE, John (fl. 1600). From Somerset, the friend of Milton's father and known to Milton's nephew, Edward Phillips, as 'a fine old Elizabethan gentleman'. He left much MS verse, including a completion of Chaucer's *Squire's Tale,* but much is lost. He published *Tom Tel-troths Message* (1600).

LANIER, Nicholas (1588-1666). From the London family connected with courtly music for several generations, he wore royal livery as a flautist. He composed music for masques by Jonson, Thomas Campion and others, and was not averse to giving a hand at painting the scenery. He was made master of the King's music on the accession of Charles I at a salary of £200 p.a. He was Marshal of the Arte and Science of Musicke in Westminster (1630), and was also an artist (who knew Van Dyck), a royal collector, and keeper of the King's miniatures.

LAUDER, William (1520?-73). From Lothian, and educated at St Andrews University, he became a minister in Perth, but devoted much of his time to writing for courtly service. There were several masques, now lost, and a series of published verse tracts which denounced immoral practices and advised the King towards a constitutional monarchy: *Office and Dewtie of Kyngis* (1556), *Ane Godlie Tractate* (1570), *Ane Prettie Mirrour, The Nature of Scotland,* and *Ane gude Exempill be the Butterflie.*

LAWES, Henry (1596-1662). Son of a vicar-choral of Salisbury, and like his brother William (killed in action, 1645) highly musical, he became a Gentleman, then Clerk of the Cheque at the Chapel Royal, and knew the family of Sir Thomas Egerton. While William wrote the music for masques by Davenant and Shirley, Henry produced and played in Milton's *Comus,* and composed for masques by Cartwright and others. He made a point of emphasising, as was perhaps needed then, that the music should bring out the sense of the lyrics. Both brothers set many songs of the period.

LEIGHTON, Sir William (fl. 1603-14). A Shropshire man, pensioner of James I, he was knighted for his *Vertue Triumphant* (published 1603). He was in prison for debt from 1608 to

1614, publishing *Teares or Lamentations of a Sorrowful Soul* (1613) of his experiences there. He also wrote songs, some with music, published in *Musicall Ayres* (1614).

LENTON, Francis (fl. 1630-40). Probably from a Buckinghamshire family, he became the friend of Sir Aston Cokayne and Sir Andrew Knyston at Lincoln's Inn. His poetry was popular with the ladies at the court of Charles I, and he became known as the 'Queenes Poet'. He published *The Young Gallants Whirligigg* (1629), *Characterismi*, imitating Overbury (1631), epigrams in 1634, and a selection of courtly wordgames including anagrams and acrostics in 1638. Much else, especially religious verse, stayed in MSS.

LEVER Christopher (fl. 1627). After Christ's College, Cambridge, he took orders but had no benefice. He published a number of religious poems beginning with *Queene Elizabeth's Teares* and *A Crucifixe* (both 1607), but we do not know if they won him preferment.

LEWICKE, Edward (fl. 1562). Nothing is known about him but his rhyming paraphrase of Sir Thomas Elyot's Boccaccio tale, *Titus and Gisippus* (published 1562).

LILLIAT, John (c. 1550-c.99). A lyric poet from Oxford, little is known about him, but some of his poetry was published in song-books, and his lovely lyrics are in MS in the Bodleian.

> When love on time and measure makes his ground
> Time that must end, though love can never die,
> 'Tis love betwixt a shadow and a sound
> A love not in the heart but in the eye;
> A love that ebbs and flows, now up, now down,
> A morning's favour and an evening's frown.

LINCHE, Edward (fl. 1596-1601). A friend of Richard Barnfield, he published verse-prose compendia, *The Fountaine of English Fiction* (1599) and *The Travels of Noah into Europe* (1601). He is the *grant auteur* of the sonnet sequence *Diella* (1596). Other poems doubtless reached print in miscellanies.

LINDSAY, Sir David (1490-1555). The earliest Scottish Renaissance poet. Neither he nor his wife Janet Douglas, a court sempstress, were of high rank. From a Fife family, he went to St Andrews University, but started in the court stables in 1508. He became equerry (really companion) of Prince James, son of

James IV, then an actor and usher, earning £10 a quarter by 1512. He was ultimately Lyon king-of-arms (1529), and the equivalent of Poet Laureate, in charge of courtly pageants and entertainments. He was the first to be thoroughly active in promoting the vernacular for poetry, law and religious services, though much of his work is reminiscent of medieval poetry and of John Skelton: *The Dreme* (1528), *The Testament of Papyngo* (1530), *Tragedy of the Cardinall* (1546) about Beaton, killed at St Andrews Castle, and the long *Historie and Testament of the Squyer Meldrum* (c. 1550). His best gifts were for narrative and satire. He was for a long time the best-known Scottish poet, hence the adage for anything irregular: 'You'll not find that in Davie Lindsay'.

He bridged, almost alone in Scotland, the medieval and the courtly Renaissance. His most important work was in drama, particularly *Ane Satyre of the Three Estaitis* (1540), though paradoxically the Reformation, which he supported, had the effect of killing off all drama in Scotland, so that there were subsequently virtually no Scottish dramatists into modern times.

Ed. D. Hamer: *Poetical Works of David Lindsay* (1931-6).

LISLE, William (1569?-1637). From a Surrey family related to Sir Henry Spelman, and Thomas Ravis, Bishop of London. His brother Edmund was at court under Queen Elizabeth, James I and Charles I. Educated at Eton and King's College, Cambridge, he wounded the Vice-Chancellor of Cambridge in 1608 in a quarrel, but this does not seem to have been held against him. He was esquire extraordinary to James I. We know him best as a pioneer in Anglo-Saxon studies, but he was also a poet, translating du Bartas (1598 and 1625), Virgil's Eclogues (1628), and Heliodorus (1631 and 1638).

LLOYD, Ludovic (fl. 1573-1610). Son of the Lord of the Manor of Marrington, and known to Hatton, Churchyard and Thomas Twyne. He produced prose-verse compilations (1573-1607), of which the first, *The Pilgrimage of Princes* (1573), is the most interesting. He dealt with military subjects, jewels, history, fables, panegyrics, all in rather a jumble. He was a barrister and Serjeant-at-Arms.

LODGE, Thomas (1558?-1625). Son of a Lord Mayor of London, he went to Merchant Taylors School and Trinity

College, Oxford, then to Lincoln's Inn (1578). He was fortunate in his friends: at university, Edmund and Robert Cary,
the sons of Lord Hunsdon, the Lord Chamberlain; in London,
Robert Greene, Samuel Daniel, Michael Drayton, John Lyly,
Thomas Watson and Barnabe Rich, who attracted him to
writing much to the disgust of his father who cut him out of his
will (although he inherited £100 from a grandmother).

A staunch RC, he found himself under Privy Council sur-
veillance, and sought to amend his fortune in two ways: he
joined the navy and served in the Canaries (1588) and in South
America (1591); and secondly by commercialising his literary
gifts, with some success. In the end, unhappy with his literary
achievements, he transferred from literature to medicine,
studying at Avignon and taking an MD at Oxford. He lived out
his life as an RC exile and GP.

His first book in 1580 was a defence of the theatre against
Stephen Gosson. He then tried writing classical drama, *The
Wounds of Civill War* (for the Lord Admiral's company, 1587)
and with Greene *A Looking Glasse* (for the Lord Chamberlain's, 1592). His other plays are lost. He wrote *An Alarum
against Usurers* (1584) to pay off debts to money-lenders.

His serious attempt at professional writing consists of prose-
verse romances. His *Scillaes Metamorphosis* (1589), dedicated
to 'the Gentlemen of the Inns of Court and Chancerie', was the
first Romantic handling of a classical theme in English, and
Shakespeare adapted it in his *Venus and Adonis*. His most
popular book, *Rosalynde* (1590), ran into ten editions by 1642
and was a source for *As You Like It*. He was Spenser's 'Alcon'.
His chief work was *Phillis* (1593), dedicated to the Countess of
Shrewsbury, 'the true Octavia of our times'. He published
satires, eclogues and epistles in *A Fig for Momus* (1595). After
that, apart from the MS poems which reached print in miscellanies, including *The Phoenix Nest* (1593), *Englands Helicon*
(1600) and *Englands Parnassus* (1600), he stopped writing.

C.J. Sisson: *Lodge and other Elizabethans* (1933).

LOE, William (d. 1645). From Kent he went to St Alban Hall,
Oxford. He was vicar at Churcham, Gloucestershire, master
of the college school at Gloucester, rector of Stoke Severn
Worcestershire, and chaplain to James I. When he fell foul of
Laud, then Dean of Gloucester, he went abroad temporarily as

pastor to the English Church in Hamburg. Later, he was vicar of Wandsworth. He is buried in Westminster Abbey.

His claim to fame rests in *Songs of Sion* (published Hamburg, 1620), remarkable because he sought to write wholly in monosyllabics.

LOK, Henry (1553?-1608?). Son of a London mercer, his mother was a literary Vaughan. After Oxford he became one of the agents of Robert Cecil, Earl of Salisbury, and was especially skilled in cipher. But his efforts did not keep him out of debt and he was jailed for debt in the Westminster Gatehouse (1606) and the Clink (1608). His century of religious sonnets, no longer extant, *Sundry Christian Passions* (1593) was an attempt at multiple patronage, dedicated to 56 different patrons, with other sonnets to 'the Gentlemen Courtiers in generall', 'the honourable Ladies and Gentlewomen attendants in the Court', and 'all other his Honourable and beloved friends in generall'. Altogether he wrote 328 religious and some 60 secular sonnets, addressed to everybody of note; a selection was published in *Ecclesiasticus* (1597).

LOVELACE, Richard (1618-58). From an old military/political Kent family: his father was killed in action in the United Provinces; his brother, the 'Colonel Francis' of *Lucasta*, was Governor of Carmarthen; his brother William was killed at Carmarthen (1645). He was born in Woolwich, and went to Charterhouse and then Gloucester Hall, Oxford, where he wrote the comedy *The Scholar* (1636), no longer extant. Known as 'the Adonis of the Court', he entered military service which was still his duty when he became the squire at Bethersden and elsewhere in 1640. His friends were the lost generation: Andrew Marvell, Sir John Suckling, Sir Aston Cokayne, Sir Peter Lely, Gideon Ashwell. He was an ensign in Scotland (1639), captain (1640), and, as a Royalist, was imprisoned in 1642 and 1648. His tragedy *The Soldier* appears not to have been acted. *Lucasta* was published in 1649, and his brother Dudley published a collected edition of his works in 1659.

LOWER, Sir William (1600?-1662). A Cornish gentleman and Royalist soldier, appointed lieutenant (1640), and lieutenant-colonel (1644); he was knighted in 1645. He wrote verse-games including acrostics, and amused himself in exile in Cologne and the United Provinces, where he was with the Princess Royal,

Mary of Orange, writing translations of French plays. He published one play, *The Phoenix in her Flames* (1639).

LYLY, John (1554?-1606). Son of a diocesan officer in Canterbury, he was educated at Magdalen College, Oxford, and Cambridge, and his noted wit brought him the patronage of Burghley and Edward de Vere, Earl of Oxford, through whose agency he became connected with the children's companies of the Chapel Royal, and, as vice-master, the St Paul's and Savoy companies. From 1581 he wrote for them eight plays, published from 1597, including *Alexander and Campaspe*, *Mother Bombie*, *Midas*, *Endymion*, and *Woman in the Moone*. He engaged in controversial prose for the bishops against Martin Marprelate (1598) under the pseudonym 'Double V'. He was MP for Hindon (1589), Aylesbury (1593), Appleby (1597), and Aylesbury (1601), but without real preferment he was in trouble with creditors. He was the friend of Thomas Watson and Gabriel Harvey.

His main claim to fame is *Euphues* (1579, 1580), a romantic novel written in the high-flown style later known as 'Euphuism'. He got the idea from William Pettie: an exaggeration of Renaissance delight in metaphor, antithesis, epigram, parallel phrases and *sententiae*. It was an abortive experiment and, although Robert Greene approved, it was attacked by Sidney, Nashe, Jonson and Drayton, as 'Playing with Words and idle Similes'.

J. Altman: *The Tudor Play of Mind* (1979); G.K. Hunter: *John Lyly: the Humanist as Courtier* (1962).

LYON, John (fl. 1608-22). Of Auldbar, his mother was a Gray, his wife the daughter of George Gladstanes, Archbishop of St Andrews. We know nothing about him apart from his debts, but he is supposed to have written the *Death of Alexander, Earle of Dunfermeling* (published 1622).

M

MACHIN, Lewis (fl. 1608). He wrote with Gervase Markham the comedy *The Dumbe Knight* (published 1608).

MAITLAND, Sir John, first Lord Maitland of Thirlestane (1545?-95). The son of Lord Lethington, educated in law in France, he was Scottish Lord Privy Seal (1567) and spiritual Lord of Session (1568). As a supporter of Mary Queen of Scots, he was the enemy of Regent Morton, whom he contrived to overthrow in 1581. With James VI, he was Privy Counsellor (1583), Secretary of State (1584), and Lord Chancellor (1587). In a long political career his principal achievement was to establish the Scottish Kirk on a Presbyterian basis (1592), but he was very much a moderate, skilled at political intrigue. Burghley, no mean judge, thought him 'the wisest man in Scotland'. He was pre-eminent in supporting courtly poetry, of which he was an able practitioner in both Latin and English; some of his poems were published in 1637.

MAITLAND, Sir Richard, Lord Lethington (1496-1586). Father of Sir John (see above). From a great Anglo-Norman family – his father was killed at Flodden – he was educated at St Andrews University and in law at Paris. Despite blindness, he was a Lord of Session (1561), Lord of the Great Seal (1562) and a Privy Counsellor. After he retired from politics in favour of his son, he concentrated on literature, building up a collection of early Scottish poems; he also wrote many himself: occasional, satirical, historical.

MARCKANT, John (fl. 1562). A vicar in Essex who contributed to the 1562 edition of the Sternhold-Hopkins psalter; he also wrote other poems, one of which was published as a broadside ballad, *Of Dice, Wyne, and Women* (1571).

MARKHAM, Gervase (1568?-1637). It is not clear whether there were one or two Markhams, but I assume only one, a gentleman from Cottam, Nottinghamshire, who served in the army in the United Provinces and as captain under Essex in Ireland, who was related to Sir John Harington and Anthony Babington. One of the first squires, writing on and practising agriculture, sport, horse-breeding and racing – he is said to have imported the first Arab horse. He was a skilled linguist in Latin, French, Spanish, Italian, and probably Dutch, but because he wrote so much for the printed-book market, Jonson dismissed him as a 'base fellow'. His published poetry includes *Thyrsis and Daphne* (1593, not extant), *The most Honorable Tragedie of Sir Richard Grinvile* (1595), *Poem of Poems, or Sion's Muse* (1595), and an extension of Sidney's *Arcadia* (1613). In drama he wrote *The Dumbe Knight* with Lewis Machin (published 1608), and *Herod and Antipater* with William Sampson (for the Queen's Revels, Red Bull, published 1622).

MARLOWE, Christopher (1564-93). The son of a Canterbury freeman and shoemaker, he went to King's School and Corpus Christi College, Cambridge, where he started writing. He joined the circle of Sir Thomas Walsingham, a cousin of the great Sir Francis, and was soon recruited as a secret agent working at Rheims, the home of many exiled RCs, and probably also in Scotland at the time of the Armada. During long spells of idleness in London he continued writing, both poetry and drama, becoming connected with the Lord Admiral's company under Henslowe and writing parts for Edward Alleyn.

Violence was never far from him: during a performance of *Tamburlaine*, an accident led to the death of a woman spectator and her child; as the friend of Thomas Watson, he was involved in a swordfight in Norton Folgate, near Bishopgate, where an assailant, William Bradley, was killed, and Watson and Marlowe pleaded self-defence. He became connected with Sir Walter Ralegh, in a group dubbed by its enemies the 'School of Night' because it endorsed Copernican astronomy; and was also associated with the Hussite heresy and the Rosicrucians, who at that time were considered atheists. A Privy Council inquiry discovered in the lodgings he shared with Thomas Kyd an essay attacking the Trinity. Kyd was found guilty of the authorship; and Marlowe was released under the probation of Sir Thomas Walsingham. One explanation of his sudden death at the age of twenty-nine was that further Privy Council inquiries drove him to suicide. A far more likely explanation is given by Leslie Hotson. While idle at Scadbury, Walsingham's home, he visited Eleanor Bull's inn in

Deptford where he met acting colleagues who had been evacuated there in the plague of 1593. A quarrel with an actor and fellow-agent, Ingram Frizer, about the payment of a bill led to a knife fight and in the mêlée he was killed by Frizer with his own weapon. At the trial Frizer successfully pleaded self-defence. Marlowe's enemies found him 'intemperate & of a cruel hart', while his friends described him as 'kind Kit'.

His contradictory character is clear in his writings. In the play he wrote at Cambridge with his friend Thomas Nashe, *Dido of Carthage* (c. 1585), the lines are full of superlatives and negative hyperboles, a characteristic which remained in his more mature plays, while the conflict between material reward and idealistic infinities mark all his poetry. It is no surprise to find in *Dido* a more harrowing account of the fall of Troy than found in either Homer or Virgil: the Greeks are 'quenchless' sadists.

His most important poetry is *Hero and Leander*, published posthumously and becoming a best-seller, and a translation of Ovid's *Amores,* which was banned, and burned by the Bishop of London. He is most esteemed for a succession of outstanding plays. Nashe identified his audience as 'Gentlemen of the Court, the Inns of Court, and the number of Captains and Soldiers about London', who, to judge from the number of repeat performances, gave a rapturous welcome to what seems today a series of remarkably bloody and rambling chronicles: *Tamburlaine the Great* (1587), *Doctor Faustus* (1588), second only to Kyd's *Spanish Tragedy* as the most popular of all Elizabethan plays, *The Jew of Malta* (1589), *Edward II* (c. 1590) and *The Massacre at Paris* (c. 1592). The texts we have are expurgated versions: the publisher confesses 'haply they have been of some vain-conceited fondlings greatly gaped at, what time they were shewed upon the stage in their graced deformities.' C.S. Lewis has described them as being about 'Giant the Jack-Killer'. Their heroes have endless power, knowledge or wealth, but are still insatiate in their ambitions. Tamburlaine, for instance, wanted to march against 'the powers of heaven and set black streamers in the firmament'; for all his great learning, Faustus seeks total knowledge; Barabas bargains his infinite material wealth against the loss of love and tranquillity; the Duke of Guise is the voice of them all:

What glory is there in a common good
That hangs for every peasant to achieve?
That like I best, that flies beyond my reach.

The conflict both fascinated and horrified his Elizabethan audiences.

D. Hilton: *Who was Kit Marlowe?* (1977); J.B. Steane: *Marlowe* (1966); P. Henderson: *Christopher Marlowe* (1952); H. Levin: *The Overreacher* (1952); M. Poirier: *Christopher Marlowe* (1951); F.S. Boas: *Christopher Marlowe: A Biographical and Critical Study* (1940); J. Bakeless: *Christopher Marlowe: the Man in his Time* (1937); L. Hotson: *The Death of Christopher Marlowe* (1925).

MARMION, Shackerley (1603-39). A country gentleman from Brackley, Northamptonshire, he went from Thame School to Wadham College, Oxford, and briefly served in the army in the United Provinces. Later, in London, he lived rather riotously on the fringes of Ben Jonson's groups, and was the friend of Thomas Heywood and Thomas Nabbes. He was in the army again in 1638 under Sir John Suckling, but fell ill at York, and retired unfit for service.

His plays, in fluent blank verse, are lost, apart from the comedies, *Hollands Leaguer* (Salisbury Court, published 1638), named after a brothel in Blackfriars, *A Fine Companion* (Whitehall and Salisbury Court, published 1633) and *The Antiquary* (Cockpit, published 1641). Of his poetry, *Cupid and Psyche* was published in 1637.

MARSHALL, George (fl. 1554). An RC writer who published *A Compendious Treatise in metre* (1554) about Christianity in England in the days of Queen Mary.

MARSTON, John (1575?-1634). Of a Shropshire family, but probably born in Coventry, his mother was a Guarsi, the daughter of an Italian surgeon; and his father was a reader at the Middle Temple. After studying at Brasenose College, Oxford, he followed his father to the Middle Temple at the age of sixteen, and they share the same grave there. However, his father recognised his son's lack of enthusiasm for the law when, leaving him his law books in his will, he expressed the hope that he 'would have profited by them in the study of the law, but man proposeth and God disposeth.'

For most of his life, Marston was drawn to the glamour of courtly poetry and drama, but his writings always had a bitter edge, and were given to satire. His *Metamorphosis of Pigmalion's Image* (published in 1598 under the pseudonym W. Kinsayder), dedicated to the 'worlds mighty monarch, good opinion', 'to detraction', 'to everlasting oblivion', 'no-body' (reminding us of the words he had inscribed on his grave-stone: *oblivioni sacrum)*, was so bitter, it gave the Bishop of London chief cause to have satire banned for a decade and to burn this and other satires and immoral books, by Marlowe and others. His enemies said he scourged villainies as 'boys scourge tops for sport on Lenten days', and certainly at first sight we can see no reason for his virulence.

He wrote chiefly for Henslowe and the Lord Admiral's company, but he was also connected with the children of St Paul's, and the Queen's Revels, in which company he had a quarter-share. He wrote pageants for guilds both in London and Ashby-de-la-Zouche. With colleagues he was gaoled twice, in 1605 and 1608, for satirical plays. The heart of his work lies in his sequence of plays: *Antonio and Mellida* (1595-1600); *The Malcontent* (1603?) a great play for the Lord Chamberlain's company and the Globe; *What you will*; and his own favourite, *Sophonisba* (1606). Several other plays were written in collaboration with members of Henslowe's group. One can see why his Malevole (*The Malcontent*) was regarded as dangerous:

> When they observe not heaven's imposed conditions
> They are no Kings, but forfeit their commissions.

This was a case against Stuart Divine Right, and for natural law and the evolution of constitutional monarchy. But what Marston, like others, transferred to Italian courts for hypothesis was more fundamental. He was concerned with man's incapacity, both tragic and comic, to escape from a fallen world, and with St Augustine's dilemma that an all-powerful God cannot be all-Good. Evil flourishes in folly where corruption is not controlled by true social justice.

He abandoned poetry and drama abruptly in 1608, leaving *The Insatiate Countess* unfinished, when he married the daughter of William Wilkes, chaplain to James I, and became vicar of Christchurch, Hampshire.

J.S. Colley: *John Marston's Theatrical Drama* (1974); P.J. Finkelpearl: *John Marston of the Middle Temple* (1969).

MARVELL, Andrew (1621-78). The son of a Calvinist Holderness clergyman who was drowned on parish duties crossing the Humber; his mother was a Pease. After Hull School, he went to Trinity College, Cambridge, a moderate college politically and his time there may have determined his stance. He avoided the Civil War by travelling abroad from 1641, visiting the United Provinces, France, Italy and Spain, and becoming polylingual. What thoughts he had about national dissension can be summed up as trust in providence to get things right in the end.

He extended his retreat in 1650 by joining as tutor the household at Nun Appleton of Sir Thomas Fairfax, third Lord Fairfax of Cameron who was as equally opposed to the execution of Charles I as to the invasion of England by covenanting Scots. Marvell managed to survive both the Commonwealth regime, becoming Richard Cromwell's Latin secretary, and the Restoration when he was MP for Hull and defended Milton. He was a latitudinarian, in the best sense, against Popish plots, persecution of nonconformists, and courtly tyranny and extravagance alike. Aubrey found him 'in his conversation very modest, and of very few words, and though he loved wine he would never drink hard in company.'

Some of his poems were published in his lifetime, but the best, written before 1650, remained in MSS. Richard Lovelace was his friend, and he was familiar with the verse of Edmund Waller, Abraham Cowley, and others. His famous beloved may have been fictional or a Royalist lady. He never married, and the Mary Marvell who published his poems in 1681 was his landlady, who used the surname purely for financial convenience.

J.D. Hunt: *Andrew Marvell: His Life and Writings* (1978); P.Legouis: *Andrew Marvell* (1965).

MASSINGER,Philip (1583-1648). He was born at the family seat of Henry Herbert, second Earl of Pembroke, where his father was house-steward and estate agent. Philip (certainly, I would think, named after Sidney) was a page at Wilton while a child.

He went to Salisbury School and St Alban Hall, Oxford, leaving on his father's death. What he did with his inheritance we do not know, for he was driven, as he says, like 'men of my poor quality' by financial necessity into the theatre with the King's company (1616-23) but chiefly with Henslowe's group, collaborating with Field, Daborne, Tourneur, and, above all, Fletcher who had the happy knack of forming close and complementary literary friendships: after BeaumontnFletcher, we have the team of FletchernMassinger and, as plague victims, they were buried in the same common grave. Outside the theatre his best friends were Sir Aston Cokayne and James Smith. He had some patronage from the St Legers, Sir Robert Wiseman, Sir Philip Knyvet and others, but chiefly from Philip Herbert, Earl of Montgomery, later fourth Earl of Pembroke, from whom he had a pension from 1624, estimated as increasing from £20 to £40 p.a. He also had his share of adversities; he was in prison with Daborne and Field, and not all his plays succeeded (Jonson was hostile, of course). Nevertheless, after Fletcher's death he was briefly the most prominent London playwright and achieved relative prosperity.

He had a hand in about forty-five plays. With Fletcher and Shakespeare he wrote *Henry VIII* (published 1623) and *Two Noble Kinsmen* (published 1634). Of the others, perhaps his chief contribution was in City comedy, notably *A New Way to Pay Old Debts* (1625) and *The City Madam* (1626).

Massinger was a moderate in politics, and there is no evidence he was ever a committed RC. He held three beliefs: that wealth ought not to be all-powerful; that rather than wealth the community should respect moral worth; that blue blood gave more hope of moral worth than upstart wealth. This can be expressed crudely in his plays – his aristocrats resort to immoral methods, sure of their own rightness; and he is apt to eliminate his villains by madness, or bolts of lightning. But he mellowed his plots with poetic justice, and he created, like Marlowe, believable monsters, lions not wolves, unscrupulous, pitiless, but full of vitality. Like Dekker's his City comedies seek enjoyable reconciliation.

D.S. Lawless: *Philip Massinger and his Associates* (1967); T.A. Dunn: *Philip Massinger: the Man and the Playwright* (1957).

MAXWELL, James (fl. 1600-40). Though from Kirkcudbright and educated at Edinburgh University, he lived in London or abroad, seeking preferment under Laud who called him 'Mountebank Maxwell', and was not convinced of his sincerity. In prose he wrote Protestant polemics, history and genealogy, and in verse he published *Carolanna* (1614, under the pseudonym James Anneson) and *The Laudable Life of Prince Henry* (1612).

MAY, Thomas (1595-1650). The son of a Surrey knight of Mayfield, his mother was a Rich. He went to Sidney Sussex College, Cambridge and Gray's Inn. He had a speech defect and concentrated on literature as an avenue to preferment. He wrote three classical tragedies and two comedies, including *The Heir* (Queen's Revels, published 1622), translations of Virgil's *Georgics* (1625), Lucan's *Pharsalia* (1627), and Martial's *Epigrams* (1629), and at King Charles's bidding two narrative poems on Henry II (1633) and Edward III (1635). He was a candidate to succeed Jonson as King's poet or Chronologer of London, but won neither post. Parliament was kinder to him and he became one of the joint secretaries at £200 p.a.

MAYNE, Jasper (1604-72). From a Devon family, he went to Westminster School and Christ Church, Oxford. While William Herbert, third Earl of Pembroke, was Chancellor of the university, he wrote much MS poetry, and tried his hand at plays ('works of this light nature . . . things which need an apology for being written at all'): a comedy, *The City Match*, (Whitehall and Blackfriars, published 1639) and a tragicomedy, *The Amorous War* (1639). He later gained a DD, and became rector successively of Cassington and Pyrton, Oxfordshire.

MEAD, Robert (1616-53). Son of a London stationer, he went to Westminster School and Christ Church, Oxford. He wrote verses at school and one play at college, *The Combat of Love and Friendship* (published 1654). After a time as a Royalist captain, he became an MD, working in Jersey, Sweden, Switzerland and Germany.

MELBANKE, Brian (fl. 1583). Educated at St John's College, Cambridge and Gray's Inn, he imitated Lyly in his Euphuistic ragbag, *Philotimus* (published 1583).

MELVILLE, James (1556-1614). The son of a minister of

Mayton, near Montrose, his mother a Scrimgeour. He was educated at St Andrews University where he was ultimately Professor of Hebrew and Oriental languages. He was very much influenced by his uncle Andrew, whom he followed to England in 1584, stopping at Newcastle as pastor of the exiled Presbyterians. He returned to Scotland with other exiles the following year and became Moderator of the General Assembly in 1589. He was bitterly opposed to Bothwell and the RC earls. James VI found him too great an extremist, putting him under restraint in 1607 in the same year his uncle was put in the Tower. He kept a diary, and wrote much poetry, chiefly religious, some of which was published in 1592 and 1598. *The Black Bastill, or a Lamentation of the Kirk of Scotland* was published in 1611.

MENNES, Sir John (1599-1671). From a Sandwich family, he was a naval commander from before 1620, commanding the Victory and Vanguard, and serving in the West Indies, Virginia and the North Sea. He later served in the Civil War. He was a friend of Sir John Suckling, and wrote much, perhaps coarse verse with James Smith, some of which was published in anthologies including *Wits Recreations* (1640) and *Musarum Deliciae* (1655).

MERCER, William (1605?-75?). Son of an Aberdeen minister, he ran away from school to serve as a soldier in Denmark and Sweden, and despite holding a royal prebend at Glenholme, he persevered with a military career, serving in Ireland in 1638 and as a captain, then lieutenant-colonel, in the parliamentary army. He wrote some elegies, but most of his work is doggerel. He published *Angliae Speculum* in 1646.

MIDDLETO1 I, Christopher (1560?-1628). From Cheshire, he was educated at Brasenose College, Oxford, and published a translation of Everard Digby's *Art of Swimming* (1595), a poetic anthology, *The Historie of Heaven* (1597), and two narratives in the style of the *Myrroure of Magistrates*, *The Famous Historie of Chinon of England* (1597) and *The Legend of Humphrey, Duke of Glocester* (1600).

MIDDLETON, Thomas (1580-1627). A Londoner from a prosperous family, he went to Queen's College, Oxford, and, like his father, to Gray's Inn. He married the sister of a fellow-actor, Thomas Marbeck, the niece of Dr Roger Marbeck,

Provost of Oriel. His earliest published work was poetry: *The Wisedome of Solomon Paraphrased* (1597), and the 'six snarling satires', *Microcynicon* (1599). He was in the theatre by 1602, after which his other interests waned. He joined Henslowe's group, writing for the Lord Admiral's, St Paul's and Prince Charles's companies, collaborating with William Rowley, Anthony Munday, Michael Drayton, John Webster and Thomas Dekker. Besides plays for the public playhouses, he wrote about twenty masques and pageants for the City of London. He became chronologer in 1620 at £6.13.4. a year, rising to £10, plus gratuities for special occasions.

He also had a hand in thirty-one plays, where oddly his undoubted gift for the heroic comes out best in his comedies; with Retiosa in the *Spanish Gipsie*, Mary Frith in *The Roaring Girle* (1611), and most notably with Captain Ager in *A Faire Quarrell* (1617) (probably his best play, despite Rowley's sub-plot). He seriously examines dishonour, the deceptiveness of reputation and the spuriousness of external codes. His ideal virtues are love, sympathy, forgiveness, self-knowledge, truth, charity and tolerance. After BeaumontnFletcher's *Philaster*, and the rise of the private playhouse, nobody could ignore the formula of romantic tragi-comedy, and Middleton's contribution to the genre include *The Witch* (c. 1626). His other noteworthy titles are *The Changeling* (a tragedy, c.1620), *A Game of Chess* (1624), his first success which earned £1500 in nine successive days, *A Mad World my Masters* (c. 1605), *Chaste Maid of Cheapside* (c. 1612) and *Women Beware Women* (c. 1622).

D.M. Farr: *Thomas Middleton and the Drama of Realism* (1973); N.A. Britten: *Thomas Middleton* (1972); D.M. Holmes: *The Art of Thomas Middleton* (1970); R.H. Barker: *Thomas Middleton* (1958).

MILTON, John (1608-74). There were, in effect, two Miltons: the poet of the Renaissance, and the Augustan: the divide in his life occurs with the outbreak of the Civil War, and I have described the conflict as between his 'Amaryllis' and 'Diomede'. He was the son of a scrivener and educated at St Paul's School then Christ's College, Cambridge, where he was nicknamed 'the lady of Christ's' because he was very hand-some. He was not attracted to a Church career under Laud nor a political career under Charles I. Instead he became a country gentleman with courtly pursuits. In his early literary career, he wrote two masques, *Arcades* (1633) and *Comus* (1634) with his friend Henry Lawes, but sought no preferment from his patrons, the brilliant Countess of Derby and the Egerton family. But he was susceptible to the ladies' charm: dainty and fastidious, like Donne, he went visiting, took an interest in the theatre, cultivated music and swordsmanship and expressed his thoughts in MS verse. Like Sidney he paraphrased psalms; like Donne he exercised his wit with puns, word-play and conceits. His verse was occasional – songs and sonnets, elegies, poems for birthdays or deaths or jubilees. He wrote beautiful verse in Latin and Italian, as well as English, but all his work, even *L'Allegro* (1632), *Il Penseroso* (1633) and *Lycidas* (1637), were to him 'triming' and 'toys': these were his Renaissance poems which he did not value highly.

All this time he was a polymath, reading a schedule harder than that of his 'tutor' Spenser. It was an unrewarding apprenticeship, it seemed:

> Alas! What boots it with uncessant care
> To tend the homely slighted shepherds trade,
> And strictly meditate the thankless Muse,
> Were it not better don as others use,
> To sport with *Amaryllis* in the shade,
> Or with the tangles of *Neaeara's* hair?

He prayed for the 'Diomedean strength' (Diomedes was the hero gifted to resist women) to prepare for epic writing: 'he who would not be frustrate of his hope to write well hereafter in laudable things, ought himself to bee a true Poem, that is, a composition, and patterne of the best and honourablest things.'

His second 'career' began in the 1640s when he made the 'grand tour', meeting Galileo, Grotius, Manso and Frescobaldi. He was particularly impressed by the academies in Italy – Gaddi's Svogliati and Coltellini's Apotisti – which fired his latent nationalism. 'What the greatest and choicest wits of Athens, Rome, or modern Italy, and those Hebrews of old, did for *their* country, I, in my proportion might do for *mine*.' He set out to find a 'fit audience, though few', a new elite based

on Parliament and the Assembly of Westminster, seeking out a
system of subscription patronage, and using print as a medium
for selected readers. He now threw off Renaissance humility;
published a collected edition of poems in 1645; abandoned his
resistance to women (rather disastrously, as was perhaps inevitable after enforced chastity); took up a political career,
serving after 1649 as Secretary of the Foreign Tongues to
Cromwell at £288 p.a.; ultimately, in addition to his epic
poems, he unearthed old MSS and printed *everything* – a
grammar, a history, a book on logic, his juvenilia. In his
revolutionary enthusiasm he attacked Charles I for reading the
'polluted trash of Romances and Arcadias', and Shakespeare
(whom he had once admired), and even sneered at 'feigning'
Spenser. He rejected masques as 'debauching our prime
gentry', rhyme as 'the invention of a barbarous Age', and all
Elizabethan drama and tragedy because it did not obey classical
rules. He thus became one of the first Augustans, preparing the
way for *Paradise Lost* and his later epics.

J.A. Wittrich, Jr: *Visionary Justice: Milton's Tradition and
his Legacy* (1979); W.R. Parker: *Milton: A Biography* (1968);
J.W. Saunders: 'Milton, Diomede and Amaryllis', *Journal of
English Literary History*, December 1955; J.H. Hansford:
John Milton, Englishman (1949).

MOFFETT, Thomas (1553-1604). Of Scottish descent, the son
of a London haberdasher, he went to Merchant Taylors
School, and then Trinity and Caius Colleges, Cambridge,
whence he was expelled for his Puritan views. Like his friends
Peter Turner, Timothy Bright and Thomas Penny, he turned
to Paracelsian medicine, taking an MD in Basle, and becoming
physician to Peregrine Bertie, Lord Willoughby, and Henry
Herbert, second Earl of Pembroke and his wife Mary Sidney
(he was a pensioner at Wilton). Later he was a distinguished
member of the College of Physicians, censor in 1588, physician
to Essex's forces in Normandy and practised in Ipswich and
London. He wrote much verse, but is best known for the
Silkewormes and their Flies (published 1599).

MONTGOMERIE, Alexander (1556?-1610?). From Hessilhead
Castle, Ayrshire, his mother was a Houston. He was at court
with Regent Morton (1577) as army captain and King's poet.
After Morton's fall James VI recognised his merit by awarding

him a pension of 500 marks p.a., on which he was able to travel in France, Spain and the United Provinces. He was an essential link in bringing the Renaissance to Scotland. In poetry he took over medieval modes in *The Cherrie and the Slae* (published 1597) and his *Flyting betwixt Montgomery and Polwart* (published 1621), but his MS sonnets broke new ground, introducing the Petrarchan form for the first time. In addition, he wrote pageants and entertainments for court, keeping alive what little drama there was in Reformation Scotland until James VI imported touring players from London and set up his own players in 1599.

MOONE, Peter (fl. 1548). Possibly a brother-in-law of Thomas Tusser, he published *A Short Treatise of Certayne Thinges abused in the Popysh Church* (Ipswich, 1548).

MORE, Edward (1537?-1620). A grandson of Sir Thomas More, who lived at one time in Buckinghamshire but died in Yorkshire. His only extant verse is his response to Edward Gosynhyll, *Defence of Women* (published 1566).

MORE, Henry (1614-87). Son of a Calvinist squire from Grantham, Lincolnshire he was not a Calvinist himself, though his uncle threatened to flog it into him. After education at Eton and Christ's College, Cambridge, he tutored Anne, Viscountess Conway. He refused all preferments (like Donne feeling unworthy and agreeing with Milton that 'God reserves his choicest secrets for the purest mind'). He liked Plato, bowls, music and conversation, started with poetry and finished in prose. He published *Psychozoia Platonica* (1642) and his collected *Philosophicall Poems* (1647).

MORLEY, Thomas (1557-1604?). From Lincolnshire and a pupil of William Byrd at Lincoln Cathedral. He was awarded an Oxford Mus. Bac., and became organist at St Giles' Cripplegate and St Paul's, and Gentleman of the Chapel Royal, later epistler and gospeller. As far as we know he was the first to use the term 'madrigal' on the title-pages of his songs (published 1593, and in four more editions until 1600). From 1597 he edited song collections. He wrote the music for *The Triumphs of Oriana* (1611) and for Shakespeare's songs 'It was a lover and his lass' (from *As You Like It*), and 'O Mistress Mine' (from *Twelfth Night*). He is one of the few musicians employed as a secret agent.

MULCASTER, Richard (1530?-1611). From a Westmorland family, he was educated at Eton under Udall, and at King's College, Cambridge, and Christ Church, Oxford. He started as a schoolmaster in London, becoming the first headmaster of Merchant Taylors School and having among his pupils Lancelot Andrewes, Thomas Lodge, Edwin Sandys and Edmund Spenser. After an interlude as vicar of Cranbrook, Kent, he became Highmaster of St Paul's School at the age of 66, not retiring until he was 78. He was a strong champion of the vernacular and taught his pupils P.E., music, singing and drama; he also wrote masques for his schools and played before Queen Elizabeth. He saw no reason why girls should not be as well-educated as boys. His English verse was written for his wife, to whom he was married for fifty years.

MUNDAY, Anthony (1553-1633). Son of a London draper (who died when Anthony was eleven), he was apprenticed to John Allde, the stationer, in 1576, but was interested in neither craft. In 1578 he was in Rome with Thomas Nowell as an agent gathering information about RCs at the English College, where the rector, Dr Morris, knew his father. Much of the material he gathered was later published in street-ballads or polemic prose. He became messenger of the Queen's chamber in about 1584.

His first known serious poetry (earlier work is lost) is *The Mirrour of Mutabilitie* (1579), but it was inevitable that the best base for a man determined to be a literary professional should be the theatre. He acted (not very well) with the Earl of Oxford's company, and toured with the Earl of Pembroke's company in 1598. He joined Henslowe's team, having a hand in seventeen plays in nine years. It seems he worked with Shakespeare on *Sir Thomas More* (not published until 1844). Only four plays are extant: *John à Kent and John à Cumber* (Admiral's, published 1595), two about Robert, Earl of Huntingdon, *The Downfall* (Admiral's, published 1599) and *The Death* (published 1601), and the play he wrote with Michael Drayton, Richard Hathway and Robert Wilson, *The True History of the Life of Sir John Old-castle* (published 1600).

Jonson satirised him as Antonio Balladino in *The Case is Altered*. His closest colleague appears to have been Henry

Chettle. He was also closely concerned with the production of pageants and entertainments in the City, especially from 1605, and was Keeper of their Properties. Perhaps his major literary work was his series of romances, beginning with *Palladino of England* (1588). He usually published in his own name, but occasionally used the pseudonym Lazarus Piot, or the identifying mottoes *honos alit artes* and *patere aut abstine*. He was a friend of John Stow, and produced a posthumous edition of the *Survey of London*.

J.C. Turner: *Anthony Munday, an Elizabethan Man of Letters* (1928).

MURE, Sir William (1594-1657). From Rowallan, Ayrshire, his mother was the sister of Alexander Montgomerie. He was educated at Glasgow University, and elected MP for Edinburgh in 1643 and became parliamentary commander in 1644. His son, also Sir William, was a leading Covenanter. He wrote a great deal of MS poetry, some in Latin, some translated, and some original English including ballads, sonnets, verse in heroic couplets, and psalms; he published a *True Crucifixe for True Catholikes* (1629).

MURRAY, Sir David (1567-1629). From Gortly, Perthshire, his mother was from another branch of the Murray family. In 1600 he became comptroller of the household to James VI, and was popular with Prince Henry, serving him as Gentleman of the Bedchamber, Groom of the Stole and Gentleman of the Robes, receiving generous gratuities – on one occasion £2000, on another £5200. He published *The Tragicall Death of Sophonisba* (1611), and sonnets and other poems in *Coelia* (1611).

N

NABBES, Thomas (fl. 1638). From Worcestershire, he went to Exeter College, Oxford, and then into service with Worcestershire families. He arrived in London about 1630, made the acquaintance of Shackerley Marmion and other Inns of Court men, and wrote plays for the Queen's company, chiefly for Salisbury Court. His City comedies include *Covent Garden* (published 1638, and dedicated to Suckling) and *Totenham Court* (published 1637); and his tragedy, *Hannibal and Scipio* was published in 1637. His high reputation was for his masques, published from 1637, most notably *The Spring's Glory* (1638), and in 1639 he published his poems including sonnets, elegies and epithalamia.

NASHE, Thomas (1567-1601). A dedicated professional man of letters, he was born at Lowestoft, the son of a clergyman, and he went to St John's College, Cambridge, where his arrogance rapidly came to the surface. The university play he wrote there apparently insulted the townsfolk, got his collaborator expelled, and led to his own departure, voluntarily, for brief foreign travel. He settled in London, and promptly used his sharp wit, in the Martin Marprelate controversy against the Puritans, in successive pamphlets, beginning with the *Anatomie of Absurditie* (1589). He took Greene's side against Gabriel Harvey, and this war of books, from *Pierce Penilesse* (1592) to *Have with you to Saffron-Walden* (1596), caused such public scandal that the Privy Council had to ban all continuation. Nashe himself tired of such 'fantasticall satirisme'. His brief incursion into the theatre was equally disastrous. *Summers Last Will and Testament* (published 1600) was a fair start, but the play which is now lost, *Isle of Dogs* (with Jonson and others, for the Lord Admiral's, 1597), had all writers imprisoned, and ended his theatrical career. His principal contribution to Renaissance literature tends to be obscured in the controversies; but he wrote lovely lyrics, finished Marlowe's *Dido Queen of Carthage* (1594) and his picaresque romance, *The Unfortunate Traveller* (1594), anticipates Defoe.

His high expectation of patronage, and his sense of power behind his skills, are extraordinary. He was supported at different times by the Cary family, who lodged him for a while; the Earls of Southampton and of Derby; and others, but he never retained patronage for long. He believed that his patrons did not respect him properly, nor deserve him.

All in vaine, I sate up late, and rose early, contended with the colde, and conversed with scarcitie: for all my labours turned to losse, my vulgar Muse was despised and neglected, my paines not regarded, or slightly rewarded, and I my selfe (in prime of my best wit) laid open to povertie.

He earned little even from his most popular works such as *Pierce Penilesse* (1592) which ran into six impressions in three years, receiving neither royalties nor an increase in the original small fee. But he also despised patronage:

give me one of my yoong Maisters a booke, and he will put out of his hat & blush, and so go his waie. . . . We want an *Aretine* here among us, that might strip these golden asses.

He greeted even kind patrons with the remark that they were exceptional in deserving immortality, whilst threatened unkind patrons with 'a living Image to all ages', 'full of *Aquafortis*, & Gunpowder, that shall rattle through the Skyes.' He was proud of the power of the pen: 'Those that care neither for God nor the divell, by their quills are kept in awe.' Yet his own position was ill-based: he claimed gentility, despised the balladists and almanac-makers, but equally condemned the scholars who wrote 'Lawiers english', 'inckehornisme', 'Hermaphrodite phrases, being halfe Latin and halfe English'.

He died, suddenly, at the age of thirty-three.

G.R. Hibberd: *Thomas Nashe* (1962).

NEALE, Thomas (fl. 1643). A travel writer, who also put together in MSS an autobiographical closet play, *The Warde*. He was the nephew of Walter Neale, the New England explorer.

NELSON, Thomas (fl. 1580). Probably educated at Clare Hall, Cambridge, he was a London stationer who published from 1583 broadsides, news-ballads, religious verses, epitaphs and accounts of pageants.

NEVILLE, Alexander (1544-1614). His family was from Nottinghamshire, his mother was a Mantell, his brother a dean of Canterbury and his cousin, Barnabe Googe. He was educated at St John's College, Cambridge and at one of the Inns of Court, where he knew George Gascoigne. He may have been MP for Christchurch (1584) and Saltash (1601). As the secretary of Archbishops Parker, Grindal and Whitgift, he wrote mostly in Latin, but English lyrics and a translation of Seneca's *Oedipus* (published 1563) also survive.

NEWMAN, Arthur (fl. 1619). Son of a Cornish squire, he was educated at Trinity College, Oxford and the Middle Temple. Besides a prose satire, he published *Pleasures Vision* (1619).

NEWTON, Thomas (1542?-1607). Son of a Cheshire yeoman, he went to Macclesfield School, and commuted between Trinity College, Oxford and Queen's College, Cambridge. He was a physician at Butley, Cheshire, and rector of Little Ilford, Essex. Besides his elegant Latin verse, he edited *Seneca his tenne Tragedies* (1581), writing the *Thebais* himself, and adding other translations by Alexander Neville, Jasper Heywood, Thomas Nuce and John Studley. He knew William Hunnis and wrote commendatory verses for him. Between 1576 and 1597 he wrote about twenty books. He seems to have been in the circle of the Earl of Essex.

NICCOLS, Richard (1584-1616). A Londoner, he served with the Earl of Nottingham at Cadiz, and then went to Magdalen College, Oxford, after which he served with Nottingham again, and James Hay, the Earl of Carlisle. A little-known Spenserian, he wrote many poems, elegiac, moral and historical, and published, under the pseudonym Infelice Academico Ignote, *Epicedium* (1606) and *The Cuckow* (1607). He edited the tenth edition of *Myrroure for Magistrates* (1610), adding his own narratives; his play, *The Twynnes Tragedie*, was registered in 1612.

NIXON, Anthony (fl. 1602). A pamphleteer who produced between 1602 and 1616 a series of verse-prose concoctions, including *The Christian Navy* (1602), *Elizaes Memoriall* (1603), *Oxfords Triumph* (an account of an entertainment for the Queen and Prince Henry, 1605), *The Blacke yeare* (1606), and *The Three English Brothers* (1607) about Sir Thomas Shirley.

NORTON, Sir Thomas (1532-84). Son of a wealthy London grocer, he started as a clerk for Protector Somerset when he was still a boy. He went to the Inner Temple in 1555 and married a daughter of Archbishop Cranmer whose stepfather, Edward Whitchurch, was the Calvinist printer for whom he did translations, including Calvin's *Institution of the Christian Religion*. He was MP for Galton (1558), Berwick (1562), and London (1571, 1572 and 1580) becoming known as 'Master Norton, the Parliament man'. As a barrister, he was counsel for the Stationers Company, solicitor to the Merchant Taylors Company, and, in 1571, remembrancer of the City of London. He was licenser of the press (1581), and 'rackmaster' of RCs including Edmund Campion. He was so fiercely anti-RC that he became dissatisfied with the compromises of the episcopal establishment and was committed to the Tower himself, briefly, for treason. He tended to equate the promoting of religion with the safety of his Prince and the good of his country.

He wrote poems, some of which were included in Tottel's *Songes and Sonnettes* (1557), twenty-eight psalms in the Sternhold-Hopkins psalter (1549), and, with Sir Thomas Sackville, the first blank-verse tragedy, *The Tragedie of Gorboduc*—one of the most cogent arguments offered for the evolution of constitutional monarchy. Published in 1565, it was played frequently at the Inner Temple from 1561.

NUGENT, Richard (fl. 1604). Son of an Irish judge, hanged as a result of the machinations of Sir Robert Dillon, his mother was a Plunket. He published *Ric: Nugent's Cynthia, containing Direfull Sonnets, Madrigalls, and passionate intercourses* (1604).

O

OGILBY, John (1600-76). An Edinburgh man, apprenticed to a dancing-master, he became the most renowned dancing expert of his time, dancing before Buckingham in London. When the Earl of Strafford became Lord Deputy of Ireland, he took Ogilby as tutor and clerk. His writing seems to have been restricted to humorous verse. His other skills were outstanding in courtly entertainments in Dublin, and he became deputy-master of the Revels. He opened the first public playhouse in Dublin, in St Werburgh Street. He lost everything in the 1641 rebellion, but returned at the Restoration to give Dublin primacy for several decades in the evolution of the theatre.

R.S. Van Eearde: *John Ogilby and the Taste of his Time* (1977).

OVERBURY, Sir Thomas (1581-1613). Son of a Welsh judge, his mother was a Palmer. He went to Queen's College, Oxford, where he became attached to Robert Carr, later Earl of Somerset, who advanced him, as sewer to the King, but whose friendship later proved his undoing. The two men enjoyed happy years in dreams of love, writing poetry in collaboration in their pursuit of Frances Howard, the Countess of Essex, and Overbury's own love, the Countess of Rutland, Sidney's daughter. Their mutual friend was Ben Jonson. King James imprisoned him for insulting the Queen. Overbury did not approve of Frances as a wife for Carr (love's game was one thing, marriage quite another) but her family, keen on the match, tried to get rid of Overbury by proposing sending him to Russia, the United Provinces and France. However, he stubbornly refused, and so they put him in the Tower, where, since his poor health would provide good cover, he was poisoned with arsenic. However, the conspirators were caught and executed, although the Somersets were reprieved.

His treatise, *A Wife* (1614), was often reprinted. It included twenty-one 'characters', verbal pictures of different people. Twenty writers commended the book, including Richard Brathwait, John Ford, John Davies of Hereford and Ben Jonson, who had not approved of his amorous pursuits but who thought he had markedly improved the cultural atmosphere at court. Among works dubiously attributed to him, the likeliest is a paraphrase of Ovid's *De Remedio Amoris*.

B. White: *Cast of Ravens* (1965).

P

PAGE, Samuel (1574-1630). Son of a Bedfordshire clergyman, he went to Christ Church, Oxford, and went as chaplain with the Earl of Nottingham to Cadiz (1595); later he became vicar of St Nicholas, Deptford. Izaak Walton and Thomas Coryat were his friends. He published sermons and devotional work, but in his youth, according to Meres, he was involved in 'the perplexities of love', and the poems he wrote then circulated in MSS, some reaching print in the collection *Alcilia* (1613).

PARKER, Henry, eighth Baron Morley (1476-1556). Son of the Marshal of Ireland, his mother was a Lovel. After an education at Oxford, he served at court as usher to Henry VIII, and as an ambassador in 1528. He was a friend of Anne Boleyn (whose brother George married his daughter, Jane) and of Thomas Cromwell, whom later it was his duty to prosecute. A perplexed RC, he was only really happy in the reign of Queen Mary. Like most courtiers, he felt he had to do some writing, but his shortcomings are seen in his translation of Petrarch's *Trionfi* (published c. 1553), and *Cupide and Dronkennesse* and his other MS relics.

PARKES, William (fl. 1612). A gentleman of Barnard's Inn whose prose-verse satire *The Curtaine-Drawer of the World* (published 1612) was particularly sharp about lawyers, usurers and scriveners.

PARROT, Henry (fl. 1600-26). A rather coarse and licentious epigrammist and satirist, he acted at the Fortune, and shared in Inns of Court society. He published *Springes to catch Woodcocks* (1613) and other collections (1606, 1608, 1615 and 1626).

PARTRIDGE, John (fl. 1566-73). Known only for his verse romances, several of which were published in 1566, including *Plasidas, Astianax and Polixena*, and *Lady Pandavda*; others followed in 1570 and 1573.

PEACHAM, Henry (1576?-1643?). Born in North Mimms, Hertfordshire, the son of a clergyman, he was 'rawlie torn' from Trinity College, Cambridge, and became a teacher at Wymondham School, Norfolk. He had many talents, in poetry, botany, music, heraldry, mathematics, painting, drawing and engraving. He travelled in the United Provinces, France, Italy and the Palatinate as tutor to the sons of Thomas Howard, second Earl of Arundel, a noted art collector. His many friends included Jonson, Selden, Drayton, Byrd, Dowland and the mathematician Edward Wright.

He first appeared in print in 1606 as a writer on art, and used his artistic skills in emblem-books, *Minerva Britanna* (1612) for example. Some of his occasional verse was published by Thomas Coryat in collections; he published in mixed Latin and English verse *Prince Henrie revived* about the Palatinate Elector's son (1615), and his collected epigrams in *Thalia's Banquet* (1620); but he is best known for his treatise, *The Compleat English Gentleman*, which was often reprinted from 1622. Poverty reduced him to writing tracts and even children's books.

PEEBLES, David (d. 1579). A canon of St Andrews from before the Reformation, he was a musician who wrote the words for his psalter, collected by Thomas Wood for publication in 1566.

PEELE, George (1558?-97?). He seems to have been one of the happiest writers of the period, catching not only popular joy but popular patriotism. He was the son of the clerk to Christ's Hospital, London, who was also a salter and pageant-maker, and was educated at Christ's Hospital and Broadgates Hall, and later Christ Church, Oxford. His university friend was William Gager, and together they were involved in theatricals, Peele writing a play translated from Euripides' *Iphigeneia*. His early marriage was fortunate, bringing him the means which enabled him to live a life of wit: some of his 'jests' were preserved in print in 1605. His lyrics were in every collection; *The Phoenix Nest* (1593), *Englands Helicon* (1600), *Englands Parnassus* (1600) and others. In London he was the friend of Marlowe, Greene and Nashe.

He settled down as an actor with the Lord Admiral's company, later the Queen's, and the Chapel Royal. He wrote plays for the companies (mostly lost) and we still have *The Arraignment of Paris*, played before the Queen by the children of the Chapel Royal (published 1593); *The Famous Chronicle of King Edward I* (published 1595); *The Battle of Alcazar* (published 1594); the first parody of romantic drama, *The Old Wives Tale* (published 1595); and *King David and Fair Bathsheba* (published 1599). He also contributed pageants for the City in 1585 and 1591, and for the Queen at Burghley's Theobalds in 1591. His long poems include *The Fall of Troy* (published 1589), *Polyhymnia*, a Spenserian eclogue (1590) and *The Honour of the Garter* (1593). He died of smallpox.

L.F.N. Ashley: *George Peele* (1970); Ed. C.T. Prouty: *Life and Works* (1952 and later years).

PEEND, Thomas (fl. 1565). An Oxford man and London barrister, he published two translations: Ovid's *Hermaphroditus and Salmacis* (1565) and, from the Spanish, *Historie of John Lord Mandozze* (1565).

PERCY, William (1575-1648). A son of the eighth Earl of Northumberland he was born at Topcliffe, Yorkshire and went to Gloucester Hall, Oxford, at the age of fifteen where he was the friend of Barnabe Barnes. His high hopes were to be disappointed: his amorous poems, *Sonnets to the Fairest Coelia*, were published in 1594, but of the six plays he wrote for the St Paul's children, only one, the comedy *Necromantes* (c. 1602), was ever acted. Little is known about his later life. Perhaps the turning point was his committal to the Tower on a charge of homicide. He disappears completely from the scene in about 1605, but in 1638 he was living a scholarly life in Oxford, 'drinking nothing but ale', and was still a bachelor.

PESTELL, Thomas (1584?-1659). After education at Queens' College, Cambridge, he became vicar of Packington, Leicestershire, and in about 1615 chaplain to Robert Devereux, third Earl of Essex, and to Charles I in the 1630s. Like his son, also Thomas (1613-1701), he amused himself with poetry. He published sermons and formal elegies, but the verse, religious and secular, stayed in MSS.

PETOWE, Henry (fl. 1598-1625). A Londoner, Marshal of the Artillery Garden, he published a continuation of Marlowe's *Hero and Leander* (1598), and *Philocasander and Elanira* (1599), in which he plagiarised Surrey, Churchyard and Gascoigne. He also wrote commemorative poems about Queen Elizabeth's death, King James's coronation, and the 1625 plague.

PEYTON, Thomas (1595-1626). From Royston, Cambridgeshire, he went to Cambridge and Lincoln's Inn, and started a long religious poem, a scriptural narrative, which he intended to publish in parts: *The Glasse of Time* (1620) deals with man's fall, and a second part (1623) took the story through to Noah. Completion was prevented by his death.

PHAER, Thomas (1510?-60). From a Flemish family in Norwich, he went to Oxford and Lincoln's Inn, publishing legal works, and then turned to medicine (MB, MD) to make the latest medical science intelligible to Englishmen in their own language. He also contributed the story of Owen Glendower to the 1559 *Myrroure for Magistrates*, wrote a ballad about Gaddes-hill, and verses of *Cupydo* (now lost), and began a translation of Virgil's *Aeneid* (first part published 1558), which was highly superior to the rival venture of Richard Stanyhurst, but which he could not complete, dying when he reached the tenth book. The work was completed by Thomas Twyne.

PHILLIPS, John (fl. 1570-91). A Queens' College, Cambridge man, and a Puritan clergyman, he published broadsides, including *A cold Pye for the Papistes* (c. 1570), and a verse romance *Cleomenes and Sophonisba* (1577); but he was chiefly a professional epitaphist, commemorating the death of a London alderman, the wife of a Lord Mayor, the Countess of Lennox, Sir Philip Sidney, Sir Christopher Hatton and others.

A John Philip published three broadsides in about 1566 on the trial of three witches at Chelmsford; just possibly it was the same man.

PORTER, Endymion (1587-1649). A fascinating key figure of the late Renaissance. He was the son of the squire of Mickleton, Gloucestershire. His mother's father had married a Spanish lady so that at the age of eighteen he was in Spain, attached to the Earl of Nottingham, and in the service of the Olivares household as page to Don Gaspar, a man of his own age and heir to the throne. It was the time of Cervantes and Lope de Vega, and Endymion, falling in love with Spain, exerted almost single-handedly through Prince Charles a pro-Spanish, anti-French influence on the Stuarts. He sought a Spanish bride for his Prince, but his effort failed, largely due to Spanish intransigence. In the pursuit of the Infanta in Spain, Porter was the leading secret agent, supporting Prince Charles and the Duke of Buckingham.

He was attached to Edward Villiers, the half-brother of the

renowned George, and after Buckingham's rise to power he was Master of the Horse and Spanish secretary. Among his friends were Balthasar Gerbier, the ex-Huguenot – they shared an interest in buying Titians – who did so much with Davenant to keep drama alive during the Civil Wars. George Gage, Sir Tobie Matthew, Herrick, Donne, Davenant, May and Edmund Bolton, who considered him an essential member of the proposed Royal Academy. All the perks came his way: he was given a Customs monopoly which was worth in rent alone £800 p.a., and then, when Groom of the Bedchamber to Charles on his accession, a basic pension of £500 p.a. plus land rent, duties, grants and sinecures, including in 1628 the Receivership of Fines in the Star Chamber, alone worth £750 p.a. It is estimated that his income amounted to £3000 p.a. in 1630, and £5000 p.a. in 1640. Soap was one of his monopolies. He put the money into trade ventures in the East Indies and elsewhere. He was MP for Droitwich (1640).

He suffered severely during the Commonwealth, since Parliament found him perhaps their principal enemy: his Spanish connections were ominous; his wife was an RC; he was blamed for the 1641 rebellion in Ireland; he lost kinsmen in war; his house in the Strand was ransacked and his paintings confiscated, but he was loyal to the end, serving as a colonel in the war and as ambassador in Paris in 1645.

There may seem little published to justify his place in an 'Academy'. We have a commemoration of Davenant's *Madagascar* and an epitaph for Donne. He was very diffident about his literary abilities, but he wrote MS poetry throughout his life, and helped Charles and Buckingham in their literary efforts, and through his membership of Gray's Inn his MS circulation was widespread, though little has survived. Most touching of all are his love-letters to his wife: seldom has a wife (and ultimately mother of twelve) received such writing.

G. Huxley: *Endymion Porter: The Life of a Courtier* (1959).

PORTER, Henry (fl. 1599). Possibly an Oxford man, he was one of the more obscure of Henslowe's team of dramatists for the Lord Admiral's company, who collaborated with Jonson and Chettle, and had a hand in six plays, only one of which survives, *The Two Angrie Women of Abington* (c.1598).

POUND, Thomas (1538?-1616?). From Hampshire, he went to

Winchester and Lincoln's Inn (1560), where he wrote masques, including one celebrating the marriage of his cousin Henry, second Earl of Southampton, and he also acted in them. As far as we can discover, his fall from grace in the eyes of the Queen was prompted by a tumble while dancing. He became an RC, and was imprisoned for thirty years from 1574 to 1604. He emerged a Jesuit, and a writer of devotional works including MS poems.

POWELL, Thomas (1572?-1635?). His Welsh family had a long tradition of service in the law, and he went to Gray's Inn, became a barrister, and was Solicitor-General from 1613 to 1622 in the Marches of Wales. During his early years he published *Love's Leprosie* (1598) and *The Passionate Poet* (1601), but thereafter his verse is only intermittent in prose works continuing to 1631, including *A Welch Bayte to spare Provender* (1603). He was a keen researcher of records in the Tower, the Chancery and the Exchequer.

PRESTON, Thomas (1537-98). A Buckinghamshire man, he went to Eton and King's College, Cambridge, becoming proctor, Master of Trinity Hall, and Vice-Chancellor (1589). As an LLD he was in the College of Advocates. He acted in a performance at Cambridge before the Queen in 1564, and wrote an important play *Cambises* (published 1569), which is described as 'a lamentable Tragedy mixed full of Mirth', a mix of allegorical and historical characters, murder and farce. Some of his ballads were published as broadsides.

PRICKET, Robert (fl. 1603). A soldier who published verse pamphlets against the RCs: *A Souldiers Wish unto King James* (1603); *Honors Fame* (1604) – this was about Essex; *Times Anatomie* (1606) – a long heroic poem culminating in an account of the Gunpowder Plot; and *The Jesuits Miracles* (1607) all to attract attention. Unsuccessful, he took orders as curate at St Botolph, Aldgate, and was a clergyman in Ireland until driven out by the 1641 rebellion.

PRIMROSE, Diana (fl. 1630). Only known for her memorial for Queen Elizabeth, written in rhymed couplets and preserved in *A Chaine of Pearle* (1630).

PROCTOR, Thomas (fl. 1578-84). Son of the first master of Tonbridge School, he was apprenticed to the stationer John Allde, becoming a member of the Stationers company (1584) and editing (and writing poems for) two miscellanies, *A gorgious Gallery of gallant Inventions* (1578) and for rather more select circulation, *The Triumph of Trueth* (c. 1585).

PULLAIN, John (1517-65). A Yorkshireman, he attended New College and Christ Church, Oxford, and was rector of St Peter's, Cornhill, until excluded under Queen Mary, when he went to Geneva, contributing to the Genevan Bible and becoming a firm Calvinist. Under Elizabeth he was rector of Copford, Essex. He started writing biblical verse as a student, but little survives except his psalm in the Sternhold-Hopkins psalter.

PUTTENHAM, George (c. 1529-90). The brother of Richard (c. 1526-1601), son of a squire from Puttenham/Long Marston, on the borders of Buckinghamshire and Hertfordshire, his mother was the sister of Sir Thomas Elyot. He was educated at Christ's College, Cambridge, and the Middle Temple. He was in prison in 1588 (like Richard, the latter for rape. He was pardoned, but adjudged it wise to disappear abroad to France, Spain, Italy, Germany, Tartary and China, writing as a peace-offering for the Queen *Partheniades*), apparently unjustly since he was given £1000 compensation. He wrote masques, interludes, and *Triumphals* for the Queen. Unfortunately virtually all of his and Richard's writings have been lost, but *The Arte of English Poesie* (published 1589), the first critical survey of English letters and more comprehensive than Sidney or Webbe, survives. It is believed to have been written by George.

Q

QUARLES, Francis (1592-1644). Son of a Romford squire who was the Queen's Surveyor-General of Victuals for the navy, his mother was a Dalton. He went to Christ's College, Cambridge and Lincoln's Inn. He attended the Earl of Arundel at the marriage of Princess Elizabeth in 1613 and was familiar with Inns of Court society, counting among his friends Drayton, Edward Benlowes and Phineas Fletcher. Later in life he was secretary to Archbishop Ussher of Armagh, returning to Essex in 1635, and becoming Chronologer of London in 1639.

He was an industrious and scholarly professional. His earliest works were heroic paraphrases from the Bible: *A Feast of Wormes* (1621), *Hadassa* (1624), *Job Militant: Sions Elegies* (1625) and the *Historie of Samson* (1631), and became increasingly meditative, taking the popular theme of the wretchedness of man's earthly existence, which his courtly colleagues found an unexciting contribution to their examination of living. In Dublin he helped Ussher with his historical research, and also wrote his first secular verse, *Argalus and Parthenia* (1629). His collected editions of 1632 and 1633 were wholly devotional. His emblem-book (1635) proved popular.

QUIN, Walter (1575?-1634?). Born in Dublin and educated at Edinburgh University, he was fluent in French, Italian and Latin after foreign travel. He became tutor to the sons of James VI, and after the King's accession to the English throne, gentleman of the household to Prince Henry at £50 p.a. and preceptor to Prince Charles in London. He wrote courtly verse for all occasions, was the friend of Sir William Alexander, Thomas Coryat and Josuah Sylvester, and wrote a biography of Lord Bernard Stuart, Lord D'Aubigny.

R

RADCLIFFE, Ralph (1519?-59). From an Ordsall family in Lancashire, he went to Brasenose College, Oxford and Jesus College, Cambridge. He opened a school in a Carmelite house in Hitchin, where he built a stage for public performances and wrote Latin and English plays for his pupils.

RALEGH, Sir Walter (1552?-1618). Writing was essential to Ralegh: Agnes Latham's conclusion was that his verses were 'a part of that strange charm with which he won the Queen's favour, a spiritual adornment, a manifestation of riches and beauty, like his pale satins and the pearl eardrops he wore in his ears.' From Devon, he took the *carrière ouverte* from Oriel College, Oxford, to the Middle Temple, and then courtly service. He was first a soldier, serving with the Huguenots 1569-74, and then ruthlessly in Ireland, becoming captain of the Queen's Guard in 1587. His military and naval service were so distinguished that the first Ark was originally named Ark Ralegh. He served with the Dutch against the Spanish, with Drake against the Armada, and with Essex in Cadiz and the Azores. He financed seven expeditions to the Americas (none of them successful) and helped his half-brother, Sir Humphrey Gilbert, fit out expeditions against the Spanish in the Atlantic, seeking, unsuccessfully, to find gold in El Dorado and the Orinoco.

He is popularly credited with introducing both the potato and tobacco into England from Virginia, but it seems that he was never in the colony himself.

At the height of his prosperity, when he was a Privy Counsellor, love blotted his record with the Queen when he seduced one of her ladies, Elizabeth Throckmorton. Both were imprisoned, and while the Queen allowed them to marry, she never forgave her former favourite. After their release, the Raleghs settled in Sherborne, Dorset; but when it seemed that he was again winning his way back into the Queen's favour, he was accused of complicity in Essex's rebellion. He had many enemies, notably Lord Cobham, and many mistrusted his group (dubbed the 'School of Night' by some, and 'School of

Atheism' by RCs) which included advanced thinkers such as Thomas Hariot, the algebraist and astronomer. Worse was to come: James I was always suspicious of anyone with an Essex taint, and had Ralegh arrested on a trumped up charge of conspiring with the Spanish to bring England under an RC monarch. Ralegh was exonerated, but nevertheless imprisoned in the Tower for thirteen years. He was finally released to lead a second expedition to the Orinoco, but, ageing and weakened, he caught fever, and left affairs to his subordinates who exceeded their orders by sacking a Spanish city. On his return to London, the Spanish ambassador demanded his life and he was executed in the Tower.

The thirty-four poems attributed to him from MS relics are archetypal Elizabethan courtly poetry: poems to the Queen; one he had slipped into 'my lady Laitons pocket'; one intended as his own epitaph, another an elegy for Sidney; literary exercises, such as his reply to Marlowe's *Come Live with me*, and *The Lie* to which other poets replied; an acrostic; commendatory verses for Spenser, Gorges and Gascoigne; lyrics which are thoughtful, wry, dry, and full of the enormous pain he saw in life. He wrote *Cynthia*, in ten books, to win back the Queen's favour. He spent his time in prison, typically, writing a *History of the World*, which went into fourteen editions between 1614 and 1687. He originated the Society of Antiquaries and the Mermaid group before Jonson, and also dabbled in chemistry.

The enormity of his execution was recognised: though Robert Carr got his large estate, his widow was awarded £8000 compensation, a pension of £400 p.a. for life – and his head which she lovingly embalmed.

S.J. Greenblatt: *Sir Walter Ralegh: The Renaissance Man and his Roles* (1973); W. Oakeshott: *The Queen and the Poet* (1960); W.M. Wallace: *Sir Walter Raleigh* (1960); P. Edwards: *Sir Walter Raleigh* (1953); A. Latham: *The Poems of Sir Walter Raleigh* (1929).

RAMSAY, Laurence (fl. 1550-88). One of Leicester's group, he was an Anabaptist, extremely Puritan and very anti-RC. He printed a number of broadsides, including *The Practise of the Divell* (c. 1571) and *Mans fatall end* (1578).

RANDOLPH, Thomas (1605-35). His father was steward in

Northamptonshire to Edward, Lord Zouche. He started writing poetry at the age of ten with *Incarnation of Our Saviour*. He went to Westminster School and Trinity College, Cambridge, writing in his university days a prose-verse satire *Aristippus* (published 1630), and a play *The Jealous Lovers*, which was performed before the King and Queen. In London, he joined Jonson at the Devil, and his friends included Sir Christopher Hatton, Anthony Stafford, Thomas Bancroft, James Shirley, Owen Felltham, Sir Aston Cokayne and Sir Kenelm Digby. When his collected *Poems* were published posthumously (1638 and bound with Milton's *Comus*) they included many fine lyrics, another Cambridge play, *The Muses' Looking Glasse*, and the Whitehall pastoral *Amyntas*.

He is sometimes called 'the younger' to distinguish him from his namesake (1523-90), the famous secret agent 'Barnabe' who was in every intrigue for Burghley, in the dynastic fighting before James VI consolidated his power in Scotland.

RANKINS, William (fl. 1587-1601). His earliest writing was an attack on the theatre, a pamphlet *Mirrour of Monsters* (1587), but later he joined Henslowe's group and wrote plays with Richard Hathway which may all have been lost, although he probably contributed to extant plays. He also published *Seaven Satyres* (1598).

RAWLINS, Thomas (1620?-70). A goldsmith apprenticed to the Mint, he became a medallist and later chief engraver. In an early play, *The Rebellion* (1640), for the Revels, he insisted 'Take note of my name, for a second work of this nature should hardly bear it, I have no desire to be known by a threadbare Cloak, having a Calling that will maintain it wholly.' He changed his mind at the Restoration and resumed dramatic writing.

REDFORD, Henry (fl. 1535). One of Henry VIII's composers and quite *avant-garde* in his music, he became master of the St Paul's children and wrote for them, words and music, and at least three moralities, of which one survives in entirety, *Wyt and Science*.

REYNOLDS, Henry (fl. 1630). Drayton's friend, a critical writer in *Mythomestes* (published 1632) and a poet in *Aminta Englisht* (1628).

RICH, Barnabe (1540?-1617). From Essex, a professional

soldier, he rose to the rank of captain, fought in France, the United Provinces and Ireland, receiving in 1616 an award of £100 as the oldest captain in the kingdom. More talented than most 'resting' soldiers, the friend of Lodge, Churchyard and Gascoigne, he published about thirty books, writing romances after Lyly, pamphlets which were most critical of vice, RCs and tobacco, and mingling poetry with prose in such works as *Mercury and an English Souldier* (1574), *Riche his Farewell to Militarie Profession* (1581), *Don Simonides* (1581 and 1584), and *The Excellency of Good Women* (1613).

RICH, Richard (fl. 1609). Another scion of the famous Essex family and soldier, who adventured in Virginia, and on his return wrote about his experiences in *Newes from Virginia* (1610).

RICHARDS, Nathanael (fl. 1630-40). A master of St Alban School in London, he published in 1630 the religious essay *The Celestial Publican*, and in 1640 the Revels play, *The Tragedy of Messalina*. Probably other poems and plays are lost.

ROBERTS, Henry (fl. 1595-1610). He served Queen Elizabeth and James I as esquire, and was envoy to Morocco in 1585. He wrote fourteen books of prose-verse, typical of which is *The Trumpet of Fame* (published 1595), commemorating the departure of Drake and Hawkins on the unsuccessful Puerto Rico expedition. He also wrote an entertainment for the visit of Christian IV of Denmark in 1606.

ROBINSON, Clement (fl. 1566-84). He edited song-books for Richard Jones in 1566, and *A Handefull of pleasant delites* (1584), which included some of his own lyrics including 'A Nosegay' (known to Ophelia), and a version of the 'Lady Greensleeves'.

ROBINSON, Richard, of Alton (fl. 1574). A Cambridge man in the household of the Earl of Shrewsbury, he published a lost tragedy and, in 1589, his poetry in *A Golden Mirrour* (where, although there seems little need, he concealed his name in an acrostic).

ROBINSON, Richard, of London (fl. 1576-1600). A freeman of the Leathersellers company, he applied to the Queen for one of the twelve 'alms-rooms' in Westminster. He collaborated with Churchyard, and published several books of religious verse, not only psalms, but also *Certain Selected Histories* (1576); a translation from Ausonius *Robinsons Ruby* (1577); and *The Dyall of Dayly Contemplacon for Synners* (1578).

ROCHE, Robert (1576-1629). A Somerset man, educated at Magdalen Hall, Oxford, later rector of Hilton in Dorset, he published didactic doggerel in *Eustathia* (1599).

ROLLAND, John (fl. 1560). A Glasgow man, presbyter of Glasgow and notary of Dalkeith. He wrote before 1560, *The Court of Venus* when he was an RC, and in 1560, as a Protestant, *The Sevin Seagis*.

ROSS, Alexander (1591-1654). From Aberdeen University he went south and, thanks to Edward Seymour, Earl of Hertford, became a master at Southampton School in 1616, royal chaplain in 1622, and vicar of Carisbrooke, Isle of Wight. He wrote a *History of the World* (published 1652), and a considerable number of poems, collected in *Mel Heliconium* (published 1642 in Latin and English) and later anthologies. He is most remembered for his Scottish ballad 'Wooed and married and a'.' He was a friend of John Evelyn.

ROWLANDS, Samuel (1570?-1630?). A friend of John Taylor the Water Poet, and like him in the lowest social class of writers for the printed-book market, he was famous for his jestbooks and news-books which were often reprinted. Among his thirty or so publications, there is some pious verse, as in *The Betraying of Christ* (1595) and *Heaven's Glory* (1628), the first and last of his run. One of his satires *The Letting of Humours Blood in the Head-Vaines* (1600) offended the authorities and was burned.

ROWLEY, Samuel (d. 1633?). The brother of William, he served Henslowe first as a script-reader, and then as a playwright for the Admiral's company, collaborating with William Haughton and Edward Juby, and a 'William Bird'. His only extant play is a chronicle of Henry VIII, *When you see me you know me* (published 1605).

ROWLEY, William (d. 1626). What he did before he joined Henslowe we do not know, though he published *The Travels of the Three English Brothers* (1607). He played the fat comics with the Prince's, the Queen's and other Henslowe companies, and was given the chance to write parts he could play. Of his fifty plays only four appear to have been written solo: *A New Wonder* (published 1632), *All's Lost by Lust* (Cockpit, published 1633), *A Match at Midnight* (Revels children, published 1633), and *A Shoomaker a Gentleman* (Red Bull, published 1638). He collaborated with George Wilkins, John Day, Thomas Heywood and John Webster; his most important joint plays are considered to be *The Witch of Edmonton* (published 1608) with Dekker and Ford, and *A Faire Quarrell* (1617) and *The Changeling* (1621) with Middleton. Some believe his contributions to the plays are very uneven and sometimes quite disastrous. Some of his poems were published with those of John Taylor, the Water Poet.

ROYDON, Matthew (fl. 1580-1622). Possibly the son of Owen Roydon, and educated at Oxford, he collaborated with Thomas Proctor in publishing *A Gorgious Gallery of Gallant Inventions* (1578). He also wrote elegies and much commendatory verse for his many friends who included Spenser, Lodge and Chapman. He knew Sir Philip Sidney, and was therefore a senior member of Ralegh's group, which included Marlowe, Thomas Hariot, William Warner and others. We know very little about him, and have little extant material of any substance, but the frequency with which his name recurs commands respect, which indeed the group accorded him. He was later with Robert Radcliffe, the fifth Earl of Sussex, but we know he was indigent in 1618-22 because on appeal Edward Alleyn sent him small gifts of 8d and 6d.

RUDYARD, Sir Benjamin (1572-1658). From Hampshire, his mother was a Kidwelly. He went to Winchester School and St John's College, Oxford, and on to the Inner Temple, becoming a barrister in 1600. He married Elizabeth Harington. He was MP for Portsmouth (1620, 1624, 1625), Old Sarum (1626), Downton (1628) and Wilton (1640). He was appointed Surveyor of the Court of Wards for life in 1618, and was awarded £6000 compensation in 1647 when Parliament forced him to resign because of his Royalist sympathies. His best friends were William Herbert, Earl of Pembroke, Jonson, John Owen and John Hoskins, though he once fought a duel with the latter. He had an interest in the Providence company. In politics he sought to exercise a moderating influence on the extremists. He tried to persuade Buckingham to join forces with a Protestant league with the Elector Palatine, and was firmly opposed to Spain and to the Irish Catholics, but he

disliked being called a Puritan, and advocated a limited episcopacy. He opposed Strafford, but did not vote for his at-
tainder. He took the Covenant and was in the Westminster
Assembly of 1643, but was imprisoned in 1648 for seeking an
accommodation with the King. Much of his poetry was written
for courtly occasions: a collected edition was published in
1660. While at the Inns of Court, he contributed to revels at the
Middle Temple.

RUTTER, Joseph (fl. 1635). Tutor to the sons of Edward Sackville, fourth Earl of Dorset, he was in Jonson's circle, lodged
for a time with Sir Kenelm Digby and knew Thomas May. He
left two published plays: the pastoral tragi-comedy for Whitehall, *The Shepheards Holy Day* (1635) and the tragi-comedy
translated from Corneille, for Whitehall and the Cockpit, *The
Cid* (1637).

S

SABIE, Francis (fl. 1587-96). A Lichfield schoolmaster, he published three volumes of verse: *The Fishermans Tale* and *Flora's Fortune* (published in one volume, 1595); a blank verse version of Green's *Pandosto*, titled *Pan's Pipe* (1596), hexameter eclogues dedicated to 'all youthful Gentlemen, Apprentises, favourers of the divine Arte of sense-delighting Poesie'; and *Adam's Complaint* (1596), scripture in heroic couplets. His son was a member of the Stationers' Company.

SACKVILLE, Thomas, Baron Buckhurst, first Earl of Dorset (1536-1608). His father, a first cousin of Anne Boleyn, was Sir Richard Sackville of Buckhurst, Sussex, and Governor of the Inner Temple. Thomas went to Shillington School and Inner Temple, becoming a barrister. He may also have attended Hart Hall, Oxford or St John's College, Cambridge (Oxford later claimed him as Chancellor). He was MP for Westmorland (1557), East Grinstead (1559) and Aylesbury (1563); he served Leicester, and then Burghley. He was an agent in the attempt for the Anjou marriage (1568), an ambassador (1571), a Privy Counsellor and a commissioner at state trials (he had the task of telling Mary Queen of Scots she was to be executed; she gave him a wood carving remembrance). He married early Cicely, the daughter of Sir John Baker of Sissinghurst. In the last years of Leicester, faced with the difficult task of fulfilling his master's wishes in the United Provinces, he met his first setbacks and was temporarily placed under house arrest. But his fortunes were restored under Burghley and he served as a tactful agent in the United Provinces and France, becoming Lord Treasurer and Lord High Steward. The king of Spain gave him a pension of £1000 p.a. for his services in securing peace in 1604. By this time he was joint Lord-Lieutenant of Sussex, and a great landowner in Sussex, Devon and Kent, where he built Knole.

Under James I he had the task of financing the King's extravagances, and though he raised non-parliamentary revenue by 50 per cent, he had to borrow at high rates of interest, and give and take bribes. In the financial crisis of 1608 he had to fight for

his life and died at the council table clearing himself of the
charge of misconduct.

He started writing while at the Inner Temple and with
Thomas Norton wrote the tragedy of *Gorboduc* (1561),
seminal as the first English tragedy in blank verse, and as one of
the clearest advocacies of constitutional monarchy. He carried
the same theme in the 1563 *Myrroure for Magistrates*, for
which he wrote the keynote *Induction* and *Complaint of the
Duke of Buckingham*, leaving development in the hands of
William Baldwin and George Ferrers. He had no faith in
democracy:

> O let no prynce put trust in commontie
> Nor hope in fayth of giddy peoples mynde.

But even the proudest and worthiest monarchs, though firm
against dread and care, pomp and greed, could not succeed: the
King should obey God's laws, and his servants should seek to
work out, in the pragmatic details, the royal will. Significantly,
it was he who commended Hoby's translation of *The Courtyer
of Count Baldessar Castilio* (1561) with the words, which
illuminate his own idea of politics:

> No proud ne golden Court doth he set furth
> But what in Court a Courtier ought to be.
> The Prince who raiseth houge and mightie walles,
> Castilio frames a wight of noble fame:
> The Kinge with gorgeous Tyssue claddes his halles
> The Count with golden vertue deckes the same.

His own songs and sonnets have nearly all been lost. He saw
himself a rude successor in descent from Wyatt, 'worthiest of
them all', and Surrey, 'that highest sittes in chair of glistering
fame'.

D. Bevington: *Tudor Drama and Politics* (1968); P. Bacquet:
Thomas Sackville (1966).

SALISBURY, Sir Thomas (d. 1643). The son of Sir Henry, of
Denbighshire, his mother was Hester Myddleton. He went to
Jesus College, Oxford and the Inner Temple. He withdrew to
the family estates on his father's death, becoming alderman and
MP for Denbigh. He was impeached for supporting the King at

Edgehill. He wrote much poetry, but all that survives is *The History of Joseph* (published 1636).

SALTONSTALL, Wye (fl. 1630-40). Son of Sir Samuel, grandson of a Lord Mayor, he went to Queen's College, Oxford and Gray's Inn, but as an indigent tutor he sought to augment his income in print. He published satires, *Picturae Loquentes* (1631), a translation of Ovid's *Tristia* in rhymed couplets (1633), and other translations from Ovid, *Heroicall Epistles* (1636) and *Epistolae de Pente* (1639). He was a friend of Robert Codrington.

SAMPSON, William (1590?-1636?). From a yeoman family in South Leverton, Nottinghamshire, he set out to serve and honour with his writings local gentry, finally becoming the secretary of Sir Henry Willoughby of Risley. He was a friend of Gervase Markham and wrote with him the tragedy *Herod and Antipater* (Red Bull, published 1622), and solo another tragedy, *The Vow Breaker* (published 1636). His heroic panegyrics of local worthies – thirty-two in all – were published in *Virtus post Funera vivit* (1636).

SAMUEL, William (fl. 1551-69). A clergyman attached to the Duke of Suffolk, he published religious verse in *The Abridgment of Goddes statutes in myter* (1551) and in other abridgements in 1558? and 1569.

SANDYS, George (1578-1644). Son of the Archbishop of York, and brother of Edwin, Treasurer of Virginia, he went to St Mary Hall and Corpus Christi College, Oxford, and the Middle Temple. He married Elizabeth Norton, of an RC family, but the marriage was unhappy and ended, after four years, in separation. He followed his brother as Treasurer to Virginia (the new Governor, Sir Francis Wyatt, had married his niece, Margaret Sandys), and while there fought in the Indian wars. On his return he was made gentleman of the Privy Chamber to Charles I, to whom he dedicated all his writings, and became the friend of Drayton, Lucius Cary, second Viscount Falkland, Sir Francis Wenman, Dudley Digges, Henry King, Sidney Godolphin, Thomas Carew and Edmund Waller. He never remarried, preferring to lodge with his niece, Lady Wyatt, at Boxley, Kent.

He wrote about his travels in France, Italy, Turkey, Egypt and Palestine, and some religious verse was generated by his visit to Jerusalem. He is best known for his translation of Ovid's *Metamorphoses* (published 1621 and 1626). His collected edition of 1632 includes a life of Ovid and a translation of the first book of the *Aeneid*. His *Ovid* went into eight editions by 1690, was read by Dryden and Pope when young, and established, with the work of Denham and Waller, the heroic couplet as *the* Augustan metre. His later work was wholly devotional, including his *Paraphrase upon the Psalmes and upon the Hymnes dispersed throughout the Old and New Testaments* (1636) and *Christ's Passion*, a heroic translation from Grotius (1540).

  R.B. Davis: *George Sandys, Poet-Adventurer* (1955).

SCOLOKER, Anthony (fl. 1604). A relative of another Anthony (fl. 1548 – the printer who translated from German, Dutch and French), he is known only for *Daiphantus* (published 1604), from which we infer that he knew Shakespeare.

SCOTT, Alexander (1525?-90?). 'Old Scott', son of a clergyman, and known most for the misfortune of losing his wife to a 'wantoun man'. His love-poems, both before and after he lost his wife, and rather coarse satires, only had MS circulation, but were preserved in the Bannatyne MS, compiled about 1568.

SCOTT, Sir Thomas (1538-94). High Sheriff and MP of Kent, he had a command against the Armada, and wrote, in very ambiguous metaphors, *Four Paradoxes of Arte, of Lawe, of Warre, of Service* (1602), and the satire *Phylomythie* (1610, 1616).

SEGAR, Francis (fl. 1549-63). A Devon man and a stationer, he versified psalms (1553) and wrote a popular *Schoole of Vertue* for children (published 1557). He came into prominence by a version of Caxton's courtesy book *The great myseries in courtes ryal*, and left in the 1563 *Myrroure for Magistrates* the definitive Tudor damnation of Richard III (written in bad verse, which William Baldwin said was fit enough for so violent a king whom, he thought, Segar had let off lightly).

SEMPILL, Robert, the elder (1530?-95). An illegitimate son of the family from Renfrewshire, he went to Paris, was a soldier, and was attached to the court of James VI. He wrote rough, reformist ballads, defending Morton and Moray, and attacking the RCs and the Hamiltons.

SEMPILL, Robert, the younger (1595?-1665?). Son of Sir James of Beltrees, he went to Glasgow University and is remembered for his elegy *Habbie Simson, Piper of Kilbarchan* (in MS c. 1640).

SHAKESPEARE, William (1564-1616). His father was a Stratford glover and whittawer, who later became a wool-stapler and dealer in other agricultural commodities, and rose in the town to be ale-taster, constable, affearor, burgess, alderman, bailiff (a combined almoner, coroner, escheator, clerk of the market and JP), and chief alderman, living till he was past 70. It is now concluded that neither father nor son were recusants, but tolerant Anglicans. Shakespeare's mother was Mary Arden, daughter of a prosperous farmer who made available a handsome dowry. A sister married a hatter, one brother became a haberdasher, another brother followed him to London to become an actor.

He went to Stratford School, but not to university, nor, as far as we know, did he ever sojourn in the Inns of Court. At first he stayed in Stratford, probably apprenticed to his father, and at eighteen he married Anne Hathaway, eight years his senior, when she was three months pregnant. Both families approved of the match, and as a farmer's eldest daughter Anne's dowry was good. The marriage had to have a special licence from the Bishop of Worcester, but this was obligatory in all marriages involving minors. It was, of course, an Elizabethan troth-plight, later regularised by the Church, as was the custom, when pregnancy was confirmed. Their daughter Susanna was born in 1583, and the twins Hamnet and Judith (named after their neighbours, the Sadlers) in 1585.

For some time scholars have agreed that Shakespeare with his wife's approval reached London with an acting company. At one time the favourite theory was that he had a connection with the Houghton and Hesketh families at Preston, who visited the Stanley home at Knowsley, where the son of the family was the theatrical patron, Ferdinando, Lord Strange. Such a link is now considered unlikely; there were so many touring companies playing at Stratford that we might as well select the most likely, Leicester's, whose base was at Kenilworth, only ten miles away, and whose leading actor was James Burbage. We cannot, however, be entirely sure about the years between 1585 and 1592 and it was 1592 before we can place Shakespeare in London with any certainty, with Warwick's company (which had inherited most of Leicester's men). His status at first must have been lowly, a hired actor who was also an odd-job man, minder of horses, and so on. But he was already an accomplished writer: like other young wits, he was circulating love sonnets in MSS, some of which reached print in miscellanies, including *The Phoenix Nest* (1593) and *The Passionate Pilgrime* (1599), but since they were private, and at least partly autobiographical, he did not print his major collection until 1609. There was no aversion to printing *Venus and Adonis* (1592) and *The Rape of Lucrece* (1594), which read like bids for attention, full of brilliant but quite extravagant metaphors. His target was Henry Wriothesley, third Earl of Southampton, and to judge from the more intimate dedication in the second book, Shakespeare was successful in winning not only patronage but affection. Much has been made, on the evidence of the Sonnets, of a love triangle between Shakespeare, Southampton, and a 'Dark Lady', identified by A.L. Rowse as Emilia Lanier, the illegitimate daughter of Baptiste Bassano, the Venetian musician in service with the Countess of Essex; when pregnant the lady was married off to a court musician from Rouen, by the agency of the Lord Chamberlain, by this time the patron of Shakespeare's company of players. Shakespeare was older than both Emilia and Henry, and the triangle, if it existed, was short-lived. (Another poet, possibly Barnabe Barnes, replaced Shakespeare in Southampton's favours.) Nevertheless, Shakespeare emerged much the richer: Sir William Davenant estimated that Shakespeare was given £1000 by his patron, and he was able to buy a share in the Lord Chamberlain's new company, which briefly had as its business manager Philip Henslowe (one of Emilia's lovers). The shares altered from time to time, but the general pattern was that the Burbages, father and son, owned half the shares, while the other half was divided between players, including Shakespeare, William Kempe, John Heminges, Augustine Phillips and Thomas Pope. With sharing, acting, playwriting and courtly gratuities, it is likely that Shakespeare was earning £200 p.a. by 1600. He was able to buy property in London, moving into a more comfortable home in 1596, buying for his father in the same

year the long-wanted title of 'esquire', and buying for his
family, with whom he constantly kept in touch, New Place in
Stratford, one of the principal properties in the town.

After 1603 the company came under the patronage of the
King and grew more prosperous: it is estimated that there were
187 court performances between 1604 and 1616, more than
those of all the other companies combined. They were ahead of
Henslowe in developing a private, enclosed, second playhouse, for a more select audience, with rewards four times
those of the public theatres: indeed, Henslowe's men flattered
by imitation. When Shakespeare's company built the Globe in
1599, Henslowe followed with the Fortune in 1600; when
Shakespeare's company opened the Blackfriars in 1609,
Henslowe followed with the Whitefriars in 1610.

Shakespeare was able to retire to his family home in 1613,
though in his last years he made occasional visits to London.
There is nothing strange about his will. Hamnet having died
young, Susanna and her husband were bequeathed the best bed
as residuary legatees; Judith's portion was guarded because he
didn't trust her husband; he remembered every relative, old
friends and the poor; and his widow, protected by her rights
and family position, got as was usual 'my second-best bed with
the furniture'.

Once we can see clearly the unexceptional lines of this story,
it is easier to see the canon of thirty-eight plays in proper
perspective, without speculating, as the Victorians were
chronically apt to do when they grouped his plays in relation to
his assumed emotional life. At no time in his life was he
exclusively concerned with a particular genre. We cannot be
sure of the exact dates of composition, and the dates below are
approximate. Some plays appeared in printed Quartos in his
lifetime, sometimes soon after the probable date of their first
production, sometimes several years later. Others were only
printed posthumously in the great Folio edition of 1623. But if
we think of him as a professional playwright, little has been
discovered by later scholars to disturb very much the order of
the canon presented by E.K. Chambers.

At the beginning of his career he collaborated, with Greene
and others; at the end, with Fletcher and others. But very
nearly all the plays written between 1594 and 1613 were all his

own work. He started by taking old plays and rewriting them, and by imitating genres then popular. There were chronicle plays: the three *Henry VI* plays – *The Contention betwixt the houses of Yorke and Lancaster* (in three parts, 1592-3) – and *The Tragedy of Richard the third* (1593). His first attempt at tragedy is as gruesome as any university play, following Seneca: *The Tragedie of Titus Andronicus* (1593-4). His first comedy again follows university plays, modelled on Terence: *The Comedy of Errors* (1593-4). He then experimented in farce with *The Taming of the Shrew* (1594); his first attempt at love-comedy in the same year was *The Two Gentlemen of Verona*. Still experimenting, he produced a pattern-play which has some of the characteristics of courtly masque: *Loves Labors Lost* (1595). Probably his first play anticipating his later genius was the tragedy founded on an Italian romance, *Romeo and Juliet* (1595); his maturity in historical plays is first evidenced in *The Tragedie of Richard the Second* (1596); his first great comic invention is Bottom in *A Midsommer Nights Dreame* (1596). *King John* (1596) evidences no important step forward – but then the occasional unsuccessful play is common in the life of any playwright. His masterpieces date from about 1597: in tragedy *Julius Caesar* (1597); in history *The Historie of Henrie the fourth* (in two parts, 1597), with the marvellous and very unclassical invention of the comic Sir John Falstaff intruding into high affairs of state, followed quickly by *The History of Henrie the fifth* (1598) – plays which address contemporary concern with the nature of the true monarch; and a curious play, serious but less than tragic, but not a tragi-comedy, *The Merchant of Venice* (1597).

There follow the three great comedies: *Much Adoe about Nothing* (1598), *As You Like It* (1599) and *Twelfe Night* (1600), plays in which Shakespeare decides true comedy is not critical, but sympathetic, an agency for reconciling human beings to the absurdities of the flesh and mind. In the same period he was able to turn his attention to the first of his great tragedies, *Hamlet* (probably 1597/8), and to respond to popular demand by describing the love-life of Falstaff in *A Comedie of Falstaffe and the merrie wives of Windsor* (1600).

There is no clear period when tragedy was his main concern – the four great tragedies, *Othello* (1603), *King Lear* (1604),

Macbeth (1604) and *Antony and Cleopatra* (1607) (the last reflecting a revived interest in stories from classical times) were written while he was also writing his tragi-comedies: *The Historie of Troylus and Cressida* (1601), *All's Well, that Ends Well* (1603), and *Measure for Measure* (1604). Three classical histories follow, but each contains elements of humour, drama and romance: *Coriolanus* (1608), *Pericles* (1608) and *Timon of Athens* (1609).

The opening of the private playhouse, the Blackfriars, in 1609 gave him new opportunities for exploiting spectacle, lighting and courtly dance, and he responded with three romances: *Cymbeline* (1609), *The Winters Tale* (1611) and *The Tempest* (1613). In his last years he collaborated in *The Life of King Henry the Eight* (1613), and, possibly, *Two Noble Kinsmen* (1614).

At all times, it seems, Shakespeare was the loyal servant of his company, responding to changes and fashions in audience taste. He had the great advantage of a homogeneous audience: the same plays could be produced at court or in the playhouse, because courtiers, university and Inns of Court men shared the same taste as the citizenry. All plays, no matter how tragic, ended with the rough-and-tumble of a farcical jig. The theatres were small by modern standards, but much more crowded, with a close intimacy between players and spectators, with stage-keepers on stage throughout to keep the audience in order. The mix of comedy and tragedy arose not from an overt defiance of classical principles, but was a natural development from the medieval mystery plays and early Tudor interludes. This mix enabled him to express the central Renaissance dilemma of how it could be possible to accept the limitations and adversities of circumstance, while at the same time rise above those limitations by heroism, his comic plays asserting reconciliation and the tragic plays aspiration.

Shakespeare's characters are never stereotypes, all have inherent contradictions. The one common element is a belief in human love as the agent of comic reconciliation and tragic redemption. *Macbeth* and *Measure for Measure* are not exceptions to the rule, but examinations of the limitations of love itself. Nearly every play has a love-problem at its centre; it brings humiliation to Malvolio, despair to Troilus, madness to

Macbeth, death to Othello, humility to Beatrice and Benedick.

J. Bayley: *Shakespeare and Tragedy* (1981); M.C. Bradbrook: *Shakespeare: the Poet in his World* (1980); M.M. Rees: *Shakespeare: His World and his Work* (1980); E. Jones: *The Origins of Shakespeare* (1977); S. Schoenbaum: *William Shakespeare: a Documentary Life* (1975); A.L. Rowse: *Shakespeare the Man* (1973); M. Chute: *Shakespeare of London* (1951); A. Harbage: *Shakespeare's Audience* (1941); E.K. Chambers: *Shakespeare: a Survey* (1925).

SHARPE, Lewis (fl. 1640). Known only as the author of the popular Salisbury Court comedy, *The Noble Stranger* (1640).

SHARPE, Roger (fl. 1610). An epigrammist, known only for *More Fooles Yet* (published 1610).

SHARPHAM, Edward (1576-1608). From Devon he went to the Middle Temple and wrote two Revels plays, *The Fleire* (Blackfriars, 1605) and *Cupid's Whirligig* (1607).

SHEFFIELD, Edmund, first Baron Sheffield (1521-49). One of the 'ghosts' of the period because all his sonnets are lost. He was in ward to George Boleyn, Lord Rochford, and then to the fifteenth Earl of Oxford, whose daughter, Anne de Vere, he married. He was killed at Norwich fighting Ket's rebellion in 1549.

SHEPHERD, Luke (fl. 1548-54). From Colchester, probably the physician friend of Edward Underhill, he was imprisoned for writing reformist pamphlets in the reign of Henry VIII, and again for denying 'the real Presence' in *John Bon the Mast Person* (1548). He also wrote psalms.

SHIRLEY, Henry (d. 1627). Son of Sir Thomas, the army treasurer, his mother was a Vavasour. He was killed by Sir Edward Bishop in a quarrel over a £2 loan. Some of his poems exist in MSS, but only one of his plays, *The Martyr's Souldier* (Cockpit, published 1638).

SHIRLEY, James (1596-1666). A Londoner, he went to Merchant Taylors School, and under Laud to St John's College, Oxford, and Catherine Hall, Cambridge. His best university friend was Thomas Bancroft. He became a clergyman in Hertfordshire, and a master at St Albans School. He turned briefly to Roman Catholicism, but in about 1625 gave up both Church and school and went to Gray's Inn, where he found his metier as a playwright. He also wrote poetry, first published in *Eccho* (1619), and later in a collected edition (1646). He had courtly connections, with George Fitzgerald, sixteenth Earl of Kildare, and later the Earl of Newcastle, but he was most at home writing for the Queen's and King's companies, gaining the support of both Charles I and Queen Henrietta Maria. His plays were chiefly written solo. He was the friend of Jonson, Webster and Massinger, whom he particularly admired, Ford, Habington, May, Stapleton, Izaak Walton and John Ogilby. He collaborated with Chapman, and possibly Beaumont.

He survived the Civil War by returning to teaching. (It is interesting to note that the dirge from his interregnum masque, *The Contention of Ajax and Ulysses*, 'The glories of our mortal state', terrified Cromwell.) What impressed his contemporaries was the 'smooth stream' of Shirley's professional Helicon, making it difficult to single out any plays, but new readers might start with the tragedy *The Traitor* (published 1635), the comedy *Hyde Park* (published 1637), and, arguably his best work, the tragedy *The Cardinal* (published 1659).

A.H. Nason: *Shirley: A Biographical and Critical Study* (1915).

SIDNEY, Sir Philip (1554-86). The son of Sir Henry Sidney, Lord President of the Marches of Wales from 1559 and a pragmatic and capable Lord Deputy of Ireland from 1565; his mother was Mary Dudley, Leicester's sister and his godfather Philip II of Spain. He spent his childhood at Penshurst, Kent. He was educated at Shrewsbury School with his lifelong friend, Fulke Greville, and at Christ Church, Oxford. On his first visit to France, in connection with the Treaty of Blois, he received a title from Charles IX. And he was in Paris at the time of the St Bartholomew's Massacre (1572) which persuaded him to turn his back on RC Spanish and French connections and join Burghley, his patron at court, and Leicester and Sir Francis Walsingham in advocating a Protestant League in Europe. His later travels in Germany, Austria, Italy, Poland, Ireland and the United Provinces confirmed him as a champion of Protestantism. At court, he opposed the Anjou marriage, and quarrelled with the Earl of Oxford who advocated contrary policies; Elizabeth never quite knew what to make of him. He voluntarily exiled himself from court from 1580 to 1581 staying with his sister Mary, Countess of Pembroke, at Wilton. He promoted not only resistance to the Duke of Alençon and the French, but support for Drake in resisting Spain and colonising America. In fact he and Greville were about to sail with Drake from Plymouth when Elizabeth made him Governor of Flushing, in support of Leicester. This led to his last mission to the United Provinces, where he died of a gangrenous wound at Zutphen in 1586. The brilliance of his state funeral in St Paul's Cathedral was unparalleled in the period.

He had two literary circles: his courtly group of friends, chiefly Fulke Greville and Sir Edward Dyer, this triumvirate reviving the leadership given at Henry VIII's court by Wyatt, Surrey and Bryan; and the 'Areopagus', a more scholarly group led by Gabriel Harvey and chiefly concerned with asserting neo-classical theories and metrification in English poetry. His support of neo-classical theory, particularly in the *Apologie for Poesie* (completed 1583) led him to attack all English drama. Without thought of publication he wrote for a MS circle psalms, a romance for his sister, *Arcadia*, and an entertainment for the Queen at Wanstead in 1578, *The Lady of May*.

His main reputation comes from the sonnet sequence *Astrophel and Stella*. Stella was certainly a real person: Penelope Devereux, daughter of Walter, first Earl of Essex, and sister of the rebel. They had known each other since childhood, and were to be married, but her father died before arrangements could be completed, and instead she was unhappily married to Lord Rich. Sidney married Frances Walsingham, daughter of the great Sir Francis.

A.C. Harrison: *Sir Philip Sidney: a Study of his Life and Works* (1977); R. Howell: *Sir Philip Sidney, the Shepherd Knight* (1968); D. Kalston: *Sidney's Poetry* (1965); F.S. Boas: *Sir Philip Sidney, Representative Elizabethan* (1955); J. Buxton; *Sir Philip Sidney and the English Renaissance* (1954).

SINGER, John (fl. 1594-1602). A comic actor with the Queen's company, and chiefly the Admiral's company, he wrote plays, but none is extant and we only have (if they are his) sallies and improvisations preserved in *Quips upon Questions* (1600) by Clunnyco de Curtaneo Scruffe.

SLATYER, William (1587-1647). A Somerset man, educated at

St Mary's Hall and Brasenose College, Oxford, he was chaplain to Queen Anne and rector of Romney and Otterden, Kent. The general opinion of his *Psalmes or Songs of Zion* (published c. 1630) was that they were improper, as they were sung to popular tunes, and his dress was described as 'not fit for a minister either'. Undeterred, he published his elegies, *Palaeo-Albion* (1621) and more psalms.

SMALLE, Peter (fl. 1596-1615). A Berkshire man educated at St John's College, Oxford. He was rector of Pinnock, Gloucestershire and published the poem *Mans May* (1615).

SMITH, Matthew (1589-1640). A Royalist barrister from the Inner Temple and a member of the Council for the North (1639). He left poems and parts of plays in MS.

SMITH, Wentworth (fl. 1601-23). One of the more obscure of Henslowe's dramatists for the Lord Admiral's company at the Rose, he had a hand in fifteen plays, collaborating with Day, Haughton, Chettle, Drayton, Munday, Hathway, Thomas Heywood and Dekker, but we cannot be sure that any of his writing is extant. A possible survivor, by 'W.S.' (it may not be his because it was acted at the Red Bull and Curtain) is *The Hector of Germanie* (published 1615).

SMITH, William (fl. 1596). The Spenserian poet whose poems were published in the miscellanies *The Phoenix Nest* (1593) and *Englands Helicon* (1600), and in a collected edition, *Chloris* (1596).

SOUTHERN, John (fl. 1584). A Shropshire man, he returned from education in France to a position as court musician. A poor poet and plagiarist of Ronsard, he published an eccentric volume, dedicated to Edward de Vere, Earl of Oxford, *The Musyque of the Beautie of his Mistresse Diana* (1584).

SOUTHWELL, Robert (1561-95). Born at Horsham St Faith, Norfolk, his mother was a Copley, distantly related to the Bacons and Cecils. He was educated as a Jesuit at Douay and Rome, becoming a priest and missionary in England and sheltered by Lord Vaux of Harrowden, Anne, Countess of Arundel, and Richard Bellamy of Harrow. He was finally arrested, tortured, put in the Tower, and executed at Tyburn. He left in MSS prose tracts, and in verse *Maeoniae, A Fourefould Meditation*, and, notably, *St. Peter's Complaint*, published posthumously in 1595, and a best-seller.

C. Devlin: *Robert Southwell* (1956).

SPEGHT, Rachel (fl. 1617-21). The daughter of Thomas (the Chaucerian editor) she was introduced to Mary Mounteford – her godmother and a physician's wife – who encouraged her to write religious verse which was included in *Mortalities Memorandum* (1621).

SPENSER, Edmund (1552?-99). The son of a London cloth-worker, he was connected with the Spencers of Althorpe, Northamptonshire, and sought the patronage of two of their ladies, Elizabeth Cary and the great Alice Spencer. He was at Merchant Taylors School, under Mulcaster, and Pembroke Hall, Cambridge, where he met Gabriel Harvey, who intro-duced him to the Leicester household and Sir Philip Sidney. He managed with great tact to avoid the worst of the Areopagus neo-classicism, and modelled himself upon the courtly group of Sidney, Greville and Dyer, whom he felt privileged to know. He made a quite extraordinary bid for political preferment in *The Shepheardes Calender* (1579), published under the pseudonym *Immerito*. (Previously he had not printed the poetry he had been writing since before university, 'least by over-much cloying their noble eares, I should gather a contempt of myself, or else seeme rather for gaine or commoditie to doe it', but now 'whiles the iron is hote, it is good striking, and mindes of nobles varie as their estates.') The impact of this one poem is probably unparalelled in English literature; its brilliance dazzled everybody. He became the 'new poet' everyone talked about: the courtiers, Sidney and Puttenham, the professionals, Nashe and Webbe, scholars like Harvey and dilettantes like John Chamberlain. When Robert Allot the printer compiled *Englands Parnassus* (1600), Spenser was given 386 quotations, with Drayton his nearest rival with 225, and Shakespeare only 95. The poem is a *tour de force,* designed to appeal in the different months to all possible audiences.

Under the patronage of Sidney, he was sent to Ireland (graveyard of so many hopes), as secretary to the Lord Deputy, Lord Grey of Wilton; but found it hard to advance further. Spenser did his best in Ireland, creating his own literary circle, including Sir Lodowick Bryskett, his senior as clerk of Munster. His post enabled him to acquire considerable estates at Kilcolman Castle. He married Elizabeth Boyle, from Towcester, Northamptonshire, a relative of Richard Boyle, Earl of Cork. (His first wife, Machabyas Childe had died shortly after the birth of two children.) Leicester, his next patron, drew him into dangerous opposition to the controversial Anjou marriage, and his later patrons, Ralegh and Essex, were not the best of allies. Burghley remained unconvinced of his political reliability, and when he was finally awarded a pension of £50 p.a., Burghley appears to have halved it.

About 1590 Spenser deliberately broke with court circles. He got Ponsonby, one of the reputable publishers, to print his *Complaints* (1591), *Fowre Hymnes* (1596), and other poems; and he rejected in *Colin Clouts Come Home Againe* (1595) the poet who goes to court, as a fool:

> all the walls and windows there are writ
> All full of love, and love, and love my deare,
> And all their talke and studie is of it . . .
> Ne any one himselfe doth ought esteeme,
> Unlesse he swim in love up to the eares.

He had long held ambitions to write epic poetry, after Tasso and Ariosto, and in 1590 set about publishing, in instalments, *The Faerie Queene* (1590, 1596), with an unprecedented multiple dedication, in seventeen sonnets, to all the important leaders of the Privy Council. He gained nothing from this beyond the meagre pension, despite the efforts of Ralegh whose estates bordered his in Cork. His castle, with, it seems, the next instalment of the *Faerie Queene* and several poems we know he wrote, but which have disappeared, were burned during the Tyrone uprising in 1598. He died in London carrying despatches. Essex paid for his funeral in Westminster Abbey.

Spenser was an extremely sensuous love poet, as is demonstrated by the marriage poems, *Epithalamion* (1595) and *Prothalamion* (1596), and the *Amoretti* (1595), the story of his courtship of Elizabeth, while in the allegory, *The Faerie Queene* he mingled many different levels of meaning – a romantic story, didactic moral and political overtones, personal identifications, and a wholly imaginative experience. At its best, the *Faerie Queene* has the charm of an expanded conceit, an extravagant, outrageous metaphor of the individualist taking arms against a sea of troubles. Though waylaid frequently into long digressions, Spenser constantly pulls his fictions back into a moral encyclopedia, where Good is predestined to overcome Evil. The moral is the invulnerability of virtue and the inevitably corrupting consequences of vice, yet often the morality contradicts the story. This dualism has been apparent to critics since the time of Rymer and Temple and other Augustan critics, a difference, as C.S. Lewis saw it, between two Spensers: one who was elfin, Renaissance, voluptuous, courtly and Italianate, and another who was Protestant, manly, churchwardenly, domestic and didactic.

H. Shire: *A Preface to Spenser* (1978); C.S. Lewis: *Studies in Medieval and Renaissance Literature* (1966); K. Williams: *Spenser's Faerie Queene* (1966); J.W. Saunders: 'The Façade of Morality', in W.R. Mueller and D.C. Allen (eds): *That Soveraine Light* (1952); A.C. Judson: *The Life of Edmund Spenser* (1945).

STANYHURST, Richard (1547-1618). Son of a Dublin Recorder and Speaker of the Irish Commons. He went to Waterford School and University College, Oxford, where he was a friend of Edmund Campion, and then to Furnivall's Inn and Lincoln's Inn. When his wife died, he went to the Spanish Netherlands and never returned. He became a staunch RC at Leyden, and spent his time, apart from writing, in rather vague plots in the Spanish interest.

He contributed to Holinshed's *Chronicles* (1586). In his translation of four books of the *Aeneid* (published in Leyden, 1582) in 'English Heroicall Verse', namely classical hexameters, he insisted on not being mistaken for an ignoramus, 'neaver enstructed in any grammer schoole, nor atayning to thee paringes of thee Latin and Greek tongue'; but the exercise proves, in unconscious burlesque, how bad neo-classical theory was.

STAPLETON, Sir Robert (d. 1669). From Carlton-by-Snaith, Yorkshire, his mother was a Pierrepoint. He was educated at a Benedictine convent in Douay and became a monk in 1625; but he abandoned his calling, turned Protestant, became a gentleman of the Privy Chamber to Prince Charles, took a DCL at Oxford, and spent the Civil War in study. In these years he wrote a play (now lost), *The Royal Choice,* and three translations: *Six Satyrs of Juvenal* (published 1644), Musaeus's *The Loves of Hero and Leander* (1645) and Juvenal's *Sixteen Satyrs* (1647).

STEPHENS, John (fl. 1615). From Gloucester, he was a friend of Jonson and Henry Fitzgeffrey. Apart from his *Satyrical Essayes, Characters, and others* (two editions in 1615) he is known only for the play *Cynthia's Revenge,* which was rather splendidly printed in 1613.

STERNHOLD, Thomas (d. 1549). Probably from Hampshire, he went to Christ Church, Oxford, and was Groom of the Robes to Henry VIII and legacied in the King's will. He was probably the MP for Plymouth (1545). Like Marot in France, and his English predecessor Miles Coverdale, he was convinced that psalms written in popular metre could and should replace songs, setting an example which many followed. His *Certayne Psalmes* (c. 1547, dedicated to Edward VI) were expanded by John Hopkins in 1549, and, after the Bible and Common Prayer Book, is the best-selling English book of all time.

STEVENSON, William (d. 1575). A Durham man, he went to Christ's College, Cambridge, where he wrote the comedy which has become regarded as typical of boisterous college tastes, *Gammer Gurton's Nedle* (published 1575). He was later prebendary of Durham Cathedral.

STEWARD, Sir Simeon (d. 1629?). Educated at Trinity College, Cambridge, he was MP for Shaftesbury (1614) and Aldeburgh (1627) and was the friend of Herrick and Thomas Fuller. He contributed the poem *The Faerey King* (1635) to a book about the kings and queens of Faerie.

STEWART, William (1481?-1550?). Educated at St Andrews University, he was a pensioner at the court of James V, his income rising from £20 to £40 p.a. before 1530. As a court poet he wrote many poems most of which have been lost apart from those preserved in the MS collections of George Bannatyne and Sir Richard Maitland. David Lindsay refers to him as one of his masters. At the bidding of James V, he wrote from 1531 a metrical version of the history of Hector Boece.

STORER, Thomas (1571-1604). A Londoner, educated at Christ Church, Oxford, he published a poem in 1599, commended by Charles Fitzgeffrey and Thomas and Edward Michelbourne: *The Life and Death of Thomas Wolsey, cardinall*. He certainly wrote other poems, but they are untraceable.

STRADLING, Sir John (1563-1637). From Bristol he went to Brasenose College and Magdalen Hall, Oxford, and the Inns of Court, and inherited his great-uncle's estate in Glamorgan. He was Sheriff of Glamorgan by 1607, MP for St Germans, Cornwall (1625), Old Sarum (1625) and Glamorgan (1626). His friends were William Camden, Sir John Harington, Thomas Leyson and Ioan David Rhys. He published several translations from Iustis Lipsius, epigrams, and *Divine Poems*, dedicated to James I (1625) and Charles I (1627). His poetical description of Glamorgan is lost.

STRODE, William (1602-45). From Plympton, Devon, he was educated at Westminster School and Christ Church, Oxford, and became public orator and proctor of the university, and chaplain to Bishop Richard Corbet, a fellow-poet. He won preferment to a canonry of Christ Church and as vicar of Blackbourton, Oxfordshire and Bradby, Northamptonshire, became a DD. He wrote plays, staged at Oxford, including *The Floating Island* (published 1655), much occasional verse left in MSS and miscellanies, and songs set to music before Charles I by Henry Lawes. He is now a neglected writer, described by Wood as 'a person of great parts, a pithy ostentatious preacher, an exquisite orator, and an eminent poet.'

STUBBS, Philip (1555?-1610?). A Puritan pamphleteer in verse and prose, educated at both Cambridge and Oxford. He had the means to travel about 'to learne nurture, good demeanour, and cyvill behaviour . . . to learne the state of all things in general, all which I could never have learned in one place.' His first religious ballad appeared in 1581, and he regularly warned about the awful judgements awaiting sinners. His most popular work was *The Anatomie of Abuses* (many editions from 1583) which at first was gentle about dancing and useful plays but which in the end damned all such courtly exercises. Another popular work was the biography of his wife, Katherine Emmes, whom he married when she was fifteen, and who died aged nineteen: *A Chrystal Glasse for Christian Women* (1590).

STUDLEY, John (1545?-90?). Educated at Westminster School and Trinity College, Cambridge, he was in trouble at college because he was a Calvinist. Paradoxically, he followed the RC, Jasper Heywood, in translating the plays of Seneca for publication. His *Agamemnon* (1566), *Medea* (1566), *Hippolytus* (1567) and *Hercules Octeus*, were collected in Thomas Newton's *Tenne tragedies* (1581).

SUCKLING, Sir John (1609-41). Son of the Secretary of State, his mother was a Cranfield. He went to Trinity College, Cambridge and Gray's Inn. On his father's death, in 1627, he inherited large estates in Suffolk, Lincolnshire and Middlesex. He was a brilliant member of the courtly society of Charles I, and the friend of Sir Tobie Matthew, Thomas Nabbes, Wye Saltonstall, Thomas Carew, Richard Lovelace, John Hales and especially Sir William Davenant. He once fought Sir John Digby in a brawl. He was leader of the circle at the Bear Tavern, seems to have invented cribbage, played bowls, dice and ninepins, and was known for his love of tobacco and reparte. He was also a soldier: blooded under the Marquis of Hamilton in the wars of Gustavus Adolphus, and commander in Scotland (1639) rising to the rank of captain; his troops were said to be the best-dressed in the army. He resisted Parliament but fled abroad after an abortive *coup*, where he committed suicide.

He was a leading dramatist, making use of scenery hitherto restricted to masques, and acting in some of his own plays. He wrote *Aglaura* (published 1638), *The Goblins* (Blackfriars, 1638) and *The Discontented Colonel* (1640). Some of his verse was published posthumously in *Fragmenta Aurea* (1646). His was the wryest, driest voice of the age.

Ed. I.A. Beaurline: *Plays* (1972); Ed. T. Clayton: *Non-dramatic works* (1972).

SYLVESTER, Josuah (1563-1618). Son of a Kent clothier who died early, he was brought up by an uncle, William Plumbe, who was married to Margaret Neville. He was educated at a select school in Southampton run by Adrian à Saravia, and then entered the Merchant Adventurers, where he served as secretary, and was sent to Middleburgh where he died. In 1606 he was Groom of the Chamber to Prince Henry at £20 p.a. He is chiefly known for his metrical translations of scriptural epics by Gascon Huguenot, and particularly for his renderings of the works of Guillaume de Saluste, seigneur du Bartas (1590, 1592, 1593, 1598, 1599, and collected in 1606). Young Milton and Dryden read him. His other published verse was chiefly elegiac or religious. Some of his poems appeared in miscellanies such as *Englands Parnassus* (1600) and *A Poetical Rapsodie* (1602).

T

TAILOR, Robert (fl. 1614). Only known for two published works: a comedy, *The Hog hath lost his Pearle* (1614), played by apprentices, who were imprisoned because it was thought 'Hog' was the Lord Mayor, Sir John Swinnerton; and a psalter, *Sacred Hymns* (1615).

TARLTON, Richard (d. 1588). Born in Shropshire, he may have been an apprentice and an innkeeper. Leicester introduced him to court as a jester, and to the theatre as a comic actor. He was a founder-member in 1583 of the Queen's company. He wrote one comedy for the company, the popular *Seven Deadly Sins,* and added improvisations and jigs to other texts. He was Master of the Fence in 1587. Philip Sidney was godfather to his son, and he knew Sir Francis Walsingham. His reputation was so high that many ballads and chapbooks appeared with his name advertised between 1578 and 1611, but they were catch-penny and probably not written by him.

TAYLOR, John, the Water Poet (1580-1653). Most people have thought of him as in the lowest strata of all in the society of professional writers in London, but even he had some claims to gentility. From Gloucester, he was educated at Gloucester School before moving to London, where he was apprenticed to a Thames waterman. He was conscripted to serve in the navy at Cadiz and the Azores (1596-7). He later became the leading waterman and collector of the wine perquisite for the Lieutanant of the Tower. He devised, for the wedding of the Princess Elizabeth in 1613, the first water pageant on the Thames. When trade began to diminish with the removal of the theatres from the South Bank, and with the growth of hackney carriages, he turned to verse for a living, and published over 150 broadsides and chapbooks between 1612 and 1653; with a folio collected edition in 1630. He pioneered subscription patronage by collecting money first for an expedition, and then undertaking and writing about it: he provoked a lucrative feud with Thomas Coryat. He set off to walk to Braemar for his *Penniless Pilgrimage,* happily for his admirers at about the same time as Jonson was walking to Edinburgh to visit William

Drummond of Hawthornden; Jonson gave him 22 shillings. He visited Princess Elizabeth in Prague. He went to York by sea. He tried to sail to Kent in a brown-paper boat.

During the 1625 plague he lodged in Oriel College, Oxford, where he wrote Royalist tracts. When we last hear of him, he was keeper of the Crown Inn in Long Acre.

THORIE, John (fl. 1590-1611). Son of a Flanders MD and born in London, he was educated at Christ Church, Oxford, where he was a friend of John Florio and Gabriel Harvey (and therefore attacked by Nashe) and where he first wrote poetry. His surviving poems are printed in the works of his friends. He is chiefly known for translations of Spanish writers.

THORNE, John (d. 1573). A musician of York Minster, he also wrote poems in MS circulation, some of which were printed in the miscellany *Paradyse of Daintie Devyces* (1576).

TICHBORNE, Chidiock (1558?-96). From Southampton, his mother was a Middleton. He paid dearly for his RC loyalties which led him into various conspiracies, including Babington's: he was disembowelled and then executed, an act so barbarous the Queen expressly forbade it thereafter. He wrote the best of all his poems on the night before his execution:

> My prime of youth is but a frost of cares,
> My feast of joy is but a dish of pain,
> My crop of corn is but a field of tares,
> And all my good is but vain hope of gain;
> The day is past, and yet I saw no sun,
> And now I live, and now my life is done.

TOFTE, Robert (d. 1620). Nicknamed 'Robin Redbreast', he was an engaging poet who translated Tasso, Ariosto and other Italians, and published love-poems – his lady was from the Caryll family – *Laura* (1597) and *Alba* (1598).

TOMKIS, Thomas (c. 1580-1634). Educated at Trinity College, Cambridge. He is known for two important plays, the comedy, *Lingua*, played before James I at Hinchingbrook (1603), one of the actors being four-year-old Oliver Cromwell; and the satire on astrology, *Albumazar*, played at Trinity College, again before James I (1615).

TOOKE, George (1595-1675). From Hertfordshire, he fought at Cadiz and wrote about his experiences in the prose-verse *The History of Cales Passion* (published 1625). He also wrote *Cansonets* (1647) for his dead wife, Anna, and some prose. His friends included John Selden and John Hales.

TOURNEUR, Cyril (c. 1575-1626). Very few details of his life are known, and even his existence has been questioned. It is now thought that his family were closely connected with the Cecils, and his father was probably the Cecil man, Richard Tourneur, appointed Lieutenant-Governor of Brill in the United Provinces. Cyril was certainly a soldier in the United Provinces and emerged as a panegyrist of Robert Cecil, Sir Francis Vere and Prince Henry. He had an annuity of £60 p.a. from the United Provinces in 1616, and was secretary of the Council of War at Cadiz (1625) under Sir Edward Cecil. After the expedition's failure, he was sent to Ireland where he died.

He wrote a satire, *The Transformed Metamorphosis* (published 1608), but is chiefly known for plays written for the King's company, some of which were written in collaboration with Fletcher and Massinger, and include *The Second Maiden's Tragedie* (1611) and *The Knight of Malta* (c. 1611). There are also two extant plays written solo: *The Atheist's Tragedie* (published 1611) and, one of the great plays of this period, notable for its horrible vision of life, *The Revenger's Tragaedie* (published 1607).

P.S. Murray: *A Study of Cyril Tourneur* (1964).

TOWNSEND, Aurelian (fl. 1601-43). From Norfolk, he was steward to Robert Cecil, first Earl of Salisbury, and later gentleman of the Privy Chamber to Charles I. He was a close friend of Jonson, Edward Herbert, Earl of Cherbury, Walter Montagu, Thomas Carew and others, whose poems he collected and edited for publication in 1640. He wrote two Whitehall masques with Inigo Jones, *Albion's Triumph* and *Tempe Restored*, both published in 1632; and his witty MS poems were printed in *Choice Drollery* (1655).

TURBERVILLE, George (1540?-1610). Born at Whitchurch Canonicorum, Dorset, his mother was a Morgan. He went to Winchester and became a perpetual Fellow at New College, Oxford, later going on to the Inns of Court. He was secretary to Thomas Randolph, ambassador to Russia (1568-9); his account *Poems describing . . . Russia* (1568) is not complimentary to the court of Ivan the Terrible: 'A people passing rude, to vices vile inclinde.' His Inns of Court friends included Arthur Broke, George Gascoigne (whose *Posies* he published), Sir John Harington, Richard Edwards and William Drummond of Hawthornden, who had published in Edinburgh in 1587 fifty special copies of Turberville's major work, *Tragical Tales* (from Boccaccio, plus sonnets). He wrote popular translations of Ovid (1567), Mantuan (1567) and Mancinus (1568), prose works on hawking and venery and, best of all, *Epitaphs, Epigrams, Songs and Sonets* (1567). He is credited with perfecting the metre of blank verse.

J.E. Hankins: *The Life and Work of George Turberville* (1940).

TUSSER, Thomas (1524?-80). From Witham, Essex, he became a chorister at Wallingford collegiate school in Berkshire, then attended St Paul's and Eton, under Udall, before going on to King's College and Trinity Hall, Cambridge. For ten years he was attached as a musician to William Paget, first Baron Paget of Beaudesert. He then married and settled down as a farmer in Cattiwade, Suffolk, and later in West Dereham, Norfolk. He introduced barley as a main crop, and wrote *A Hundreth Good Pointes of Husbandry* (1557), which was a best-seller. However, his farming ventures failed, and he had to resume his work in the choirs of Norwich and London, drawing Henry Peacham to write of him:

> Tusser, they tell me when thous were alive
> Thou, teaching thrift, thyself couldst never thrive.

He died in the debtors' jail, Poultry counter.

TWYNE, Thomas (1543-1613). Son of a master at Canterbury School, he went to Corpus Christi College, Oxford, and later to Cambridge becoming an MB and MD, a practising physician and member of the College of Physicians. He was a friend of John Dee. As well as his prose works and translations, he completed Thomas Phaer's *Aeneid* (1573).

TYE, Christopher (1497?-1572). Educated at King's College, Cambridge, he became master of the choir at Ely (1543) at £10 p.a., a Gentleman of the Chapel Royal, canon of Ely and rector of various Fen parishes. He presented music and song before Edward VI, and was a distinguished writer of part-songs for which he wrote his own lyrics. He versified the last fourteen chapters of Acts (1553) and published a metrical translation from Boccaccio, *Nastagio and Traversari* (1569). His tunes have come to accompany some of Burns's poems and Christmas carols.

U

UDALL, Nicholas (1505-56). From Hampshire, he went to Winchester and Corpus Christi College, Oxford. He was the friend of John Leland, and an accomplished Latin poet; (he also wrote a few poems in English). In 1534 he became headmaster of Eton, writing Latin and English plays for his pupils, including the famous comedy *Ralph Roister Doister* (1541). He was a strict man: his pupil Thomas Tusser recalls receiving 53 stripes for a 'fault but small, or none at all'. He was dismissed for homosexual offences against his pupils.

He then became vicar of Braintree, Essex, was helped by Princess Mary in a translation of Erasmus's *Apothegms* (1542), served Catherine Parr, and published other translations, including his own version of St Luke (1548). During Edward VI's reign he became a Reformist controversialist, but when Queen Mary, his old collaborator, succeeded to the throne, she did not penalise him. He wrote dialogues and interludes for her. He was tutor to Edward Courtenay (a prisoner in the Tower), rector of Carisbrooke, Isle of Wight, and a tutor in the household of Stephen Gardiner, Bishop of Winchester. Finally, he returned to teaching and was appointed headmaster of Winchester (1554), where he wrote more plays for his pupils, including *Ezekias* (published 1564).

UNDERDOWN, Thomas (fl. 1566-87). He was educated at King's College, Cambridge, and was in the household of Sir Thomas Sackville. He translated Heliodorus, in prose, *An Aethiopian Historie* (1569), and in fourteener verse, *Ovid his invective against Ibis* (1569).

V

VALLANS, William (fl. 1578-90). A salter from Hertfordshire and antiquarian friend of William Camden, he published a hexameter description of Hertfordshire, *A Tale of Two Swannes* (1590).

VAUGHAN, Henry, the 'Silurist' (1622-95). From Brecon, (hence his nickname), the cousin of John Aubrey, he went with his twin brother Thomas to Jesus College, Oxford, where he studied medicine, becoming a physician in Brecon in 1645. He contributed to the Renaissance *Poems, with the Tenth Satyre of Juvenal Englished* (published 1646), and *Olor Iscanus* (the chief poem about the Usk, published 1647). His more devotional poems were written after 1650.

J. Bennett: *Five Metaphysical Poets* (1964).

VAUGHAN, Thomas (1622-66). Henry's twin, he became rector of St Bridget's, Brecon, but as a Royalist he was deprived of his living during the Commonwealth. He turned instead to alchemy, and probably died of mercury inhalation. He wrote on alchemy under the pseudonym Eugenius Philalethes, and circulated poems, in Latin and English, in MSS. Some were published after 1650.

VAUGHAN, William (1577-1641). From Carmarthenshire, he went to Jesus College, Oxford, and later became Sheriff of Carmarthen (1615). He is chiefly known for his promotion of the colonisation of Newfoundland, which he visited. He published some quaint mixtures of prose and verse: *The Golden Fleece* (1626, with the fleece turning up in Newfoundland), *The Golden Grove Moralised*, *The Church Militant* (published 1640) and *The Soules Exercise in the Daily Contemplation of our Saviours Birth, Life, Passage and Resurrection* (1641). He seems to have turned entirely to religious verse after his wife was killed by lightning.

VAUX, Thomas, second Baron Vaux of Harrowden (1510-56). He was educated at Cambridge but started courtly service at the age of thirteen with Cardinal Wolsey. He was one of Henry VIII's most faithful servants, but his only public office was that of captain of the Isle of Jersey. He was a member of Wyatt's group, and we find some of his poems in later miscellanies such as Tottel's *Songes and Sonnettes* (1557) and *Paradyse of Daintie Devyces* (1576). Perhaps his most famous poem is 'Brittle beauty', interesting in its mix of homely medieval similes and Renaissance metaphors.

VENNAR, Richard (d. 1615?). From Salisbury, he was educated at Balliol College, Oxford and Barnard's and Lincoln's Inns; he also travelled in France and Germany. Queen Elizabeth suspected he was a double-agent when he was received so well in Scotland at a time when his mission there should not have been popular. He was notorious for taking money for masques which were not written – *Englands Joy*, supposedly for the Swan in 1602, and another for the Lord Mayor, for which he elicited £500 from Sir John Spencer. His actual writing was very meagre. Nevertheless, his debts mounted, and he died in the Wood Street counter.

VERE, Edward de, seventeenth Earl of Oxford (1550-1604). A very wayward, petulant man, his mother was the sister of his tutor Arthur Golding. When he was twelve, his father died and he succeeded to the title and all its courtly emoluments. He was educated at Queens' and St John's Colleges, Cambridge, and an MA of both universities. He was the ward of Sir William Cecil, Burghley, who married him to his daughter Anne. He had a scheme for rescuing the Duke of Norfolk from the Tower, and when his father-in-law stopped him, in petulance he set out to spend his wife's fortune of £12,000 and from 1575 to 1577, as Burghley discovered, 'prodigally spent and consumed all even to the selling of the stones, timber and lead'. He fled abroad, and brought back from Italy powdered gloves and jerkins, rare perfumes and sweet-bags, and was indeed the perfect Osric. The Queen did not know what to make of him: she liked him for his 'valiantness' and skills at dancing and jousting, but he was jealous of Sidney, wanted to duel with or murder him, and indeed nearly killed Thomas Knyvet in a duel and was placed under house arrest. Burghley finally disowned him. He served under Ralegh against the Armada, and his second marriage to Elizabeth Trentham was more successful. He sat on the trials of Essex, Southampton, and Mary Queen of Scots.

He was patron of an important company of players, writing

plays now lost. He supported Lyly, Spenser, Munday, Underdown, Twyne and John Southern. His love of music and lyric poetry was genuine, and his MS poetry appeared in several miscellanies, including *Paradyse of Daintie Devyces* (1576), *Phoenix Nest* (1593), *Englands Parnassus* (1600) and *Englands Helicon* (1600).

VICARS, John (1580?-1652). He was educated at Christ's Hospital, and Queen's College, Oxford, returning to Christ's Hospital to be an usher there almost all his life. He published translations, including an *Aeneid* (1632), and some Presbyterian anti-episcopalian verse-prose concoctions, including *Mischeefes Mysterie* (1617), *A Prospective Glasse* (1618) and *Babels Balme* (1624).

W

WADESON, Anthony (fl. 1600). One of Henslowe's playwrights known for two plays about the Earl of Gloucester who conquered Portugal, and one of which, *Looke About You* (published 1600), survives.

WAGER, Lewis (d. 1562). The rector of St James's, Garlickhythe, who wrote an interlude which was performed at universities and published in 1566 as *The Life and Repentaunce of Marie Magdalene*.

WAGER, William (fl. 1566). A writer of interludes, known for: *The longer thou livest, the moore foole thou art*, and *The Cruell Debtor* (1566).

WALLER, Edmund (1606-87). He was from Hertfordshire, and his mother was a Hampden, who sent him, after his father's death, to Eton, King's College, Cambridge and Lincoln's Inn. When he was sixteen he was already MP for Amersham, later representing Ilchester, Chipping Wycombe and St Ives. He married Anne Bankes, the rich heiress of a mercer, who died three years later in childbirth. Her dowry was £8000. He wooed his 'Sacharissa', Lady Dorothy Sidney, daughter of the Earl of Leicester, but did not win her and married instead Mary Bracey in 1643, the daughter of a wealthy Thame family.

He was probably the richest English poet ever. Even after the massive fine he received at the hands of Parliament for his part in the 'peace party' conspiracy (see below), with Lord Jermyn he was the only exile able to 'keep a table' — even if he had to sell his second wife's jewels to do so. In politics he was in the group with Lucius Cary, Viscount Falkland. At first, because he was related to Cromwell, he supported Pym and the populist cause, objecting sincerely to the notion of the Divine Right of Kings and absolute episcopacy; but he also disliked innovation, was fundamentally *laissez faire*, and was against the extremists. He remained in London defending Royalist interests, and engaged in the abortive plot in 1643 to seize London in the name of the 'peace party'. Many of the conspirators were hanged, but Waller, abject in court, and making a full confession, was fined and imprisoned in the Tower whence he escaped abroad. Cromwell allowed him to return in 1655 and made him Commissioner for Trade. Charles II also thought highly of him.

He was highly acclaimed by his contemporaries and later writers. On his tomb the words 'Inter poetas sui temporis facile princeps' were inscribed; the 1766 *Biographia Britannia* called him 'the most celebrated lyric poet that England ever produced'; Dryden said of him 'Unless he had written none of us could write.' And Sir Thomas Higgins, in 1688 concluded:

> The English he hath to perfection brought;
> And we to speak are by his measures taught.
> Those very words that are in fashion now,
> He brought in credit half an age ago.

While spearheading the Augustan revolution against the Renaissance, Waller also reflects the groundswell of continuity; as in politics, his poetry stood in both camps. At first he wrote, 'only to please himself, and such particular persons to whom they were directed', poems about a naval victory, the death of a Prince, the illness of a Queen, a royal visit, and so on. His love-poetry, though good, was rarely drawn directly from his own experiences, though one poem seems to have been addressed to *both* Lady Dorothy Sidney and Lady Anne Cavendish. Sixteen poems appeared in the anthology *Witts recreations* (1645); but underlying his fluent triflings were serious concerns: he wanted to civilise English verse: 'Methought, I never sawe a good copie of English verses; they want smoothness; then I began to essay.' He developed the heroic couplet and the panegyric – the metre because of its plain dignity, the form because he wanted to restore poetry of praise – and built on the Renaissance acceptance of the immortality of poetry, seeking a national art. His first poem, 'Of the danger his Majesty escaped', written in 1623 about Prince Charles's feat at Santander, was written when he was only seventeen, and its style heralds the rational, humane and ironic voice that was to dominate English poetry for 200 years. His collected *Poems* (1645) a miscellaneous collection which came by accident into the hands of a publisher, are thus a complete mix of old and new.

J.W. Saunders: 'The Social Situation of Seventeenth-

Century Poetry' in D.J. Palmer and M. Bradbury (eds): *Metaphysical Poetry* (1970).

WALSINGHAM, Edward (d. 1663). Not of *the* Walsingham family (who only produced prose) but from the Warwickshire family related to George Digby, second Earl of Bristol, whose secretary he was in 1643. After taking his MA at Oxford, he became an RC exile and secret agent, but apparently a poor one: according to Sir Edward Nicholas he was 'a great babbler of his most secret employments'. He commemorated in prose and verse Royalist worthies.

WALTON, Izaak (1593-1683). From a Staffordshire yeoman family he became an ironmonger in London, in the parish, St Dunstan's, where Donne was priest. Besides Donne, his friends included Jonson, Drayton and Wotton. We know him as the author of *The Compleat Angler* (1653), but probably more important are his biographies and editions of poets, and his own poetry which he was writing by 1619.

WARD, John (fl. 1642-3). A Puritan from Tewkesbury, he served in the parliamentary forces and published verse commentaries on the moral and theological shortcomings of the Royalists in 1642: *The Taking of Winchester,* and *An Encouragement to Warre.*

WARMESTRY, Gervase (1604-41). Son of the diocesan registrar of Worcester, he was educated at Worcester School, Westminster School, Christ Church, Oxford, and the Middle Temple, succeeding his father as registrar in 1630. He published a verse tract, *England's Wound and Cure* (1628).

WARNER, William (1558?-1609). A Londoner, educated at Magdalen Hall, Oxford, he later became an attorney. His friends were Marlowe and Drayton under the patronage of the Hunsdon family. Besides prose tales, he wrote several plays, including a version of Plautus's *Menaechmi* (published 1595). His main work was his long poem in fourteeners, *Albions England,* published in instalments (1586, 1589, 1592, 1596, 1602 and 1606) with a posthumous complete edition in 1612. Drayton found his poems

> so fine, cleere, new
> As yet they have bin equalled by few . . .

and in Robert Allot's *Englands Parnassus* (1600), an anthology of quotations and as such an index of the times, the principal three poets who emerge are Spenser (386 entries), Drayton (225), and Warner (171) (Shakespeare was placed eighth and Chapman ninth). His reputation has since declined.

WARREN, Arthur (fl. 1605). He wrote of his experiences in debtor's prison in six-line stanza poems, *The Poore Mans Passions* and *Poverties Patience* (both published 1605), and was the 'A.W.' who contributed 77 poems to Francis Davison's *A Poetical Rapsodie* (1602).

WARREN, William (fl. 1581). Known only as the author of a lost book, *A pithie and plesaunt discourse, dialoguewyse* (1578), and in fourteeners, a book about Englishwomen, *Nurcerie of Names*, published in 1581 by 'Guillam de Warrino'.

WASTELL, Simon (d. 1632). From Cumbria, he was educated at Queen's College, Oxford, and became headmaster of Northampton School where, to reinforce his teaching, he published, after John Shaw, a verse summary of the Bible, published in 1621 as *Biblia Summula*, and in 1629 as *Microbiblion*.

WATSON, Thomas (1557?-92). An important Elizabethan whose work has been much neglected. A Londoner, at Oxford he was a classical scholar and at the Inns of Court a legal. He was imprisoned with Marlowe in 1589 for killing William Bradley in Shoreditch, but pleaded self-defence and was exonerated.

His Latin poems were first esteemed in France, where, on the whole, he was thought more highly of than in his own country. His talents caught the attention of Sir Francis Walsingham, and through him that of Sir Philip Sidney. He was the friend of Lyly, Peele, Nashe and Marlowe, and William Clerke observed that Shakespeare was 'Watson's heire': he was Spenser's 'Amyntas'. He was the first sonneteer of Elizabeth's reign, giving new life to the verse forms of Wyatt and Surrey, before Sidney. He published in 1590 a collection of Italian madrigals, gathered on foreign travels, together with the music.

His most important book *Hecatompathia* (published 1582), consists of sonnets (with an elaborate *apparatus criticus*, like E.K.'s in Spenser's *Shepheardes Calender*), in which with great skill he imitates poems by Petrarch, Strozza, dell'Aquila,

Ronsard, Firenzuola, Forcatulus, Parabosco, Aeneas Sylvius, Sophocles, Theocritus, Apollonius of Rhodes, Virgil, Tibullus, Ovid, Horace, Propertius, Seneca, Pliny, Lucan, Martial, Valerius Flaccus, Poliziano, Baptista Mantuanus, Sepinus of Saumur, and others. In 1587 Abraham Fraunce published an English verse translation of his Latin version of Tasso's *Aminta*. He also wrote tragedies, now lost; and he left many poems in MS, some of which were published posthumously in *The Teares of Fancie* (1593), and others in miscellanies, *The Phoenix Nest* (1593), *Englands Helicon* (1600), *A Poetical Rapsodie* (1602) and *Englands Parnassus* (1600).

A.L. Rowse: *Christopher Marlowe* (1964).

WEBSTER, John (1577?-1634?). Son of a London merchant taylor, he was apprenticed to the Merchant Taylors, but soon joined the theatre, writing for the King's company but chiefly for Henslowe and the Queen's company, for whom he wrote fourteen plays in twenty-four years, though sporadically since the plays accumulate in the periods 1602-5 and 1609-14. He may have started as an actor, but he was not one of the best. He wrote at least one pageant for the City, *Monuments of Honor* (published 1624). He collaborated with Drayton, Middleton, Munday, Chettle, Thomas Heywood, Tourneur, Wentworth Smith, and particularly with Dekker – in *Westward Hoe* (for St Paul's children) and *Northward Hoe* (also St Paul's) in 1604-5. But he is most respected for his solo plays: *The White Divel* (Queen's, at the Curtain, published 1612), a revenge tragedy written after the success of Tourneur's *Revenger's Tragaedie*, another tragedy, *Appius and Virginia* (Queen's, about 1609), *The Duchess of Malfy* (the King's, at the Globe and Blackfriars, published 1623) and the tragi-comedy *The Devil's Law Case* (published 1623).

He was an intensely serious dramatist, revealing in his prefaces that he was disappointed by failures in the public playhouse, claiming kinship with Euripides, Horace, Martial and Shakespeare, and hoping for immortality himself. He interfered with his sources to whitewash and blackwash his characters and make the moral points he desired. A wealth of animal imagery seems to reveal his fear of a chaotic society; there is a general fear of death and an obsession with the triviality of human values. In love with the playhouse, he threw all its assets at his audience: antic dispositions, dumb-shows, ambassadors who dress up twice in one play (to show off costumes), ghosts galore, and on occasions all the action stopped for lectures on natural history; but one forgives him much for his poetry, characteristically at its best when his characters are facing death.

M.C. Bradbrook: *John Webster – Citizen and Dramatist* (1980); P. Berry: *The Art of John Webster* (1972); P.B. Murray: *A Study of John Webster* (1969); C. Leech: *John Webster: a Critical Study* (1951).

WECKHERLIN, George Rudolph (1584-1653). From Stuggart, he was educated in law at Tübingen University and was em-ployed in diplomatic service for Wurtemburg. He married an Englishwoman, and was employed as a drafter, translator and decipherer of foreign correspondence, becoming Milton's pre-decessor as Secretary for Foreign Tongues in 1644, and there-fore the first of a long line of Foreign Secretaries. He wrote with equal facility poems in German, French and English, notably *Triumphal Shows* (1616), *Panegyricke to Lord Hay* (1619) and the MS psalms and imitations of Daniel and Wotton published in 1641 and 1648.

WEDDERBURN, James (1495?-1553). One of three sons of a Dundee merchant he was educated at St Andrews University, and in Dieppe and Rouen before returning to his father's business. He wrote two plays for performance in Dundee – both directed against RCs – one about St John the Baptist, the other about Dionysius the Tyrant. With his brothers (see below), he wrote *The Dundee Psalms*, sacred parodies of popular ballads published as broadsides from 1542 and col-lected in 1567. He was forced into exile as an extreme reformer considered a heretic, and died in Rouen.

WEDDERBURN, John (1500?-56). The second of three brothers, (see above), he was chaplain of St Matthew's, Dundee, but like other extreme reformers was forced into exile and died in England.

WEDDERBURN, Robert (1510?-57?). The third of three brothers, (see above), and like them a graduate of St Andrews University, he became vicar of Dundee, went into exile like them, but returned to die in Scotland.

WEELKES, Thomas (fl. 1602). A B. Mus. from Oxford, he was

organist at Winchester and Chichester Cathedral, and a gentleman of the Chapel Royal. He published very popular madrigals and anthems in 1597, 1598, and twice in 1600.

   D. Brown: *Thomas Weelkes* (1969).

WEEVER, John (1576-1632). From Lancashire, he went to
Queens' College, Cambridge, and published *Epigrammes* in
1599, in which he made observations about Shakespeare and
other poets and men of the theatre. He also published *The
Mirror of Martyres* (1601) about Sir John Oldcastle; an erotic-
satirical poem *Faunus and Meliflora* (1601) ; and a popular
thumb-book (size 1½ inches) versifying the story of Christ,
An Agnus Dei (1606). After travels in Liège, Paris, Parma and
Rome, he became an antiquarian. He was the friend of Sir
Robert Cotton, Sir Henry Spelman, John Selden and Sir
Simonds d'Ewes.

WEST, Richard (fl. 1606-19). Known only for his published
verse, *News from Bartolomew Fayre* (1606), *The Court of
Conscience* (1607), and the second part of Francis Segar's
School of Vertue (1619).

WHARTON, John (fl. 1575-78). A Puritan schoolmaster who
castigated 'abhominable Caterpillers', including Chaucer, in
Whartons Dreame (published 1578).

WHETSTONE, George (1544?-87?). His father was a Lincolnshire squire, related to William Fleetwood. In London, he was
extravagant with his patrimony (which added force to his later
attacks on the depravities of city life), and fled from his respon-
sibilities as a soldier to the United Provinces in 1572, and with
Sir Humphrey Gilbert to Newfoundland; he was also with
Sidney at Zutphen in 1586. He was taken up by various
patrons, including Sidney, Thomas Radcliffe, Earl of Sussex
and Francis Russell, Earl of Bedford, all of whose deaths he
commemorated in biographical elegies. He was a friend of
George Gascoigne, whom he commemorated in *A Remembrance* (1577). He pioneered Italian romances in *The Rocke of
Regard* (1578), and is best known for his play, never acted,
Promos and Cassandra (published 1578) which was the main
source of Shakespeare's *Measure for Measure*.

   T. C. Izard: *George Whetstone: Middle Elizabethan Man of
Letters* (1942).

WHITNEY, Geoffrey (1548?-1601?). From Cheshire, he was

educated at Audlem School and Magdalene College, Cambridge, after which he took up a legal career, studying at Leyden and becoming eminent in the United Provinces; he was later under-bailiff at Great Yarmouth. He is best known for *A Choice of Emblemes* (published 1586), based on the emblem-books of Italy and France and consisting of 248 poems with woodcuts and mottoes. His sister Isabella was also literary, and published 'phylisophicall flowers' in *A Sweet Nosegay* (1573).

WHITTINGHAM, William (1524?-79). From Chester, he was educated at Brasenose College, All Souls' College and Christ Church, Oxford, and became an army chaplain, chaplain to Francis Russell, second Earl of Bedford, and Ambrose Dudley, Earl of Warwick. He was made Dean of Durham (1563). He was an early reformer, travelling to Orléans, Germany and Geneva. He was in exile at Frankfurt in the reign of Queen Mary, a supporter of Knox and his successor as minister in Geneva. He helped to translate the Geneva Bible, the main Elizabethan Bible, and wrote much religious verse: metrical psalms, revising the work of Sternhold and Hopkins and published in Geneva in 1556; metrifications of the Ten Commandments, The Song of Simeon, and the Lord's Prayer; and psalms for Scotland.

WHYHORNE, Thomas (1528-96). His MS poetry, often accompanied by music for virginals and lute, was always autobiographical: his poetry was about lovemaking or grief, with the boundaries indistinct.

WILBYE, John (1574-1638). Born at Diss, Norfolk, the son of a teacher, he became a lutanist and musician in the family of Sir Thomas Kytson of Bury St Edmunds; he was later with Lady Rivers at Colchester. The most prominent of all English madrigal composers, publishing 64 in 1598 and 1609; they include 'Sweet honey-sucking bees' and 'Draw on, sweet night'. He wrote his own lyrics.

J. Kerman: *The Elizabethan Madrigal* (1962).

WILKINS, George (fl. 1607). From Shoreditch, but little is known of his life. He was a pamphleteer from 1604, and wrote a 'novel' *The Painful Adventures of Pericles, Prince of Tyre* (1608); but he is chiefly known for his plays. He wrote for the King's and Queen's companies. Some of his collaborations, with Dekker and Thomas Heywood, are lost, but we have *The*

Travels of Three English Brothers (1607), written with Day and Rowley, his solo play *The Miseries of Inforst Marriage* (1607) based on a Walter Calverley who murdered his wife and children at Wakefield, and the play he probably wrote with Shakespeare, *Timon of Athens* (1609).

WILLOUGHBY, Henry (1574?-99?). From West Knoyle, Wiltshire, he was educated at St John's and Exeter Colleges, Oxford, and then served in the army abroad. Because he was connected by marriage with a friend of Shakespeare, Thomas Russell, his book *Willobie his Avisa* (published 1594, reprinted 1596 after Peter Colse's imitative *Penelopes Compaint*) has aroused more interest than it merits. It is a poetic account of the siege of a hard woman's heart, in which the poet is advised by a 'W.S.' It was published by Hadrian Dorrell, about whom nothing is known, and was very popular, rapidly running into six editions. Although there may be a dark meaning in the poem (possibly an attack on Southampton by the Ralegh group) it is doubtful if 'Avisa' is the Dark Lady, 'W.S.' Shakespeare, or 'H.W.' a 'new actor' of importance.

WILMOT, Robert (fl. 1569-1608). The Essex rector of North Okenden and vicar of Horndon-on-the-Hill, he was educated at the Inner Temple, and maintained his links there for twenty-four years. While there he wrote for performance before the Queen in 1568, the oldest known play taken from Italian novella, *The Tragedie of Tancred and Gismund*.

WILSON, Arthur (1595-1652). An extraordinary character respected for his physical strength. He was born in Great Yarmouth, and travelled in France in 1609. On his return he took it upon himself to learn writing 'court-hand' with John Davies of Hereford, and became a clerk in the Exchequer under Sir Henry Spiller, a post he lost in 1613 for satirising Sir Henry's wife. He was then taken up by Robert Devereux, third Earl of Essex, attracting his attention by saving a laundry maid from drowning. He served Essex in the Palatinate (1620), the United Provinces (1621-4) and Cadiz (1625) again leaving service (but with a pension) after a quarrel with the new Countess of Essex.

At this point he took himself to Trinity College, Oxford, and read mathematics, theology and science, proving it seems a highly innovative scholar. Afterwards, having turned Puritan, he joined Robert Rich, second Earl of Warwick, serving in Breda (1637). He wrote a history of Britain up to the reign of James I, published in 1653, and several plays, but only one is extant, *The Inconstant Lady* (c. 1640).

WILSON, Robert, the elder (d. 1600). An original member of Leicester's company in 1574 he became famous as a comic, becoming with Tarlton a founder-member of the Queen's company, later joining Lord Strange's and thus the Lord Chamberlain's company. He was known for his extempore wit and improvisations. His tragedy *Catiline* is lost but four plays are extant: *Three Ladies of London, Three Lordes and Three Ladies, The Coblers Prophesie* and *The Pedlars Prophesy,* all published between 1584 and 1594.

WILSON, Robert, the younger (1579-1610). Probably the son of the elder, he joined Henslowe's group of writers, collaborating with Drayton, Chettle, Munday and Hathway, and writing twenty plays in twenty years – sixteen of them crowded into three years. Only one is extant: *Sir John Old-castle* (1599).

WISDOM, Robert (d. 1568). Educated at Oxford and Cambridge, under Henry VIII he was curate at Stisted, Essex, but was too extreme a Protestant and was imprisoned in the Lollards Tower in 1540. He recanted in 1543, and with a similar heretic, Thomas Becon, he retreated to Staffordshire. Under Edward VI he was vicar of Settrington, Yorkshire; went into exile in Frankfurt during Mary's reign; and after Queen Elizabeth's accession was Archdeacon of Ely. Besides theological prose, reflecting the changes in his life, he published *Postill . . . upon every Gospell* (1549), and other religious poems in 1551.

WITHER, George (1588-1667). He was born at Bentworth, Hampshire, and educated at Magdalen College, Oxford and Lincoln's Inn, where he became the friend of Drayton, William Browne and Richard Brathwait. He was a favourite with the young Princess Elizabeth, celebrated her brother Henry's *Obsequies* (1612) and her marriage (1613), but satirised courtly extravagance and corruption and the whole monopoly scandal in *Abuses Stript and Whipt* (1613), for which he suffered the first of his spells in prison, until the Princess secured his release. From him we have the best description of prison conditions at the time: solitary confinement, paper and friends forbidden, food stopped and even kept for 24 hours 'without so much as a dropp of water'. But the Marshalsea proved, in the end, the place where he wrote much of his best poetry, veiling his satire in eclogues to beat the censor, as in *The Shepherd's Hunting* (1615), and writing love poems in *Fidelia* (1615).

When released, he found some patronage with the Earls of Southampton and Pembroke, and later he visited his Princess in Bohemia. He was now more concerned with abuses among publishers than courtiers: his brave *Wither's Motto, Nec Habeo, Nec Careo, nec Curo* (1621) earned him another term in the Marshalsea as 'too busy and satirical'. He found that the press, which should have afforded him professional security, fed on writers like 'the third plague of *Aegipt*', used unscrupulous catchpenny wiles to cheat authors, and most shamefully wanted to pay him for 'matter injurious to the person of the King': 'I have been offred a larger yearely stipend, and more respective entertaynments, to employ my selfe in setting forth hereticall fancies, then I have yet probabilitey to hope for, by professing the Trueth.'

As his writings become more Puritan – though not Calvinist – with psalms written in 1620 and 1621, he took on the stationers who could sell 20,000 copies of his works without paying him a penny, and his winning of a privilege for *Hymnes and Songs of the Church* (with music by Orlando Gibbons) was the very first claim for copyright. His *Brittans Remembrancer* (1628) inspired by the 1625 plague had to be self-financed because the stationers would not support him.

He served Charles I as a corporal against the Scots but, rejecting Royalist extremists was the parliamentary commander of Farnham Castle in 1642, saved from death by Denham when the Royalists won the battle there. When Parliament was victorious he was made a JP, promoted to major, and given £2000 for his plundered estates. But he was still unhappy about the balance of power, warning of calamities to come in *Prosopopoeia Britannica* (1648). His earlier imprisonment by the Royalists was repeated with another three years in Newgate and the Tower at the Restoration.

WOODHOUSE, Peter (fl. 1605). Known only for his *Conten-*

tion between the Elephant and the Flea (published 1605).

WORTLEY, Sir Francis (1591-1652). A son of a Warwickshire knight, his widowed mother married William Cavendish, Earl of Devonshire. He was educated at Magdalen College, Oxford, and became MP for East Retford (1624) and Yorkshire (1625). He fought a duel with Sir John Savile in 1626. Surprisingly, he was the friend of both Ben Jonson and John Taylor, the Water Poet. He was a Royalist commander, but was defeated, arrested and put in the Tower, from which he was released in 1649, much the poorer. He published in the 1640s *His Duty* (for Queen Elizabeth of Bohemia), *Fame and Truth* and *Characters and Elegies,* biographies of dead Royalists.

WOTTON, Sir Henry (1566-1639). A distinguished courtier, intimate with many writers and noblemen, including Essex, Jonson, Donne and most of the Inns of Court men. From Kent, he was educated at Winchester and New College, and Queen's College, Oxford, where he wrote a tragedy, and he travelled widely in Austria, Germany, Switzerland and Italy before entering the Middle Temple. He was with Essex as a secretary and agent, and after Essex's fall attended Ferdinand I of Tuscany, serving him on a secret mission to James VI. This mission made him welcome in England when James acceded to the English throne and he served as ambassador in Venice and Germany. He was also an envoy in France and the United Provinces, and MP for Appleby (1614) and Sandwich (1625). In 1624 he became Provost of Eton (a post he held till his death) taking orders in 1627.

He wrote about architecture, but was chiefly a prolific poet, leaving letters and poems in *Reliquiae Wottoniae,* from which a collected edition, with Walton's biographical preface, was published in 1651. Though he was not by nature a despondent man – too realistic for self-pity – his best lyrics reach towards an impossible ideal of 'honest thought, And simple truth'. He wrote fine lines for James I's brilliant daughter, Elizabeth; and no man knew better how to comment 'upon the sudden restraint of the Earl of Somerset, then falling from favour, 1615':

> Dazzled thus with height of place,
> Whilst our hopes our wits beguile,

No man marks the narrow space
'Twixt a prison and a smile.

If Ralegh was the archetypal Elizabethan courtly poet, Wotton
was the archetypal Jacobean.

L.P. Smith: *The Life and Letters of Sir Henry Wotton*
(1907).

WROTH, Lady Mary (1586-1640?). Eldest daughter of Sir
Robert and Barbara Sidney, and niece of Sir Philip Sidney, she
married Sir Robert Wroth, who had large estates in Essex, but
who squandered his wealth, leaving debts of £23,000 on his
death a month after their son was born. Mary never succeeded
in clearing the estate of debt and her son died aged three. She
acted in Jonson's *Masque of Blackness* in 1605, and published
in 1621 *The Countess of Montgomerie's Urania*, in imitation of
her uncle's *Arcadia*, but her satiric bent offended Buckingham.

WYATT, Sir Thomas (1503?-42). We have to sort out his poems
from MS collections where they lie cheek-by-jowl with poems
by Henry Howard, Earl of Surrey; Howard's father, Lord
Thomas Howard; Howard's sister, Queen Catherine
Howard; Wyatt's brother-in-law, Sir Antony Lee; Sir Francis
Bryan; Anne Boleyn's brother George, Viscount Rochford;
Thomas Vaux; and others. But it is clear that he was the leading
poet of the court of Henry VIII.

He was the son of Sir Henry Wyatt, an accomplished
courtier loyal to the Tudors since 1483, living at Allingham
Castle, Kent. He was educated at St John's College, Cambridge – where he knew John Leland – and later at Oxford. He
brought back to England from travel abroad, the MS of
Castiglione's *Il Cortegiano* in 1528. At the age of seventeen, he
was married to a Howard lady, Elizabeth Brooke, daughter of
his neighbour Lord Cobham, but after the birth of their son,
Thomas, the marriage disintegrated and ended in separation.
(Attempts at court, even as late as 1541, failed to make him take
her back.) He was involved in many love-affairs: Anne Boleyn
was his mistress for two years. Later in life he settled with
Elizabeth Darrell, who was one of Queen Catherine Howard's
attendants. After the Queen's execution, and though he sur-
rendered Elizabeth, he was imprisoned by the King, who
unjustly suspected his loyalty. Many of his friends were

executed: George Boleyn (accused incredibly of incest), Francis Weston, Henry Norris, William Brereton and, of course, Anne herself.

In 1524 he was Clerk of the King's Jewels, by 1525 Esquire of the Body, and from 1529 High Marshal of Calais, a suitable place in which to lie low after being Chief Ewer at Anne's coronation. He fought against the northern rebellion, the 'Pilgrimage of Grace', and was unshaken as Privy Counsellor from 1533. He established himself in Kent as Sheriff and then High Steward of West Malling and was in Parliament as knight of the shire in 1542. He was also Commissioner of the Peace for Essex. He managed to survive the fall of Anne Boleyn, and even more remarkably the fall of his last patron, Thomas Cromwell – this time because of his wife's connections with the Howards. He was also a navy captain. He was appointed, first as ambassador, then as envoy, to Spain where he died of fever.

None of his poems was published in his lifetime. His *Certayne Psalmes* reached print in 1549, and much of the rest – sonnets, epigrams, rondeaux, and satires in heroic couplets – in Tottel's *Songes and Sonnettes* (1557). He had an extraordinary gift for expressing, often in irregular scansion and vivid vocabulary, the central dilemmas of Renaissance lovers. He was probably not really intimate with the younger Henry Howard, Earl of Surrey until 1540, by which time, although still only thirty-seven, he would have been regarded as a veteran of the court and of poetry. If one tries to identify those who might have influenced his poetry, there is the scholar John Mason and, of the courtiers, Sir John Russell, Earl of Bedford, his companion in Italy. Another intimate was Sir Francis Bryan with whom he shared another interest – jousting at court displays – but little is known about their relationship.

P. Thompson: *Sir Thomas Wyatt and his Background* (1965); K. Muir: *The Life and Letters of Sir Thomas Wyatt* (1964); J.W. Lever: *The Elizabethan Love Sonnet* (1956).

WYKEHAM, William (1539-95). With Richard Corbet and Henry King, the most literary of the churchmen. He was educated at Eton and King's College, Cambridge, and became royal chaplain and vice-provost of Eton. Later he worked his way through the ranks of the Church: as prebendary of Westminster, Lincoln and Lichfield; canon of Windsor; Archdeacon of Surrey; Dean of Lincoln; and finally Bishop of Lincoln, then Winchester. His MS devotional verse accompanied this career.

Y

'YARINGTON, Robert' (fl. 1601). This may be a pseudonym used for the publication of *Two Lamentable Tragedies* (1601), in one book Haughton and Day's *Tragedy of Thomas Merrye,* and Chettle's *Orphanes Tragedie.* The plays have been lost, so we shall never know.

YATES, James (fl. 1582). Known only for the poem *The Castell of Courtesie* (published 1582).

YOUNG, Bartholomew (fl. 1577-98). A Middle Temple man who travelled in Spain, translated Boccaccio, and is chiefly known for the translation of Montemayor's Spanish romance *Diana* (1598), used by Shakespeare in *Two Gentlemen of Verona.*

Postscript

Many of these biographies could be enhanced by further attention: some important writers still lie dormant; and general studies are also needed. We need, for instance, a book about the writers who exploited their language and other courtly arts as secret agents. Another fascinating subject would be the 'sports and games of my lady's chamber': it might well transpire that Queen Henrietta Maria, whose attempt to regularise courtly adultery in a code of love, so wittily examined by John Ford and others, was building on a practice already existent. Deciphering fiction from truth in the affairs of the 'Stellas' and the 'Annes', and 'Gloriana' herself, would be well worth while. But the greatest need is for a *complete* examination of hierarchy, to which both the Elizabethans and Jacobeans were instinctively loyal, but for which we have no adequate survey.

It is relatively easy to work out sectional hierarchies, but we have nothing about the interfaces and interstices which made subtle alterations in the sections. The Church of England today is still a good guide to the Church then: we can identify promotion through prebendaries, archdeaconries and deaneries, to the bishoprics, and we notice the order there – how outer sees like Chichester, Oxford, Lichfield and Exeter, and indeed Durham which had not then achieved its later primacy, were stepping-stones to Lincoln and Norwich, Winchester and London, and so to York and Canterbury.

We have some foothold in studies of local government, but its complex subtleties need further examination.

It is not too difficult to establish precedence in heraldry: from 1483 there were six heralds, Windsor, Lancaster, York, Somerset, Chester and Richmond, followed by the *poursuivants* ranked in their colours, and then the Kings of Arms, headed by Garter and Bath. Army and navy appointments follow familiar lines, although the normal sequence is disturbed from time to time by those with particular power over recruiting, transportation and pay.

With Oxford or Cambridge, it is important to be aware of the regional policy and political affiliation of individual colleges. The Inns of Court were hierarchical, with minor Inns including Barnard's and Thavies' surrounding the big four, the Inner Temple, Middle Temple, Gray's Inn and Lincoln's Inn, whose primacy seems to vary. It is not difficult to establish how a man progressed in a legal career: he became a member or student of an Inn; if he were there long enough without qualifying for the Bar, he became an ancient; otherwise he became a barrister, MP, Serjeant-at-Arms, Recorder, Justice of Petty Sessions, Justice of High Courts, Chief Justice (not always in this order, and bearing in mind the difference between Chancery and Exchequer posts). MPs were recruited chiefly from this career-line, and constituencies, like Church benefices, were largely in the hands of royalty and the nobility, so that some seats were more important than others.

One finds similar hierarchies everywhere: in the Chapel Royal for musicians, in the College of Physicians, and so on.

Talent was exploited in this complex of systems in a dozen different ways. What is needed is a study of the interfacing where the different professional lines coincide in the retinue of a monarch or a nobleman, because here the power exercised varied very much according to personality and favour, the importance of posts rising and falling without any absolute rules applying. We have a modern respect for anyone called Lord Chancellor, Chancellor of the Exchequer, or Secretary of State, but posts with a specific political context like these were not always as powerful then as now. And the heraldic orders had their own courtly Chancellors, who might or might not be influential. In a purely courtly context there seems little doubt that the chief four offices were the Lord Chamberlain (sometimes called the Lord Great Chamberlain to prove the point), the Lord Steward, the Master of the Horse, and the Earl Marshal, in that order. Others, like the Lord Keeper of the Privy Seal, the Lord Treasurer, the Lord Privy Seal (sometimes a different person than the Keeper), and the Lord President of the Council were in a second grade.

The total court structure might employ as many as 1000 people, each holding a desirable pension: the 'inner cabinet' seems to have consisted of the gentlemen of the Bedchamber, sometimes headed by the Groom of the Stole, surrounded by the gentlemen of the Privy Chamber, with their grooms,

ushers, pages and messengers, all under the control of the Lord
Chamberlain – perhaps 300 in all. And the Queen's ladies,
whether or not the monarch was a queen, could exert strong
influence here, too. They were defended chiefly by the royal
bodyguard, of maybe 80 Esquires of the Body. In this outer
system were all kinds of professionals: as many as five
physicians, four apothecaries, five surgeons, a herbalist, a
dentist (the in-fighting in this group alone is fascinating); the
royal chaplains; the royal musicians; the librarian and picture-
keeper, Master of the Revels (or Pastimes), and others who
were given from time to time special titles, like regius orator,
regius antiquarius or historiographer-royal, King's poet, and
even the licensed jester. Further removed were the many cup-
bearers, carvers, servers, embroiderers, sempstresses,
launderers, shoemakers, spurriers, goldsmiths and jewellers,
bellringers, wood-bearers, porters, vermin-killers, and the
special hierarchy of the kitchen.

   Nor is this all. The outermost defences were manned chiefly
by the serjeants-at-arms, the yeomen of the guard and their
pensioners, some of whom had specialist roles in making bows,
gunpowder, or whatever. Then there were equerries, footmen,
coachmen, littermen and farriers, at one time forty-four water-
men, with a barge-maker and joiner under the Master of the
Barges, thirty falconers, twenty-four huntsmen, sixteen
harriers, and special keepers for the royal cormorants and
spaniels. It is difficult to establish exactly where the frontiers of
the court finally end.

   There is one final thought. The literariness of the
Renaissance seems dependent on a high level of literacy, and
according to the method used, research shows different levels.
I think we can safely assume that in London, the adjacent
Home Counties and extending into East Anglia and parts of
Nottinghamshire, there was a literacy rate of about 80 per cent.
Women were less fortunate than men, but even so in this
region, we may assume that the majority of women were
literate; perhaps in 1560-80 London was the only city in
Europe where this was so. The figures from the south-east are
quite remarkable, higher for instance than they were three
centuries later in the squalor of the Industrial Revolution. But
outside this privileged corner figures tail off, and it would be

unsafe to assume more than a 15 per cent literacy rate in
Cornwall, Wales, Scotland, and the north-west and north-
east.

Index